THE REAL DOMESTIC PRODUCT

THE REAL DOMESTIC PRODUCT

HOW BIRTH CONTROL BUILT EQUALITY (AND WHY THE FUTURE OF THE ECONOMY AND THE PLANET DEPENDS ON IT)

ELIZABETH GREGORY

THE MIT PRESS CAMBRIDGE, MASSACHUSETTS LONDON, ENGLAND

The MIT Press
Massachusetts Institute of Technology
77 Massachusetts Avenue
Cambridge, MA 02139
mitpress.mit.edu

The MIT Press would like to thank the anonymous peer reviewers who provided comments on drafts of this book. The generous work of academic experts is essential for establishing the authority and quality of our publications. We acknowledge with gratitude the contributions of these otherwise uncredited readers.

This book was set in ITC Stone and Avenir by New Best-set Typesetters Ltd. Printed and bound in the United States of America.

Library of Congress Cataloging-in-Publication Data

Names: Gregory, Elizabeth L., 1957- author
Title: The real domestic product : how birth control built equality (and why the future of work and care depends on it) / Elizabeth Gregory.
Description: Cambridge, Massachusetts : The MIT Press, [2026] | Includes bibliographical references and index.
Identifiers: LCCN 2025048310 (print) | LCCN 2025048311 (ebook) | ISBN 9780262051682 hardcover | ISBN 9780262051699 pdf | ISBN 9780262051705 epub
Subjects: LCSH: Birth control—Economic aspects | Child care—Economic aspects | Women—Social conditions | Women—Economic conditions | Women's rights
Classification: LCC HQ766 .G725 2026 (print) | LCC HQ766 (ebook)
LC record available at https://lccn.loc.gov/2025048310
LC ebook record available at https://lccn.loc.gov/2025048311

10 9 8 7 6 5 4 3 2 1

EU Authorised Representative: Easy Access System Europe, Mustamäe tee 50, 10621 Tallinn, Estonia | Email: gpsr.requests@easproject.com

For my grandparents:
Mildred Dager Theis, Édouard Jean Emile Theis,
Emilie Rebecca Craven Gregory, and John Charles Gregory Sr.

Resistance Is Fertile!

CONTENTS

The bibliography is online at https://mitpress.mit.edu/real-domestic.

PREFACE

For decades, I've researched shifting fertility dynamics—especially the intersection of economics, reliable birth control, family structure, and women's movement into civic life. But growing up, I watched that change progress for years earlier.

In 1991, as a young professor, I recall standing in my university's central plaza processing with amazement the news that, suddenly, I lived in a place with a female governor (Ann Richards), a female mayor, a female university president, and a female police chief. In none of the cities or states I'd operated in previously, and just one of the schools (a women's college), were any of those roles filled by women. Now the better world where women had an active role in running things had arrived—and it was here, in Houston, Texas!

Fast forward to spring 2024, where the Feminist Theory seminar I was teaching looked out on the same plaza. Although the *Roe v. Wade* decision won by Texas lawyer Sarah Weddington in 1973 had been overturned two years before, and we no longer had women in three of the roles they'd filled on that day in 1991, we did have a (second) female university president. We also had a striking statue on display on that plaza—an idealized eighteen-foot gold female figure called Witness representing women's progress in the judiciary, by Pakistani American artist Shahzia Sikander.

The piece—a streamlined body with roots for arms and legs[1] and a lattice hoopskirt/metal frame from the waist down—had been co-commissioned by the university with New York City's Madison Square Park. There it had been displayed in 2023 along with a similar but skirtless figure called NOW by the same artist, which had been placed atop the nearby Manhattan Appellate Court building—the only female figure among nine others that had long stood there representing great legal minds from across history and cultures (Confucius, Moses, Zoroaster, Justinian, Manu-smriti, St. Louis, Solon, Lycurgus, and Alfred the Great).[2] The Witness statue's presence in NYC and then in Houston testified that while the movement toward equity was challenged, it was still underway.

The seminar met in the evening, and over the term, our sessions coincided with a series of protests—against the statue. The marchers, from an anti-abortion group called Texas Right to Life, had decided (following the logic of a *New York Times* op-ed published during the statue's New York run) that the figure was "satanic" because its thick braids resembled rams' horns (though the artist saw them as "universal symbols of strength and wisdom") and because it wore a jabot—a lace legal collar like those worn by Supreme Court justices Sandra Day O'Connor and Ruth Bader Ginsburg.[3] The protesters took the nod to Ginsburg, an abortion-rights supporter, as "honoring abortion," so they invested many hours circling the plaza, shouting. Although the statue didn't directly reference abortion, having women's voices represented in the public square (literally) after millennia of exclusion has been the direct result of their ability to control their own fertility, and the protesters connected those dots—disapprovingly. Their signs called the statue "ugly," and they carried a shrouded figure of the Virgin Mary with only the face and praying hands visible as a counterexample of appropriate representation of women. Although officials didn't feel they could eject protesters exercising free speech, they posted guards 24/7.

The dynamic produced an intense semester—as the amazing and diverse group of twelve graduate students from many disciplines read and discussed a wide range of feminist works, connecting them to their own lives and research, with the protesters howling outside. On two occasions, several students—including one who'd recently exited a Christian cult, after experiences of sexual predation and harassment—went out to protest the protesters during the break. The semester ended positively, with hope for future progress.

Fast forward two months more to July 8, 2024, at 2:00 a.m., at the same plaza. Hurricane Beryl was barreling through, the guards were sent off site for safety, and someone with a face cover seized the chance to climb up the lattice hoopskirt and decapitate the statue, and then ran off, leaving the head shattered in the grass—all caught on video. It was a particularly salient representation of the backlash from the patriarchal crew to the increasing presence of women in the public sphere. The statue became a performance piece, and the artist called for the head to remain unrestored, leaving the statue to stand as "a witness to the fissures in our country," until its installation ended four months later.[4]

This book explores those fissures: the movement toward real democracy that women's control of their own fertility has enabled, the pushback to that change, and the pushback to the pushback. The struggle continues!

INTRODUCTION

Tipping Point: The Econo-Politics of Fertility

For decades, Americans have pussyfooted around what's at stake in the abortion debate: most basically, that's women's status as equal citizens in our democracy, able to fully participate and represent themselves. Over the past thirty-five years, women around the globe have moved into civic life in significant numbers—for the first time in recorded history. That revolution was directly enabled by the availability of reliable birth control (aka RBC, defined here as *contraception backed up by safe, legal abortion if needed*), a transformative, almost evolutionary development for our species.[1] In contrast, as recent events have made clear, efforts to deny access to RBC aim to push everyone with a uterus back down the ladders they've been climbing and out of the polity. In response to this attempt to suppress, now is the time for plain speaking.

Beyond the harm to women, all people are wounded when denied the ability to control their own reproductive decisions. Historically, our inherited economic model has actively blocked both men and women from thriving—in large part through fertility manipulation. Our economy has depended on the desperation of poor parents, who've been propelled by unplanned, early births into filling multiple low-wage jobs to feed their kids and, simultaneously, deprived of educational opportunities and civic voice. Early childbearing has also forced women of all classes and race/ethnicities into dependent roles within patriarchal families, where their unpaid labor has provided employers and governments with a steady stream of workers and soldiers, and their husbands and families with household service, "for free."

Although fertility and its intimate partners gender and sexuality are typically viewed as matters of personal autonomy or morals, I argue, like feminists prior, that they are fundamentally labor issues. They involve work in themselves, while also shaping the kinds of work that individuals may do in society. By limiting the numbers of unplanned births (and thus of desperate workers), RBC has directly undermined old gender-, class-, and race-based labor and pay structures and allowed many young women and young men who aren't parents to complete their schooling, raise their wages, and move into jobs formerly blocked to them, bringing new skills to market and new perspectives to our discourse.

Not surprisingly, among those new perspectives are demands for change to our socioeconomic model—to allow all Americans a real chance to thrive. Recent clampdowns on RBC, on diversity efforts, and on LGBTQ+ rights aim to push the genie of labor systems change back into the bottle and return us to an abusive past.

In 1970, the average age at first birth for US women was 21.4, but by 2024 it was 27.6: similar rises globally have transformed human society. Although the pace of change has varied across nations, and some backlash has followed, patterns have shifted steadily toward degendering jobs, moving more women into paid work and policymaking, and growing their social status. In many lands, "women's concerns" like childcare, domestic violence (DV), and wage inequity have begun to be addressed, where before demands for change were spurned as "unrealistic."

In the United States, those who oppose women's progress have fought back, using a sentimental and inaccurate discourse of fetal personhood to divide people and bring out voters for conservative candidates, who when elected have filled the courts with like-minded judges. That paved the way for the 2022 *Dobbs v. Jackson Women's Health Organization* decision, which switched the direction of change. Dobbs took a hard-won constitutional right of all women to control their own fertility and reduced it to a revocable privilege, dependent on address.[2]

Post-Dobbs, abortion bans sprang up in twenty-four states over 2022–2023—based overwhelmingly on votes cast by conservative male state legislators, many in gerrymandered districts, whose standing to dictate women's choices was never debated. Although bans have since been overturned in several states (abortion is legal up to at least twenty-two-weeks in thirty states and Washington, DC, in January 2026),[3] Dobbs demoted people with uteruses to secondary citizens, endangered their lives and health from puberty to menopause, and traumatized the nation.

Although anti-abortion activists assert that fetuses have a "right" to be carried to term no matter what circumstances they would arrive into or how their arrival would affect the women who carry them, as a group we haven't discussed who benefits from such births when they are unwanted (hint: it's not the children, women, or families involved).

Simultaneously, bans restricting the rights of LGBTQ+ Americans (including Don't Say Gay rules, gender-affirming care [GAC] bans, and attacks on trans people) have also divided us. I'll argue that the efforts to restrict the rights of women and LGBTQ+ people are linked—through their fertility effects, since same-sex love is effectively in itself contraceptive,[4] and through their shared challenges to the old social order. The bans and conservative pronatalist rhetoric of our moment together aim to push both women and LGBTQ+ folk out of the civic sphere they've just begun to enter in order to block their ability to substantially alter it, for the better.

These bans and clampdowns on speech attempt to reimpose a "traditional" fertility pattern—of early births and compulsory heterosexuality. This pattern is often discussed in relation to patriarchal religious concepts (a factor, it must be acknowledged, in the thinking of the current Supreme Court majority of conservative Catholics) and to racist fears about "replacement" of white Americans as the national racial majority. But while such narratives may bring out voters, they are not the full or even the main story. *The Real Domestic Product* explores both who stands to benefit from forced childbirth—economically and otherwise—and who is harmed.

While technical and legal changes around RBC in the 1960s and 1970s introduced important societal and economic shifts, only recently have the full force of those changes begun to be felt. The admission of women's voices to civic debates challenges longstanding patterns of *discounts* for employers and *deferences* to male householders created by unpaid or underpaid gendered care work, done largely by women who are or are likely to become dependent mothers. Both the discounts and the deferences involve employers getting labor for less than it's worth, due to workers' limited bargaining power (including both men and women in the workplace, and women in the home). The context in which childbearing occurs and its timing (not just the numbers or rates of births) shape the ways that a person can participate in society, in private life, and in the economy. The radical changes in timing and context created over the past fifty-plus years by RBC have enormously altered all three spheres—hence the current conflicts.

These changes have expanded opportunities for long-term thriving, but they alarm old-school (unfettered) capitalists, who don't see profit in shared thrive. On the other hand, fettered capitalism—aka a mixed economy or social democracy—combines some market freedom with government supports for the populace, which involve both taxes and regulations. The United States has operated with a limited version of such a system (including basic services like disaster assistance; weather alerts; some subsidizing of health care, elder care; food stamps/SNAP; and a few other services for underresourced groups), but many developed nations offer a much fuller array of supports, within a capitalist frame.

The women's rights revolution of the past 180 years and especially the past four decades has brought us to a *tipping point*. Women have much more knowledge, clout, and influence than previously, which they and their allies can use to continue America's movement toward a more inclusive power structure (aka democracy paired with an economy built to give everyone a real chance to thrive). Or they can watch that power erode, and even aid in its erosion, as a minority elite doubles down on the exploitative model through forced births and the increased desperation of the many (aka autocracy/oligarchy and patriarchal capitalism).

While polls show that large majorities of Americans disapprove of abortion bans, and while majorities voted to protect abortion rights in fourteen of the sixteen states where a referendum on a state constitutional amendment protecting abortion was held between 2022 and 2024, that sentiment did not sway the 2024 presidential election.[5] The question going forward is whether Americans have the will and vision for a real dialogue about what's at stake, what's desired, and what's possible—and to continue to evolve a democratic society where people of all genders, races, and classes can thrive. Recent history shows that that depends on which fertility policies the group endorses going forward.

PATRIARCHY: THE BACKSTORY

Analysis of our moment requires some understanding of the patriarchal framework we inhabit, which directly links gender, fertility, and sexuality to economics and workforce. That's complicated, since so much of that framework developed before the invention of writing, and doubtless many different dynamics played out across our prehistory. If patriarchal history is old hat to you, skip ahead—but if not, here's a simplified summary.[6]

Scholars date the establishment of widespread patriarchal socioeconomic systems between 4000 and 3000 BCE—roughly 6,000 years ago—just the blink of an eye in planetary history.[7] "Modern" homo sapiens stabilized in their current physiology about 250,000 years ago, though our trademark ability to speak appeared only 50,000–70,000 years back—a big leap forward, speeding information exchange and new-idea formation.

Archaeological evidence suggests that our early ancestors lived in mobile bands of fifty to two hundred kin-linked people, cooperating to hunt, gather food, and raise children.[8] The combination of bipedality and bigger brains means human infants have to arrive early to fit through the birth canal. Human maturation depends on extensive postnatal care, making up for the shortened time in womb. Back in the prehistoric day, like now, if a mother had more than one child close together, she needed help tending them. While she nursed her youngest, archaeologists deduce that everybody else would have been additional caregivers ("alloparents") for the older kids—part of the village that raises all children together.[9] Without romanticizing the early days or assuming there were no divisions, we can understand a core need for cooperation and recognition of the contributions of all.

But things changed in the Neolithic period (10,000–3000 BCE),[10] when cattle breeding and then agriculture replaced hunting and gathering. Farming and herding both created the possibility of surpluses, which spurred trade and the development of money, the concept of private ownership, a legal system to enforce property rules, and hoard-able wealth. The stationary farming life enabled the accumulation of objects, creating new demand for goods. Steady supplies of food could support more children, who as they grew older could be put to work in the fields and then as warriors as needed to protect the family's goods or—in less friendly mode—to seize the goods of others.

All of this coincided with the development of labor hierarchies linked to who had surpluses and of differential pay and growing social inequality. The first of these hierarchies seems to have been patriarchy, a gendered labor system whose name—meaning *rule of the fathers* (over the mothers, the children, and the childless adults of both sexes)—underscores its root in fertility dynamics.

Patriarchal society developed as a fertility-claiming system, built around defining women as a special form of property, claiming the fruits of their fertility through marriage or concubinage, requiring women's chastity, and policing their sexuality through social censure to ensure that they (or most of them) slept and conceived with their assigned mate exclusively. Women's work, which provided their group with laborers, warriors, and caregivers, earned them food and shelter and ensured that men could fairly confidently leave their goods and funds to their own genetic heirs—their next-gen selves. Men of wealth took the lead in civic forums, building the early kingdoms around class systems with a patriarchal core, while women, tied to home by frequent births and nursing, became responsible for all the care work, but they got no pay for that endless effort. Because they couldn't trade that care work for cash, they depended on their spouses' earnings and status and were denied most public roles and voice.

Thus developed the premodern version of what we know as *gender*—essentially a work-assignment system with pay scales. Feminist Friedrich Engels called this transition "the World Historical Defeat of the Female Sex."[11] By using women's fertility as the catalyst for locking them into positions of dependency, service labor, low or no wages, and child production, men in power have systematically profited from women's work. But they've obscured that dynamic by calling it "instinct"—and women had no forum to dispute that claim. With limited options, women have accepted this system and perpetuated it by teaching it to their children as the way of the world.

Many men at lower ranks in the social and pay hierarchies have also been negatively affected by the patriarchal labor structure, but their resistance to it has been suborned in exchange for power over the women in their homes such that even the poorest man may be understood to operate as a boss—of his wife/housekeeper. As Heidi Hartmann explains, "Hierarchies work at least in part because they create vested interests in the status quo. Those at the higher levels can 'buy off' those at the lower levels by offering them power over those still lower. In the hierarchy of patriarchy, all men, whatever their rank in the patriarchy, are bought off by being able to control at least some women. . . . [Thus m]en are dependent on one another (despite their hierarchical ordering) to maintain their control over women."[12]

Thus even in situations in which men are exploited, they can expect more pay and status than female workers from their male employers to ensure that they won't join up with the women to revolt against the bosses who oppress them both.

Since reproduction of the workforce is both the means and a goal of control, heterosexuality is required (with varying levels of exclusivity), and men who don't play by that rule have historically been punished by other men.[13] Not because gay love itself is inherently objectionable to them but because it threatens the system of enforced fertility. To work effectively, patriarchy requires that all or most men be on board. Although today many men consider themselves nonpatriarchal, most still reap at least some of the system's benefits, along with its harms.

After the gendered labor hierarchy, others emerged—including tribe- or race-based hierarchies, involving the enslavement of rival populations, and class-based hierarchies based on income and caste. While within a given group women had lower status and decision-making power than the men, women aligned with men in higher-status groups also benefited from the labor of those in lower-ranked groups.

This power redistribution across class, group/race, and gender hierarchies didn't happen all at once or the same way everywhere, but over time things coalesced into the post-Neolithic Patriarchal Age.[14] We still operate within a version of that. Stories, framed within new religious narratives, were developed to both make sense of things for people and to convince most of them that taking a lower status was what their god intended, and that inequitable suffering on earth would lead to bliss hereafter. Religious communities also provided sources of strength for dealing with those inequities.

Before the end of the Neolithic, evidence suggests that women were active in civic and religious life.[15] Although they sound parallel, matriarchy isn't patriarchy in reverse: before chastity rules, only mothers could be surely known, so families were defined around women, though men also had valued roles. Feminist archaeologists and scholars have documented evidence of prepatriarchal cultures in Europe and around the globe. For instance, Marija Gimbutas documented fertility goddess worship in the seventh-century BCE, when early potters sculpted female statuettes featuring "supernatural buttocks" and highlighting pubic areas to indicate regenerative power.[16] Additionally, ancient burial sites include many female skeletons buried with high-status items, indicating rank and power.[17] Heide Goettner-Abendroth has documented that some matriarchies continued around the globe,[18] but they have largely been marginalized.

The contagion of patriarchy led to the exclusion of women from most divine theologies and from leadership: while the plethora of antique female sculptures indicates that prior cultures worshipped female divinities, the Abrahamic religions (Judaism, Islam, and Christianity) and most others current today pointedly do not, replacing fertility goddesses with a solo male creator who, contra all visible signs around who gives life, is credited with generating humanity.

Yet another of the innovations of the Neolithic was the human ability to communicate through writing, which emerged around 3400 BCE in Sumer (Iraq)—initially as a means of recording expenditures in the new market economies. So while the majority of human history involved shared power, most of the stories we have access to come from patriarchal contexts. Before writing, the evolution of speech had expanded human capacity to network brains through conversation (more perspectives, shared at greater speed) and to spread new ideas across communities. Writing (a technology but also effectively a form of externalized evolution) connected thinkers across greater distances and time. It allowed humans to increase their sharing, collection, analysis, and refining of thoughts and information of all kinds (scientific, technological, historical, and personal, among others).

But writing also had the effect of fixing in static form versions of what had previously been fluid spoken texts. Before writing, people memorized stories and evolved them on retelling to fit their moment.[19] Written texts can give us insight into the organization of social structures and technologies of their time, and they can preserve wisdom a group has developed, for generations to come. But conversely, they also allow versions of prescriptive social rules that were operative at the moment they were recorded to take on a long-term authority they wouldn't previously have had.

Patriarchal origin stories like those introduced in the Old Testament, and then reaffirmed in the New Testament and Qur'an, are viewed as themselves coming from an origin because earlier origin stories for the same groups weren't recorded, for comparison. While prescriptive texts may pass down wisdom, they may also inhibit development of new ideas and systems.[20] Such has been the case with the prescriptive, patriarchal stories we've inherited. The apparent authority of the written texts and the embeddedness of patriarchal systems in so many parts of our lives make them hard to stand back from and critique. Nonetheless, as society has evolved democratic values, scholars have begun to name and address the many problems with the undemocratic systems that have shaped us.

While the absence of records of social systems from before the Neolithic has also inhibited our imagination of pre- or nonpatriarchal worlds, one foundational Western story tracks the transition. The *Iliad* recounts a ten-year battle to recapture a woman who thinks she can change partners at will. Helen, a demigoddess (daughter of Zeus and Leda in the Greek pantheon, evolved from a prior-phase fertility goddess), dropped King Menelaus of Mycenae for Prince Paris of Troy, assuming she had that option.[21] But if she had it previously, the story documents the abrogation of her right of choice.[22] As you've heard, Helen lost that battle—and in the sequel, Odysseus's loyal wife Penelope absorbs that lesson of required acquiescence, serving as a surrogate for all women who hear Helen's story. Western civilization to date has been built on that defeat. Although Homer's two poems take place over a twenty-year period, we can read that long time in individual lives as a metaphor for change over millennia in human societies. With past as prologue, we can use that example of cultural change as a basis for envisioning and enacting more equitable change now.

CAPITALISM VERSUS DEMOCRACY

Although we don't widely acknowledge patriarchy's role in our society (being taken for granted is part of its success), Americans do proudly pledge allegiance to democracy. We talk about equality and fairness, but we've enacted those very gradually and incompletely. Instead, we get wound in the inequities of capitalism, the other concept to which Americans understand ourselves devoted, claiming it enables all to thrive (if only they try) and thus supports democracy. Except that promise has never been kept either: while a few succeed, a system of identity-based labor discounts or direct wage thefts ensures that many people cannot succeed, as unfettered capitalism requires their poverty and ensures that poverty through unplanned fertility.

Nonetheless, the goals of full democracy and economic prosperity for all have been lodestars leading America's social evolution since 1776. I define *full democracy* as a social structure that seeks to help all community members thrive; which, instead of using power over some to their harm, uses its power to enable all present—so that all insights and skills feed the collective. One that rather than exploiting people so the economy thrives along with a few at the top, instead puts the economy to work to help people thrive. The economy thrives too, but differently.

In much of our history, socially constructed identities have been linked to labor categories—effectively as castes, as Isabel Wilkerson has shown regarding race.[23] But rising status for historically disadvantaged identity groups had occurred gradually with more equitable redistribution of resources, so that some can build good lives. Investment in the thriving of currently underresourced groups—by putting all brains on the problems, expanding markets and jobs, and building an ethos of community trust and support—can benefit all.

This is very different from the current model, in which competition between individuals spurs some innovation and a lot of harm and mistrust. Efforts to expand American civic life to include historically underresourced groups on a level playing field—through diversity, equity, and inclusion (DEI) programs that aim to rectify past and ongoing labor injustice by affording equitable access to jobs to those previously excluded—have spurred backlash. Those losing privileged access to good jobs resent having to compete against a bigger pool than previously and find it inconvenient to acknowledge either the past injustice or the possibility of addressing its consequences in the present. Many also believe that some must be miserable for others to thrive because that's all they've seen. But there are alternatives, as we'll see.

Since all groups experience suffering of various kinds, no one position is fully "privileged." To create a democratic economy of mutual thriving and care will require real discussions that lay bare old assumptions and open them to challenge and innovation. These discussions can explore both how the full economy works now and how it could be strengthened to supply all Americans with the resources for at least a baseline decent life, upon which each can build. That would include fully and equitably funding education, health care, and other care needs—as we'll see, there is enough to go around if those at the top aren't allowed to hoard. In so doing, such a care economy can generate even more prosperity. But the deadlines created by climate change and corruption at the top require fast action to allow that.

As I write, the economy is threatened by oligarchs and patriarchal ideologues behaving as what economists variously call "bandits" (people who steal from the system outright through embezzlement, corrupt legislation, insider trading, fraud, and related practices), "free riders" (people or organizations who get outsized benefits relative to their contributions), and "top riders" (leaders who skim more profit off the top than they deserve, in the form of high salaries, stock options, low taxes, and similar perks)—all known colloquially as *grifters*. Such actors often aim to limit or destroy government regulation systems to increase their profits and to reimpose steep wage discounts and direct wage theft. Tax breaks for oligarchs and cuts in the federal workforce at the expense of basic services for the rest of the population both operate like the vampiric private-equity firms that suck the value out of small-town companies to benefit shareholders (through value extraction, predatory lending, or leveraged buyouts), soon leaving the businesses bankrupt and unable to generate jobs and services for their communities.

Political economist Mancur Olson predicted such a development in initially stable democracies where entrenched interest groups ("distributional coalitions") can manipulate regulations to develop outsized wealth and power, buy influence, and protect their own privileges, because the larger group (the people!) is not sufficiently organized or agile to advocate effectively in its own defense. In the process the interest groups destabilize the democracy, pillage its coffers, and slow innovation.[24] Economic prosperity requires both political order and an impartial legal system to hold leaders in check, protect individual rights, and discourage predation (hence the United States' tripartite government). Undermining the rule of law by advantaging particular parties in disputes or through lobbying weakens economies, since businesses and individuals can't plan ahead reliably. Connections to our moment are clear. Supreme Court overrides of constitutional precedents have undermined individual rights (including those of women and voters) in order to advantage privileged parties. Per Olson, such actions set in motion economic and societal decline. Conversely, affirming and expanding those rights enables economic and societal stability and health.

Opposite to a value-extraction approach to an economy is one that invests in communities and creates jobs. These include jobs in businesses and in government-supported roles in education, health, and other services (federal, state, and local) that build value for individuals and the community. This investment-versus-extraction tension defines our moment, and our decisions around it will determine democracy's fate.

If the nation survives the current corruption crisis, and in the growing shadow of climate change, the interests and concerns of all groups must be addressed to create a fair and viable national economy going forward. When the pendulum swings, if the excesses of the oligarchs spur deep conversations and activate real commitments to one another, that's some compensation for harm done.

The hard work to follow will involve overcoming the divide-and-conquer mechanisms through which people in diverse sectors have been made to see others as competitors, rather than as cooperators whose insights and efforts can assist one another. Although cooperation has historically been a very difficult nut for humans to crack, we can break the pattern by focusing on the pressing global goal of climate care and repair, for which cooperation is essential.

Only when all citizens have access to civic voice and the ability to represent themselves will the twin goals of equitable social and economic opportunities that inspire many Americans be realizable. Reliable birth control and childcare are key to making that happen.

PRESENT TENSE

As we'll see, the expanded availability of reliable birth control in the United States since the introduction of the Pill in 1960 has enabled many women to delay or forgo marriage and first births in order to complete their education and establish themselves at work, before starting families if they chose—as Goldin and Katz have shown.[25] Consequently, unprecedented numbers of women—of all backgrounds—have gained civic voice, both directly and indirectly, through elected female representatives and women who've advanced in business and policy roles. That huge advance toward full economic participation and real democracy, paired with parallel advances for queer voices, has destabilized the patriarchal socioeconomic model. But the forces of yesteryear haven't given up on re-creating old patterns.

Key to this effort is child poverty: though politicians often claim to want to end it, somehow they never do. That's because exploitative economic structures draw power directly from it: impoverished workers are tied to bad jobs *by the need to feed their hungry kids*. Acknowledging this fact reframes current efforts to deny women access to abortion and, increasingly, to contraception,[26] while also explaining the new administration's shutdown in March 2025 of free lunch programs that fed millions of school children, and subsequent further defunding of supports for poor families.[27]

Though the anti-reproductive rights movement often overlaps with white supremacist messaging around more white births, it's also deeply invested in expanding the number of Black and brown children—and their poverty levels. It's no accident that the abortion-ban zone includes all former slave states (except Virginia, the most northerly)—the economy of the American South having been structured around the extraction of severely discounted labor for centuries, with fertility-linked and race-based poverty systems operating long after slavery (see the appendix). Likewise, it's no coincidence that all Southern ban states, along with the South-adjacent and Midwest states in the ban zone, have also passed restrictions on LGBTQ+ rights.

As Loretta Ross, Dorothy Roberts, and others in the Reproductive Justice Movement have argued, a just system would honor all women's choices to have children or not and provide safe and healthy environments for parenting.[28] Such a system could undo the low-wage worker pipeline and create fruitful social and economic outcomes, but that's not the system operative. Instead, race/ethnicity and gender are still utilized within a hierarchized work-assignment system, as they have been historically.

The current debate about access to reproductive services is fueled by a small but powerful minority. A 2025 Gallup poll found that *only 13 percent of Americans felt abortion should be illegal in all cases*; 49 percent (including 56 percent of women and 41 percent of men) felt it should be legal in all or most cases; and 35 percent "only in a few."[29] Against that backdrop, I'll demonstrate that in our society the age at which people have (or do not have) children shapes the workforce participation of two generations simultaneously: adults in the near term, and children later on.[30]

For millennia, lack of both contraception and family-support infrastructure in a context of compulsory heterosexuality fed "traditional" patterns of paid and unpaid labor, which reproduced not just individuals but also the class structure. Babies are the workforce of the future, but they're also the glue that keeps parents stuck to their respective grindstones in the present, often for low pay for men and even lower pay for women. Un-contracepted hetero sex, and the dependency of women on men's wages to support kids that often follows upon it, have for ages had the effect of locking both genders into patriarchal hierarchies of financial power and status.

Reliable birth control's reduction of the number of unplanned births has broken that lock, dissolved that glue, meaning that young workers (of both sexes) don't have to take any job available to put food on the family table—because they don't have a family yet! In recent decades, women have radically challenged old economic models that depend upon both

- a continuous stream of babies, many of them unplanned, to supply a steady and often economically precarious workforce
- and a care system wherein women to do most of that essential work, uncompensated.

When that basis for workers' commitment to low-wage jobs disappears, it directly impacts employers who counted on that desperation to create workers willing to take undervalued jobs, increasing business profits but living hand to mouth themselves, and raising their children in the trauma of poverty. In addition to challenging patriarchy, reliable birth control also radically challenges the regnant class system. Whether it leads to its world-historical defeat, TBD.

Instead, newly able to finish their educations and get good jobs of their own, women don't have to kowtow to the men in their lives, and men don't have to support families they didn't intend to take on (or feel guilty if they don't), opening new chances for peer marriages based on shared interests down the line (not just mutual obligation) and for forming families when and if couples or individuals feel ready.

Whether or not those forgoing unplanned births now choose to have planned children when they're older will depend on whether society makes family formation seem affordable and responsible. Or, it has occurred to some, you could try to force them to have unplanned kids now, by blocking access to abortion and contraception. So far that's been ineffective.

The battles around limiting access to reliable birth control must thus be understood not as moralistic efforts to save unborn souls or "fetal persons," but as policies forwarded by those with economic interests in ensuring more births. This clearly includes unplanned births among low-wage workers, but middle-class births (planned or not) also create a committed, if slightly less desperate workforce, as may babies who provide the rich with someone to "carry on the name." Recent changes to society's patterns and rules around fertility, gender, and sexuality undercut established financial interests and social hierarchies that count on those duty-bound parent workers.

Contra the anxieties that change spurs in those invested in old ways, RBC's transformations of national and global economies are widely beneficial, for two reasons. First, because "equity grows the pie"—since more workers with a decent wage to spend create more demand and expand both the workforce and the economy. Second, because the inclusion in civic debates of the voices, insights, and concerns of people of all genders and backgrounds is essential to expanded understanding and innovation on all fronts. Today, such voices are especially key to addressing the climate change emergency.

While both environmental education and increasing weather catastrophes have raised climate change awareness, if women—historically the ones assigned the gendered job of caretaking—are pushed into early pregnancies and out of civic power, and consequently are excluded from climate care policy decisions, the likelihood of positive change around climate falls markedly.[31] As Janet Yellen has described, if we don't include women's insights, "we will squander the potential of many of our citizens and incur a substantial loss to the productive capacity of our economy."[32]

Though conservatives lashed back against women's progress in 2024 and after, that progress has already occurred and cannot be quickly erased. Many people of both sexes who are committed to the advancement of democracy and to building a society and economy that values care work still hold influence, so we remain at a tipping point. It's a use-it-or-lose-it emergency, and the next few years will be pivotal.

THE GDP AND THE CARE ECONOMY

Turning again to our Greek cultural roots, I'll note that the root of the Greek word *oikonomia* ("household management") is *oikos* ("household"), while *domos* (the root of our word *domestic*) means "house."

As feminist economists have long emphasized, gross domestic product (GDP)—the standard measure of the health of our national economy here at home (not including imports and exports)—distorts the picture of what and who contributes to the nation's thriving because it only counts the annual cash value of the nation's expenditures on goods and services—the economy's *exchange value*.[33] It doesn't include the value of the huge volume of unpaid care work, done mostly by women at home (including the work of biological reproduction and of child-rearing and daily maintenance of families), even though that work creates enormous value for the families and is also the basis of all paid production and consumption, benefiting business.

The GDP views a family's investment of labor and love into the workers of today and tomorrow as a donation to employers, having only *use value*, which is recorded in no ledger since there's no payment involved. Although use value and exchange value are accounted for differently, and modern economics concerns itself largely with the exchange side, paid and unpaid work are interdependent. Together they add up to the *real* domestic product, the sum of all labor that contributes to the functioning of the economy. Simultaneously, and more literally, babies, families, and individual workers are also *real domestic products*, whose lives comprise the fabric of the nation. All those lives are of great value, though less quantifiable than labor, and our moment demands that we evolve our socioeconomic model to much better recognize and support all contributors.

Until recently, home and market work have been heavily gendered, but we all contribute to both. This book explores the shifting categories of gendered work—including aspects elided in standard discussions of GDP and the national economy—and it recognizes identity-based status and imposed deference as additional nonpecuniary forms of compensation that are often more highly valued than money by their beneficiaries.

Over time, feminist economists' arguments have gained influence, pressing to get care work acknowledged in the national accounting and in some cases monetized (aka paid for).[34] Multiple alternatives to GDP that do include care have been proposed—including the United Nations (UN) Human Development Index, which adds up average life expectancy, levels of schooling, and standard of living to gauge whether a society is doing well, and the Organization for Economic Co-operation and Development (OECD)'s Better Life Index, which measures a society's resources, including housing, income, jobs, community, education, environment, civic engagement, health, life satisfaction, safety, and work/life balance.[35]

As birth control has enabled women to move into policymaking roles, many bring an ethic of care with them—both because care has been women's assigned realm and because care serves their needs: childcare especially enables women's civic participation.[36] As a result, a primary concern for feminist policymakers has been building a care infrastructure, which could include universally affordable childcare, after-school and summer care, health care, elder care, a child allowance/tax credit, and solid education for all. Such infrastructure would outsource and pay for some of the care work formerly done at home without pay, though much would remain for families to do after work hours.[37]

Figuring out how to fund this in the United States—or "who pays for the kids?" as feminist economist Nancy Folbre succinctly framed it—has been the underlying effort and source of tension around care dynamics for the past thirty years, not because it's hard to figure out (other nations have systems that could serve as starting points) but because it involves reductions in patriarchal privilege (which, again, also harms most men). Rather than explore the range of possibilities, the discussion has been limited to what's been viewed as "possible" in the US context. But over time efforts to build a care infrastructure have had increasing success—creating economic and social gains and expanding women's civic voice. This progress has sparked the recent backlash against RBC. The closer women get to making real change in this realm, the more vehement the response from those who benefit from the status quo ante.

That backlash whipped loudly in 2025—scary for all who counted on public services or the ability to plan their families. But in their haste to clamp down on change, the Project 2025 team detailed their plan in writing, revealing their hand, which had benefited previously from deniability. Following that up with a tax cut for the wealthy and major cuts in services for the rest only added to the revelatory effect, opening the way for those in opposition to respond.

FERTILITY, JANUARY 2026

Since Dobbs, untrackable numbers of women in ban states, most of them poor or otherwise unable to travel, have been forced to bear babies they didn't want or can't support, while hundreds of thousands have hit the road, trekking long distances for abortion care,[38] after struggling to organize childcare, time off from jobs, and funds for the journey. Many others have accessed medication abortions at home. Still others whose planned pregnancies developed complications were forced to carry nonviable pregnancies to term (contributing to the rise in stillbirths and infant deaths post-2022) or were turned away from emergency rooms because the new bans forbade care until they were at death's door.[39] Some died, while others faced medical horrors and trauma as their doctors refused them service when most needed because they feared imprisonment for doing their job.[40] Emotional stress was highest for pregnant women, but in all ban states, women of childbearing age reported heightened levels of depression, stress, and anxiety—while women over age forty-five in those states (with postmenopausal privilege) and all men made no such reports, nor did women or men in ban-free states.[41]

As I write, women have different status in ban and ban-free sectors, though denial of rights to others also affects US women overall. The two sectors have varying access to OB-GYN services of all kinds, as many doctors migrate into ban-free states where they can practice medicine without state interference.[42]

But despite the bans, the US fertility rate continued its seventeen-year decline post-Dobbs, falling 2.6 percent in 2023 and 1.3 percent in 2024—a 22.4 percent decline since 2007. Fertility rates fell in all fifty states in 2023 and in thirty-seven states in 2024 (rising slightly in thirteen, including seven ban states).[43] The number of abortions rose in both years.[44] If the bans were intended to reverse the fertility rate declines bemoaned by conservative pronatalists (discussed in chapter 2) and/or to reduce the number of abortions, they seem to have worked oppositely (though without the bans, the declines might have been steeper). In a time when concerns about economics, climate change, and more were already limiting births, the new knowledge that even a wanted pregnancy might kill them meant that many women (and their partners) who could choose were deciding not to risk it. As a Texas woman framed things on a 2024 Zoom call, and I paraphrase, "I'm thirty-eight with one child—we want another and the clock is ticking, but I'm also more at risk for complications, so we can't take the chance." Millions of women are making similar calculations.

Levels of stress have also been raised recently by widespread bans on GAC for minors and on gay rights generally (Don't Say Gay laws and LGBTQ+ book bans), and prohibitions on mentioning transgender people in public schools. Together these constitute additional fertility-and-sexuality-linked interventions into the private lives of American citizens.

Anti-gay laws are in effect in twenty-seven states, including all of the twenty states with abortion bans or gestational limits before twenty-two weeks, in January 2026.[45] These laws impact LGBTQ+ people of all genders and are deeply worrying for their families, who have been threatened with prison in some states. Some families have relocated, and others have refused jobs in ban states or didn't apply because they didn't want their kids growing up there, whether or not those kids were LGBTQ+[46]—decisions that also affect workforce and more.

Stunned by the rapid changes, the nation took a while to register the many harms unrolling. The 2024 election and the presidential candidacy of Kamala Harris shone light on the stories of women suffering and dying due to lack of access to abortion care. In GAC-ban states, conservative candidates focused their ads not on issues affecting most people but on stoking fears about biological boys on girls' sports teams (though few), leaving unexplored the stresses trans kids face or how trans sports issues might actually be addressed fairly. Post-2024, targeting of trans people continues—as a distraction from the many other harms being done nationally and because they challenge the patriarchal agenda.

When the 2024 election showed an eleven-point gender divide among voters aged eighteen to twenty-nine voting for Trump (males 49 percent; females 38 percent),[47] some women felt betrayed by their peers' apparent unconcern about their loss of rights. Some renounced hetero sex (the 4B movement) as a sure way to avoid unplanned pregnancy—a trend that may further lower fertility. Likewise, the threat of economic recession may further undermine pronatalist efforts, since historically recessions are contraceptive (fewer jobs, fewer babies). If by the time you read this the scene has changed radically, the principles I outline still apply.

THE WAY FORWARD: INVESTMENT, NOT EXTRACTION

The arrival of RBC has transformed all aspects of human society, because now, if people who have heterosexual intercourse don't want to have kids, they don't have to. Access to RBC means our love lives no longer funnel us into gender and class positions and roles as workers and consumers through the conduit of parenthood, often unplanned.

Whereas before human lives rotated around child-rearing largely by default, we're now discovering whether, when, and in what context people want families, and what that means. Such foundational change requires deep discourse and innovation to create new social models built around investment in, not extraction of, individual and community value.

This book pursues that mandate, exploring the ripple effects of new patterns of family formation and of investment in individuals, families, and communities—also characterizable as real domestic products. It analyzes our history and our moment, and outlines a way forward to what feminist political scientist Joan Tronto calls a *caring democracy*, where all can thrive. Backlash from those who've profited from old models is predictable and ongoing. But the pendulum swings both ways.

The chapters that follow track shifts in old fertility, gender, and sexuality models that are transforming inherited ideas of work, family, and society—analyzing their effects on political representation, wages, civic status, and our job-assignment processes. They show that democratizing access to civic voice and to jobs has been and can continue to be hugely positive for the families and individuals cared for in our homes, for the economy, and for the future of our planetary home as well.

Chapter 1 explores both how RBC and changing fertility patterns have transformed women's progress in political representation and the workforce, and the movement toward universal affordable childcare.

Chapter 2 offers detailed analysis of how fertility patterns have shifted due to RBC, and of the progressive degendering of work as a result. It explores both the interaction of recent fertility declines with the "tempo effect"—as young women and men wait a beat before starting families—and the pronatalist response.

Chapter 3 outlines the historical role played by lack of fertility control in reproducing poverty among both parents and children, tracks the recent huge decline in teen births and its transformative and positive effects as teens grow into adulthood, and analyzes the history and present of our capitalist economy's reliance on an exploitable, impoverished workforce, especially in the South.

Chapter 4 considers the historical division of work and wages through identity categories of gender and race that operate as castes, the challenge to old labor discounts and deferences created by recent efforts to degender work and pay, and the backlash against efforts to equalize opportunity.

Chapter 5 examines the evolving status of women's legal citizenship in recent decades and the devolution represented by the Dobbs and related judicial decisions that support undemocratic interests and a patriarchal religious agenda.

Chapter 6 explores the economics of gendered violence and coerced sex, their interaction with patriarchal capitalism, and their exclusion from most economic discourse.

Chapter 7 analyzes the impact of expanded claims to and acceptance of queer and nonbinary identities on shifts in gendered work dynamics (including procreation), and explores the possibilities of *gametogenesis*, a technology that could reshape LGBTQ+ (and all human) reproduction.

Chapter 8 is a case study of Texas, a leader in "care-less-ness," where competition for interstate business investment drives efforts to limit state services and impoverish large sections of its own populace, while also seeking to increase population—to grow cheap labor and census count.

Chapter 9 connects the dots between the recent expansion of human longevity and fertility declines, and observes their effects on workforce and the polity. It argues that the expanding labor demand from retirees who are living long while not reciprocating with their own labor is a new dynamic among humans. Supporting that dynamic requires the construction of a paid care infrastructure, which would both allow currently sidelined people of working age into the labor force and meet the growing demands for care and other forms of labor that longevity in retirement entails.

Chapter 10 proposes a way forward through building a national mixed-market care economy (a Wages for Care program) in which all can thrive, before it's too late. It provides a clear and hopeful plan for responding to the multiple challenges we face, identifying changes needed and demonstrating their feasibility.

Chapter 11 notes that without RBC, the already huge load on earth's environment would be much greater, and it argues that effective climate care requires input from women—long assigned the work of care—and other historically sidelined groups to organize global and local cooperative responses to the crisis. Caregivers were pointedly excluded from the businesses that made this crisis of care-less-ness, and only if they are not just at the decision-making table but also prominently involved in running it do we have a chance to save the world.

Everyone with a job, a sex life, a family, or hope for the future has an interest in the nexus of issues raised here and in our options for addressing them going forward from this tipping point.

1

STEPPING IN

Fertility Control, Representation, and the Childcare Gap

We must bear in mind the possibility that the greater opportunities open in the twentieth century to women may be quite withdrawn, and that we may return to a strict regimentation of women.
—Margaret Mead, *Sex and Temperament* (1935)

For millennia, women's traditional maternal functions—childbearing, child-rearing, and family management—have been widely used to define and exclude them (or us, as the case may be) from participation in both civic life and the paid economy. Instead, women have been expected and often compelled (each in her separate enclosure!) to conceive, bear, rear, and then deliver to their employers' doorsteps the workers of tomorrow—the most valuable of products—without compensation. For "free." This extraction of women's care labor at no cost to employers is the core dynamic of patriarchal capitalism's free riding. For most of that time, women, though acknowledged as citizens, have had little say in the rules of the society they steadily reproduce and no funds of their own to influence change.

The arrival of increasingly reliable birth control (RBC) over the past two hundred years has played a big role in changing that by reducing the overall number of births and shifting their timing in women's lives (a switch with environmental benefits too—see chapter 9). The ability to control their own fertility, rather than having it controlled by others, has allowed women to devote more time to activities other than child-rearing, including education and the paid labor force, where they fill spots their unborn additional children would have filled (a huge efficiency), increase the funds available to their families, raise their own status, join the polity, and in so doing move us closer to real democracy.

Contra the alarms raised lately around declining fertility rates, these changes have many positive effects on the workforce—both present and future. Adding into the public dialogue women's insights and perspectives around care—the realm of work to which they were long limited—in itself challenges old economic models designed specifically to exclude caring, as does their need of a family-support infrastructure in order to combine childbearing and careers. Such challenges have triggered transformative discussions of work and class (forwarded by organizations like the National Domestic Workers Alliance) and of how a care approach can mitigate human harms to the planet (led by ecofeminists like Vandana Shiva). All of these topics require input from all sectors of the American community, in hard-to-build forums where funds don't outweigh logic.

It's not a surprise that such change has spurred pushback from those invested in established hierarchies. As Margaret Mead noted nearly a century ago, women's rights could go either way in the years ahead (e.g., Iran in 1979), and the same is true for other long-excluded groups. Which way things go will depend on women's and their allies' use of the civic power they've accrued to date. Against a backdrop of rising climate pressures, there's much for the full community to discuss in order to find the best way forward to a future of mutual thriving. This book aims to forward dialogue on imagining and building that better future.

SCAFFOLDING THE TRANSITION INTO CIVIC LIFE

Until recently, women who were pushed into early childbearing (which was most) were denied both education and control of their own time, a combination that barred them from climbing the rungs of power into roles in government and business where they could represent their own concerns (see figure 1.1).

Locked into the private sphere, their insights and perspectives have not informed national debates until lately and still in limited ways. Likewise, people of color and diverse sexuality were long silenced, also for reasons linked to workforce and fertility exploitation, as we'll see. While society loses from these exclusions, those excluded lose most since, as Texas governor Ann Richards famously noted, in politics, "if you're not at the table, you're on the menu."

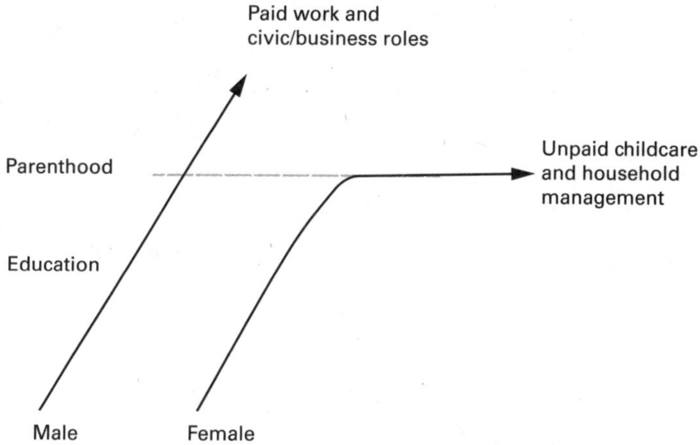

Figure 1.1 Historical effects of early fertility on gendered life roles. Source: Author.

Although women won the vote in the United States in 1920, that didn't guarantee that they would be participating actively in civic life anytime soon thereafter.[1] Instead, several more developments were needed, as suffragist Crystal Eastman predicted: she called for a degendering of work so both men and women combine housework with careers, reliable and accessible birth control (aka voluntary motherhood), and a motherhood stipend for those who step out of careers to raise kids.[2]

By 1990, seventy years after suffrage, women still held only 5.8 percent of the seats in Congress. But their representation there began to shift notably upward shortly thereafter, as figure 1.2 documents. That moment came in 1992, "the year of the woman," so-called because four new female senators raised the total to six (1 R, 5 D), following the national outcry over Anita Hill's revelations about sexual harassment at Clarence Thomas's Supreme Court confirmation hearing.

By 2024, just thirty-four years later, the proportion of women in Congress had risen to 28.4 percent. That recent figure is still far from women's 51 percent of the population, but it's a vast increase over 1990.

Although not the sole factor, advances in RBC played a huge role in spurring that upward shift—specifically the development of the Pill in 1960 (enabled by activist Margaret Sanger and philanthropist Katharine McCormick)[3] and access to safe, legal abortion in 1973 (after the *Roe v. Wade* decision). The upswing in representation began once these

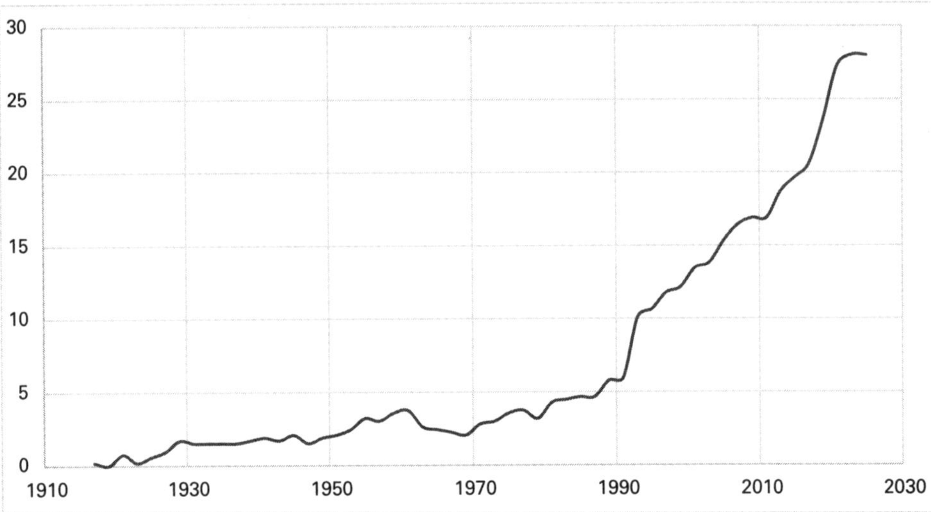

Figure 1.2 Percentage of women in Congress, 1917–2025. Data source: "History of Women in the U.S. Congress," Center for American Women and Politics, Eagleton Institute of Politics, Rutgers University-New Brunswick.

transformations had been in place long enough to allow sufficient numbers of women to delay or forgo having kids; progress through law school, local political offices, and/or policy jobs; and begin to win federal-level elections (figure 1.3).

As a Supreme Court majority acknowledged in its 1992 *Planned Parenthood v. Casey* opinion, "the ability of women to participate equally in the economic and social life of the Nation has been facilitated by their ability to control their reproductive lives."[4] Recently, several congresswomen have made clear that their ability to represent their constituents was enabled by their access to abortion.[5]

The growth of legislation providing access to education and legal equity also contributed, including the Equal Pay Act of 1963 and the Civil Rights Act of 1964, which prevent employment discrimination; Title IX (1972), which prevents discrimination based on sex in education; and the Equal Credit Opportunity Act (1974), which gives women access to credit. Such laws have eroded barriers to employment, as Eastman advised. Likewise, the gradual processes of building acceptance of women candidates over thousands of losing campaigns and of developing patronage channels

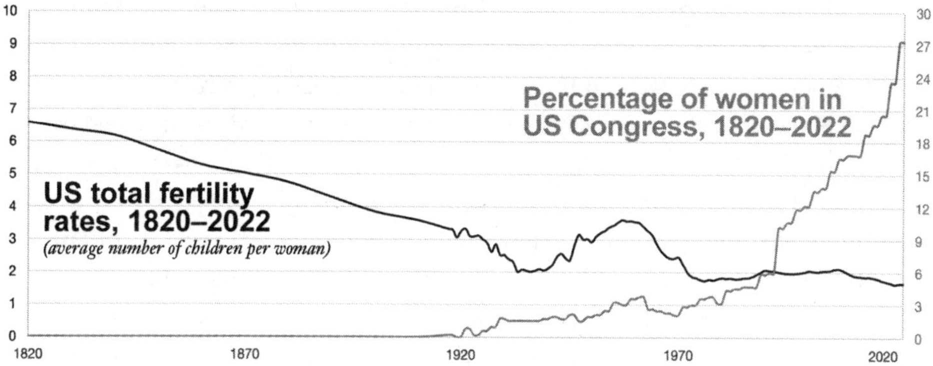

Figure 1.3 Percentage of congressional seats held by women and US total fertility rates, 1820–2022. Data source: Center for American Women and Politics, Eagleton Institute of Politics, Rutgers University and Our World in Data. Credit: Gabby Barucci/The Nation.

through women's-rights fundraising political action committees[6] created an infrastructure for female candidates' advancement into electoral politics (a process aided by women's expanded earnings). Women's political representation today is a direct effect of all these framework changes, pivoting around the freedom to choose whether and when to be a parent, enabled by RBC.

Of course, it's not only in elected office that women appear now in greater numbers. They've also risen in the ranks in all spheres of professional and civic life across the United States, and access to RBC has been key there too (see figure 4.1).[7] But elected officials set the rules for employment and create the supporting infrastructure, so having more voice in government for any group can herald change in other realms.

THE CHILDCARE PARADOX

Just as the right to vote wasn't enough on its own, the addition of RBC and legal supports didn't fully remove all barriers to women's labor force participation. While RBC has allowed many women to delay children in order to progress in careers, once they start families, they need good, affordable childcare to continue to work consistently (as in life, this will be a recurring refrain across this narrative).

While some childcare spots are available to some low-income families in the free federal Head Start program (begun in 1965) and through federally funded state-administered childcare subsidies (which partially cover costs),[8] childcare has been largely available only to those who could self-finance. Since it's pretty expensive (the 2024 national average was $12,000 per child), many new mothers who would have preferred to continue working have had to step out to provide care themselves, often derailing their careers and long-term earnings. Until recently, the lack of universal sliding-scale childcare combined with few women in government enforced a vicious cycle: because most women who started families did so in their teens or twenties, and because many of them didn't earn sufficient funds to access the full-time childcare that would let them focus on career or school while raising kids, there were too few women moving from graduate school into government and policy jobs and then into elected office—to build a family-support infrastructure.

Because they lacked a childcare infrastructure, they couldn't create one: a paradox. That lack has also barred women from participating fully in other industries.

The failure to create a childcare system wasn't because the United States didn't know how—an effective national system was developed quickly during World War II to allow women to staff factories. Although women petitioned to continue it postwar, President Truman refused, aiming to reduce competition for returning soldiers, though jobs were soon plentiful. Twenty-three years later, in 1968 President Nixon campaigned on a plan for free universal childcare for three- and four-year-olds so mothers could work. However, once the Comprehensive Childcare Development Act passed Congress, he faced conservative pushback (it was portrayed as a communist plot and anti-family), and he vetoed his own suggestion. A few years later, the US military built an extensive childcare system to provide for the families of soldiers, which still functions brilliantly. But despite many efforts since, no such national program has emerged, and families still struggle to find and afford childcare.

Instead of equitable support for all kids and families, the United States offers those who can manage it the right to pay in full for private childcare, while poor families battle over the limited subsidized spots. Those who can't do either often rely on relatives to fill in or on moms to stay home—cutting family income, often increasing household stress, and making them more vulnerable to DV, since they can't afford to leave if a partner becomes abusive.[9]

The dearth of affordable, good childcare in the United States led Danish sociologist Gosta Esping-Andersen to call the American women's liberation movement an "incomplete revolution," arguing that women's progress into civic life would be limited without a system similar to the one in his home country (a much smaller place, where free childcare began in the 1820s), which has had two female prime ministers to date.[10] More than a century before him, feminist Charlotte Perkins Gilman in her groundbreaking *Women and Economics* similarly observed that lack of childcare infrastructure would hobble women's economic independence.[11]

But despite that lack, over the past thirty-five years the delay of childbearing to later ages enabled by RBC has allowed some US women to move, at rising rates, into positions where they can begin to build that infrastructure, which can in turn allow still more women to participate in public life. RBC has served many as a shadow benefits system, allowing them to delay arrival of their first child until they earn enough to pay for childcare.[12] That was the case for the overwhelming majority of the women I interviewed for *Ready*, a book about later motherhood that I wrote a few years back.[13] Not that the delay pattern itself is desirable for all—many who wait encounter infertility and some would have preferred to start families sooner. But delay has proved a successful strategy for advancing both individuals and women as a group into civic life in our family-unfriendly context, with an aim to create a more family-friendly context with better options for all down the line.

RBC has reshaped the patriarchal scene, as more women of diverse backgrounds have completed their educations, established themselves in careers, and trickled up into policymaking roles in government and business. Their perspectives often turn out to be different from those of the men who have previously claimed to represent them, on the assumption that a woman's interests replicate those of the men around her. Their new and diverse insights contribute importantly to solving the many problems our world faces. But for many women, including those who had children earlier, access to both good childcare and good jobs has remained elusive.

If the more-complete feminist revolution that Gosta Esping-Andersen called for is to occur, the responsibility now falls to those women who could delay, to represent the interests of those who could not and to create that family-friendly next phase that can further expand democratic access. This would follow the "lifting as we climb" philosophy of African American women after the Civil War, a mutual aid effort whereby individuals who make advances for themselves use them to speed the progress of and expand the options available to the community. That is already happening at some localities: women with clout and their allies in New Mexico, Minnesota, Massachusetts, Oregon, Pennsylvania, Vermont, New York City, Seattle, and Washington, DC, among others, have instituted state and local funding mechanisms to expand federally funded childcare access in programs of varying sizes and pay structures.

But much remains to be done to create a full national family-support infrastructure, which could include not just childcare but also after-school care and summer care for older kids, day care and long-term care for the elderly and disabled, paid parental and sick leave, and paid in-home care where needed. While these involve up-front cost, they also generate value, profits, taxes, and economic growth, as we'll see in chapter 10, to cover the initial investments.

Expanding childcare remains a focus for many women leaders in order to expand women's participation in civic life, but anti-feminists oppose such measures using the opposite logic because they don't see democracy as an advantage. As the Boston Tea Partiers understood, crucial to getting any group's issues heard and acted upon is representation in government by sufficient numbers of its own members, not just others who claim to speak for them. Because in struggles for resources (essentially every political conversation) they rarely do.

Which isn't to say that all women agree on all or even most issues. Some women, whether or not they recognize problems with the status quo, see their interests as best served through allegiance to the patriarchal powers that still be, doubting that change will occur or, if it does, that it will bring benefits for their families and seeking to maintain what they have. Across all cultures, women have often been patriarchy's enforcers based on similar logic.[14] As with both 1970s antifeminist activist Phyllis Schlafly and the Aunts in Margaret Atwood's *The Handmaid's Tale*, being a mouthpiece for restrictions on women's rights can allow some women opportunities for status they wouldn't otherwise have. Others endorse the patriarchal guidelines they've grown up with, if their lives are satisfying, or don't want to leave even if they do see problems because they love their communities or can't imagine change. Some have felt their life choices are belittled by expanding women's choices outside family formation and so oppose such choices for others. Conversely, the resignation of Rep. Marjorie Taylor Greene (R-GA) in late 2025 over the efforts of what she called "a lot of weak Republican men" to "always try to marginalize the strong Republican women" and similar displeasure expressed by her peers with their treatment by Speaker Mike Johnson (R-LA) suggest that further shifts may occur.[15]

Often those who fight hardest for change are women who face bias on multiple fronts and don't have the same option that others may have to endorse the gender status quo in exchange for other privileges. But reliance on those with the most to lose to do the hard work of change is unfair, dispiriting for them, and finally ineffective. As in all labor fights, only unity across class, race, gender, sexuality, and party positions can bring together sufficient numbers from all sectors to pitch in with resources and energy to enable real change. That only becomes possible when divide-and-conquer narratives are replaced with clarity on how mutual thriving serves all.

ACROSS THE AISLE

Convincing people to invest in new patterns involves providing them with both escape from immediate harms and a vision of long-term improvements. Increasingly, the benefits of including the voices of women of all backgrounds across society are clear to many, and over time their presence in public life has become more normalized. But as elections and recent history have shown, people may support reproductive rights but still vote for candidates who oppose them, if other concerns take precedence.

Nonetheless, by definition, women with caregiving responsibilities bring structural challenges to the status quo when they enter the public sphere, which must be addressed if they are to remain there in substantial numbers. So historically, economically and politically conservative women have sometimes collaborated with progressive women across party lines on gender-linked issues.

Such was the case in 1973 when Kay Bailey (R) and Sarah Weddington (D) coauthored the first anti-rape bill in the Texas Legislature. In Washington in 1977, the bipartisan Congressional Caucus for Women's Issues, founded by fifteen female representatives, committed to improving the lives of women and families and to putting their differences aside to do so. Among their accomplishments are the following: the Pregnancy Discrimination Act (1978), the Retirement Equity Act (1984), the Civil Rights Restoration Act (1987), the Women's Business Ownership Act (1988), the Breast and Cervical Cancer Mortality Prevention Act (1990), the Child Support Enforcement Act (1992), the Mammography Quality Standards Act (1992), the Family and Medical Leave Act (1993), the Violence Against Women Act (1994), and the Commission on the Advancement of Women and Minorities in Science, Engineering, and Technology Development Act (1998). But as yet, no national childcare act.

In the twenty-first century, partisanship has grown, but nonetheless, five South Carolina female state senators stood together across party lines against the abortion bans put forward there in 2023. Although they lost their effort to block it, the six-week ban ultimately voted into law by an all-male majority was not a total ban due to their efforts. The three Republicans among them were then primaried in 2024, all losing to male challengers.

Over the past few decades, as the presence of female policymakers in the rooms where things happen has increased, many of them (and their male allies) have named and worked to further address the needs of women and their families. For example, the Paycheck Fairness Act was first proposed in 1997 by Rep. Rosa DeLauro, and she and partners have proposed it in every session since. That bill following up on the 1963 Equal Pay Act to ensure that there are enforcement mechanisms by which "women can challenge pay discriminations and hold employers accountable" still hasn't been enacted. But as the numbers of women in the legislature have grown, it has received increasingly attentive hearings: it passed in the House in 2007, 2009, and 2019; in 2021 it passed again and for the first time was referred to a committee in the Senate. (It helps that the growing numbers of women are largely Democrats, as that party is historically more receptive to equal pay and to female leadership, so it is more likely to pass in times when Democrats, and their larger proportion of women, control the House.)

AT THE THRESHOLD OF CRITICAL MASS

As women's voices have grown more numerous in policy discussions, they approach what group-dynamics theorists call "critical mass" (ballparked as roughly 30 percent)[16]—the point at which they could gather support both from their own ranks and from allies, who suddenly see women's concerns in a new light of possibility because they're endorsed by a sufficiently large portion of the group. That's what happened with the universal sliding-scale childcare proposal in the Build Back Better Act of 2021, which lost by just one vote, when Joe Manchin (a coal business owner) broke with his party, arguing that he couldn't support the "entitlement mentality"[17] that would result (assuming Americans aren't entitled to a chance to thrive and disliking the act's clean energy focus).[18]

And indeed, dynamics have shifted as many women of all backgrounds have brought an ethic of care into the civic sphere.[19] Such an ethic has long been instilled as part of women's "job" description as members of their gender, though its principles frequently conflict with an economic status quo that depends on exploitative profiteering, often involving direct harm to women and children—most frequently in the forms of poverty, denial of resources, and physical assault. In daily life, unpaid, caregiving women are expected to provide some balm for capitalism's harms, as Jessica Calarco has noted.[20] But they can only treat symptoms.

The extent to which poverty and living in impoverished neighborhoods full of desperate people are not just "hard" but also directly traumatizing to all who suffer through them has been too little acknowledged in discussing American capitalism. Although male family members are accountable for any violence they impose on relatives, they too may be traumatized by poverty, stress, and violence, spurring violent reactions. Efforts to build a care infrastructure aim to counter that exploitation and trauma in order to expand women's access to jobs that can help support their families and move them out of dependency and also to increase the services and resources available to men.

To date, most such efforts have met with resistance from the business community, specifically because many companies don't like the idea of paying (through taxes) for the care work so long provided by women for "free" or for sharing more of the fruits of their success with their workers. Business's commitment to the status quo translates to keeping low-income workers and their families in poverty—despite claims to want to help everyone succeed. Likewise, many business leaders don't want care-focused individuals in policymaking roles, where they might offer critiques of and solutions to the care-less aspects of current systems, which they believe benefit them.

But companies aren't the only resistant ones; men who feel they benefit from it may also resist changing the model of female dependency on and service to men. The 2025 campaigns by Christian nationalists to rescind the nineteenth amendment and push women out of the workforce reflect this attitude. Although in the best cases marriages have operated as partnerships, often they have not been—and even when they were, there have been clear role and status differences. Many women have suffered disrespect, expectations of servitude (the housework that's "never done"), and DV (the rampancy of abuse by intoxicated husbands spurred the temperance movement and Prohibition [1920–1933]).

Women have also been required to perform public and private gratitude. As feminist theorist Silvia Federici explained in 1974, "We [women] are all in a servant relation with respect to the whole male world. . . . ('Smile, honey, what's the matter with you?' is something every man feels entitled to ask you.)"[21] This is different from common civility. Having half the world as your acknowledged inferiors, obliged to dress to please you, to anticipate your desires in advance, and to recognize your superiority in every encounter with a submissive smile signaling acceptance of the status quo, is a luxury that accrues to *power over* others that some men seem unready to relinquish. Since no one behaves submissively unless they have to, maintaining women's dependency is key to ensuring that this continues.

Deference from all lower-ranked groups supports a feeling of superiority in those deferred to that is in itself experienced as compensation,[22] tallied on the same kind of nonpecuniary patriarchal balance sheet where care work has operated for ages, within a social economy of status. When a woman is not compensated for her home labor, her husband's paycheck reflects the value of that work as does his employer's bottom line, and both husbands and employers win status through contrast with the unpaid women.[23] Although the balance sheets for unpaid work are invisible, they're part of the real economy. The current pushback against women's progress is a last gasp attempt to preserve the old deferences and discounts, before the balance shifts entirely.

2

TIMING CHANGE

Delayed Motherhood, Workforce Gains, Fertility Declines, and the Pronatalist Response

Save for the possibly relevant fact that not one of them had a child, four more incongruous characters [than Jane Austen, George Eliot, and Charlotte and Emily Brontë] could not have met.

—Virginia Woolf, *A Room of One's Own* (1929)

To better understand contemporary dynamics around reliable birth control (RBC), let's start with a look back. Between 1800 and 1900, what was initially a high US birth rate relative to many European nations declined notably, from an average of 7 babies per woman to an average of 3.5. Since then it's fallen further—to 2 in 2000, and to 1.6 in 2024. Over the past two centuries, RBC has become markedly more effective: where previously condoms made of sheep bladders assisted some, they weren't fully reliable (or comfortable) or widely available. Charles Goodyear's vulcanization of rubber in 1839 led to the development of better-functioning "rubbers" and later of cervical caps and diaphragms. But these also weren't available to all. For couples in the nineteenth century, abortion by various means (purgative botanicals, poisons, douching, surgery, falls, and other methods) was also widely used to end pregnancies before what was called *quickening*—the point when a fetus could be felt moving and before which it was considered nonviable.

Physicians of the time estimated that one in every five pregnancies in the United States was being aborted previability between 1840 and 1890.[1] While in 1820 abortion was legal in all states, an active campaign to ban it was conducted from 1857 onward by medical doctors (mostly male) focused on ousting their "quack" competitors (many of them female), defining fetal life as starting at conception, blocking women from the profession, and keeping America majority white Protestant (most of the women aborting were of that group). The doctors' efforts succeeded, and by 1910 abortion was illegal in all states.[2] The fertility rate did not rise as a result, however, because over the same time span, contraception and other means of preventing conception had become more effective, more available, and more widely understood by couples, whether married or not. And many people still accessed abortion despite its ban, sometimes fatally.[3] Abstinence from hetero sex, by choice or happenstance, by increasing numbers of women who stayed single also played a part.

WOMEN IN THE WORKFORCE

The reduction in births enabled some progress for women in the workforce over the nineteenth and early twentieth centuries, as did the expansion of women's education. But when the suffrage amendment passed in 1920 after seventy-two years of struggle, some of the energy around feminist progress abated. While women's labor force participation grew somewhat through the Depression, it rose sharply during World War II when women assisted the victory by subbing for soldiers in US factories. Then when soldiers returned, many women were pushed out, often unwillingly.

From the mid-1950s through the 2000s, women's labor force participation took off again (rising from a trough of 38.9 percent in January 1955 to a twentieth-century high of 77.3 percent in April 2000, for women twenty-five to fifty-four years old) whereas the participation of men twenty-five to fifty-four declined (from 97.5 percent to 91.7 percent) in the same span, in large part due to reductions in manufacturing jobs gendered male. Women's twenty-first-century rate then stayed fairly steady, reaching a low of 73.3 in September 2015 but then trending up (excluding COVID); it was 77.7 in August 2025. Men's labor-force participation continued to fall from 2000 to 2014 (to 87.9) but has risen since then to 89.8 percent (August 2025).[4] In this age group, 6.1 percent of men and 15.7 percent of women were part-time workers in 2023—with the lack of affordable childcare again affecting the difference.[5] So what changed to allow that big change in the second half of the twentieth century?

FERTILITY RATE SHIFTS

Recent fertility stats can help frame the workforce discussion. The chart in figure 2.1 represents the number of children born per one thousand "fertile women" (a demographic term for women aged fifteen to forty-four) for each year from 1910 to 2024: the General Fertility Rate (GFR).

Diverse factors have impacted the shifts demonstrated below. Starting at 126.8 in 1910, the period of decline to about 1940 includes World War I, the 1919 pandemic, and the Depression, all of which affected births. After World War II, the baby boom (1946–1964) rebuilt the workforce and the economy, zooming to its peak of 122.9 in 1957 (my birth year). That boom had already lost steam when the hormonal birth control pill was introduced on Mother's Day in 1960 (the year my sister and sole sibling arrived). The rate continued to fall sharply—to 87.9 births in 1970, 81.6 in 1971, 73.1 in 1972, and 65 in 1976 (nearly halving the peak)—and then remained fairly steady until 2007, when it again began declining nearly every year, down to a new low GFR of 53.8 in 2024.

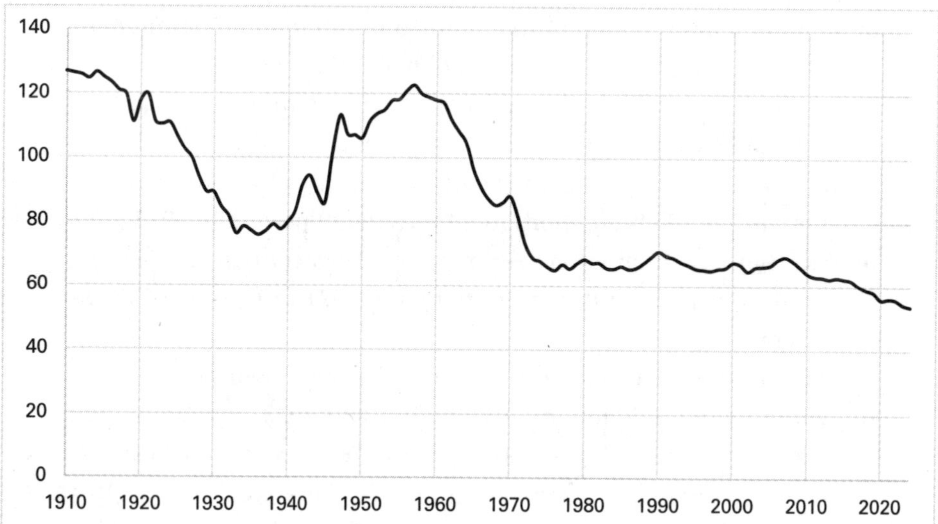

Figure 2.1 US general fertility rate, 1910–2024. Births per 1,000 women, aged 15–44. Data source: CDC Birth Data. (See online reference list for details on CDC documents consulted, and see https://wonder.cdc.gov database for online data from 1995 through 2024.)

As we'll see further on (figure 2.4), the reduction in births since the baby boom (along with expanding longevity) paved the way for many women from all groups to join the labor force and for those women and many men of color to compete for good jobs formerly held almost exclusively by white men. That's not just because women with no or fewer kids were able to work; the smaller group of workers aging up into the labor force also meant there were not enough skilled white men to fill the open positions, since the demand for labor to provide services in all fields remained high, due both to the size and wealth of the boomer generation and to retirees' increasing number and longevity. Women and people of color filled the need, and their own increased earnings then further expanded demand for labor.

The change in the steady birth pattern after 2007 began with the Great Recession (December 2007–June 2009), a contraceptive in itself, followed by improvements in the effectiveness and delivery of hormonal contraception—including the expanded availability of long-acting reversible contraception (LARCs), Plan B emergency contraception, and, though not reflected in the data in the chart, the 2024 introduction of the over-the-counter Pill (Opill). The Food and Drug Administration (FDA) approved Mifepristone as safe for use in medication abortions in 2000—in clinics only. Remote provision via mail for pregnancies of up to ten-weeks' gestation became available during COVID, proving its safety. In 2021 the FDA lifted the restrictions permanently, and medication abortions rose to 63 percent of all US abortions in 2023, from 39 percent in 2017.[6] The number and rate of abortions also rose post-Dobbs, from 11.6 per one thousand women aged fifteen to forty-four in 2021 to 15.9 in 2023 (versus 29.3 in 1981).[7]

Sterilization (permanent contraception) has also risen post-Dobbs—with tubal ligations doubling between 2022 and 2023 and vasectomies tripling, though women's rates remain higher.[8] Rises occurred in all states but were greater in ban states.[9] In one study, some subjects' fear that access to sterilization might be blocked spurred them to action. Another study found that users included people who had previously expressed lack of interest in children and those who previously wanted them.[10] Although both procedures may sometimes be reversed, any such births would be planned. Both increased abortions and increased sterilizations undercut pronatalist goals to raise birth rates.

Globally, fertility rate declines over the past two centuries were due not just to improved birth control but also to lessened demand for births, caused by

- improved public health—so more children survive and fewer births are needed by families and society;
- improved technology, lowering need for farm and other manual laborers;
- the democracy movement, which led women to challenge their subordination; and
- expanded longevity, allowing women to have children later and freeing them to enter the paid workforce.

Against the backdrop of a world in which the population has exploded from one billion in 1825, to two billion in 1925, then eight billion in 2025, declines in births have had positive effects on the workforce, on democracy, and on the climate—for starters. That is not the narrative you hear from contemporary pronatalists, many of them conservative. Their discourse forecasts an underpopulated next generation with too few young workers to support Social Security checks for the future's many retirees. It also frequently plays on racist fears of "replacement," as the non-Hispanic white proportion of the population has declined from 90 percent in 1950 to 56 percent in 2024.[11] To change these trends, it aims to push women of all races into bearing more babies, earlier (though with public emphasis on white women), and, not coincidentally, out of civic life.

But the data cited by those who claim that the world is heading toward a lonely hell in a low-birth-rate handbasket speak more complexly. While it's true that over the seventeen years between 2007 and 2024 the US fertility rate declined by 22.4 percent (after three fairly steady decades between 1975 and 2005), the fall is largely due to women in their teens and early twenties using RBC to delay the birth of their first child in order to finish their schooling and establish careers (as we'll see in more detail in chapter 3). Similar dynamics are occurring in other developed nations (though in some less developed nations, rates remain high).

Many of those who delay are likely to have children later, and they'll likely be better situated to support them. But many considering whether and when to have kids still hesitate, as demographer Peter McDonald outlines, due to "the high cost of children, the risk of making long-term

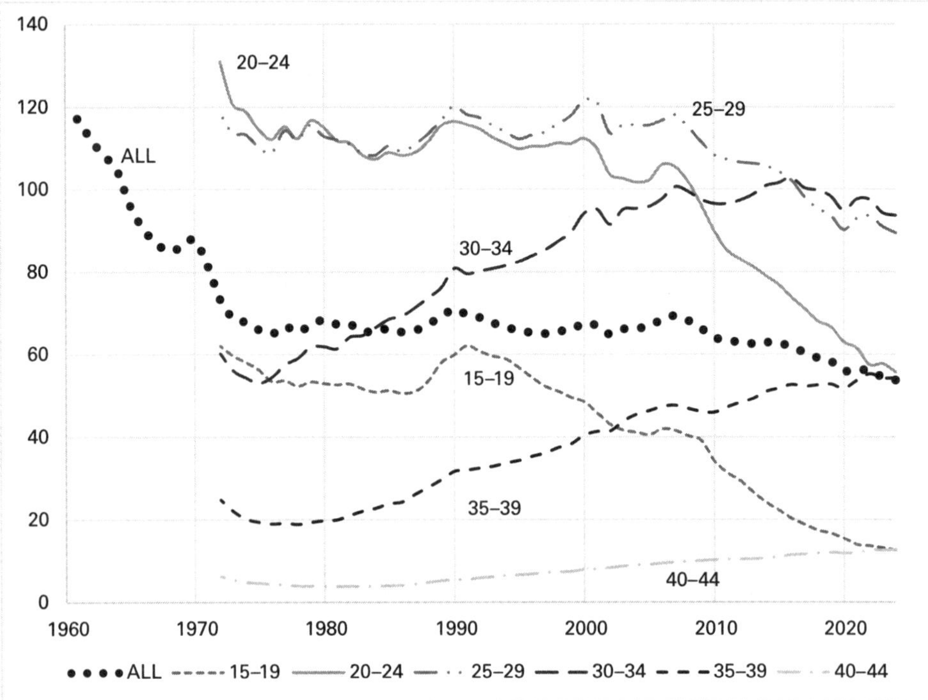

Figure 2.2 US fertility rates: GFR, 1960–2024; and by age of mother, 1972–2024. Births per 1,000 women, aged 15–44. Data source: CDC Birth Data. (See online reference list for details on CDC documents consulted for data prior to 1995, and see https://wonder.cdc.gov database for online data from 1995 through 2024.)

commitments in the face of an uncertain future, and the uneven nature of gender equity."[12] Others just don't want kids, and now have that option while maintaining an active hetero sex life, or have still other worries. Unless these concerns are effectively addressed soon, we can anticipate low fertility rates for a while to come—calling for innovations to fill the coming gaps in worker supply, which we'll explore further on.

Figure 2.2 breaks out US fertility rates by age of mother from 1972 on, indicating that the timing and rate of births has changed substantially over that time period. As noted, in 2024, US women overall had 53.8 births/one thousand women aged fifteen to forty-four, down from 118 in 1960.

Demographers also track what's called the annual "total fertility rate" (TFR)—the total number of children the average US woman would have if

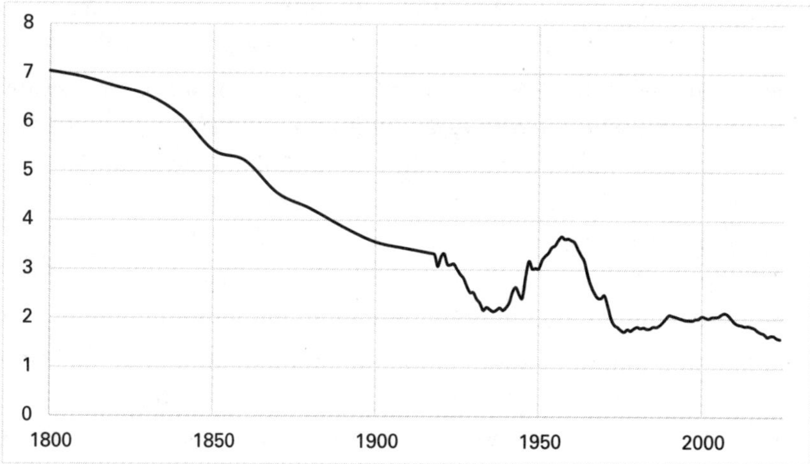

Figure 2.3 US total fertility rates, 1800–2024. Data source: CDC Birth Data. (See online reference list for details on CDC documents consulted, and see the CDC WONDER database https://wonder.cdc.gov for online data from 1995 through 2024.)

she procreated at that year's rate for each age band, across her life.[13] While in 1800 the average US woman had 7 children, she had 1.73 in 1976, 2.12 in 2007, and 1.59 in 2024 (figure 2.3).

TFR doesn't report the number of babies women in these years actually had over their lives (their "completed fertility"), just the average of the age-specific fertility rates in a given year. While in the past the TFR has fairly accurately predicted the number of births per woman long term, its ability to forecast may be less reliable when the age bands in which people have children are altering markedly, as now. We won't know until roughly fifteen years on how many young women who delayed births between 2008 and 2024 (lowering the TFR) will end up having babies—perhaps bearing the same total as if they'd started earlier (which would raise both the TFR in that year and their completed fertility)—or fewer, or more.

DEGENDERING WORKFORCE

While figures 2.1, 2.2, and 2.3 show declines (fewer births and smaller families), that hasn't meant that the proportion or even the numbers of paid workers are down commensurately. Instead, even though the fertility rate declined, the population overall has grown steadily (from 180 million in 1960 to 340 million in 2025)[14] due to the many baby boomers and their children (fewer but still many), the expanding elder population (living longer, while working less—see chapter 9), and immigration. That means that demand for workers to serve that population has grown too (expanding the labor force from 70 million in 1960 to 170 million in 2025).

So, given the decline in births, who filled the extra labor-force spots over the decades in between?

Since the 1960s, millions of US women of all backgrounds using RBC were among those who did (while some US men formerly sidelined by racism and immigrants also accessed a wider range of jobs).[15] Many women crossed old gendered work lines and effectively filled the place of at least one of their unborn sons or brothers in the paid workforce, a huge efficiency—and given tech advances, one well-trained worker could complete increasingly more tasks than previously. Simultaneously, men have also crossed old gender lines to do increasing proportions of unpaid home care work.

Figure 2.4 summarizes the change in the gendering of paid market work and unpaid family care work, and the effect of that change on need for workers in both categories. On the left, across two generations, a family supplies the workforce with four paid workers under the old gendered-work model—the father and three sons (who may work simultaneously for several decades)—and four unpaid home-based caregivers—the mother and three daughters. On the right are three variations of a family with

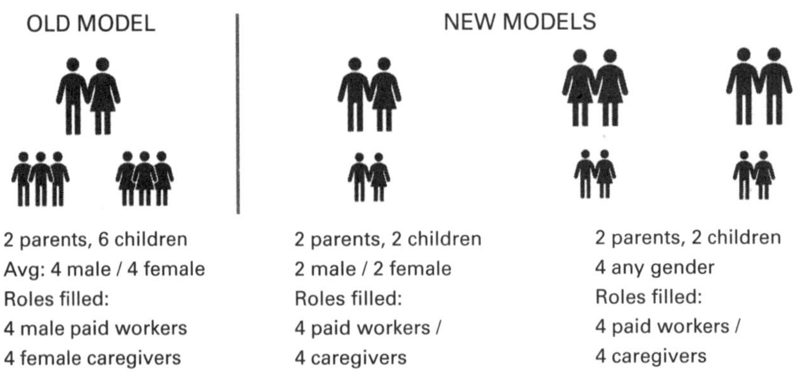

Figure 2.4 Gendered and degendered work assignments for paid and unpaid workers over two generations: Four family scenarios. Source: Author.

two parents and two children, all of whom also supply four paid workers over two generations, but under the new model in which both parents work in the market for pay and share unpaid care work at home after hours, while hiring childcare during the day. The new model lessens the inefficiencies and inequities of the old gendered task model, in a context where RBC is available and additional children are not needed to work on a farm or at a small business.

Historically, lower-income women have often worked for pay in addition to covering care work at home, anticipating current dynamics, though many in all income levels worked at home for no pay, exclusively. This chart portrays the shift from the exclusive unpaid care work model to the degendered paid work model, across income levels.

Whereas the old model expands population over time, the new model does not, thus lowering the burden on planetary resources. (If families produce two workers in each generation, the overall population of workers would remain roughly static, though altered career lengths could shift totals.)

As tasks are increasingly degendered, having two children today can accomplish roughly the same workforce effect as having six previously—at least in theory, since the number of paid workers generated from the family unit remains the same (that's four in the examples in figure 2.4, assuming overlap of generations in the workforce, ongoingly).

While in 1975 about 20 percent of US children under age five were in some form of nonparental childcare, in 2024 it was much higher.[16] While many are in unpaid care with grandparents, the increased funds exchanged for those in paid care now go directly into GDP, growing the economy and beginning to articulate in cash the value of the work that was being done all along, unacknowledged, part of which is now available as exchange value in addition to its use value. The new funds earned both by caregivers (most of them women currently) and by the women whose children are now in care, freeing them to work in other fields, provides those women with increased funds of their own and increased social status. Further expanding the affordability of care would substantially increase its use and these effects.

Of course when families access childcare during the workday, even with fewer children born, lots of family care work remains after work hours.[17] Historically, much of that has been done by working mothers, who had either part- or full-time jobs with varying levels of childcare and then worked a "second shift" after hours.[18] While fathers now share more of the second shift, it remains an uneven split,[19] an issue cited by women hesitating to have kids now.

But the core problem for many caregiving parents who would like to work remains the total unaffordability of childcare. As one young mom on a subsidized childcare waitlist put it when asked if more affordable spots were needed, "Oh my god, yes!"[20]

Were childcare to be made affordable to all, the additional caregiving jobs involved could be filled in part by the 22 percent of women who are not currently in the workforce (there would be childcare-center positions for roughly 14 percent of those new workers released into the workforce by childcare).[21] If making families more affordable led to more births among women currently working, still further childcare positions could open. The process would further the documentation of the value of care work in the GDP; expand state, local, and federal tax bases; give the new childcare workers a good wage to help their families; and raise women's status across the board.

While the movement of women into the workplace where they can earn has been a necessary step in the process of their acquiring civic status in the contemporary context, work need not be an end point in itself; some people would prefer to stay home with their kids, especially while they're small. A motherhood stipend of the kind Crystal Eastman outlined in 1920 (terms to be determined through public dialogue) could be another form of paid childcare in addition to childcare in centers; it would allow some women to stay at home with young children with less loss of independence and civic status than is currently associated with that. However, without firm guardrails it might also create long-term negative economic effects for those women, as previously.

THE RIPPLE EFFECTS OF DELAY

The Pill introduced the possibility of reliably delaying births, but how long women would want to delay has been a learning process for everyone. In the interviews for my study of later moms, it became clear that women feel "ready" for family at different points, often depending on when and whether they've completed their educations, found a partner for the long term or given up that search, seen enough of the world that they don't feel shortchanged staying home with kids—and can afford good childcare. Public health advances have increased longevity and allowed many people, male and female, to reschedule their lives to start their families later, through birth or adoption. The increasingly acceptable option of single motherhood (linked to women's greater ability to support children) has also played in.

Since 1970, the average age at first birth for women has increased steadily, from 21 to 27.6 in 2024, with many waiting late into their thirties and even forties (a smaller cohort) to start families, taking the risk of increasing likelihood of infertility with advancing age between 35 and 42, after which very few have children without aid.[22] As a consequence of that delay and planning, new parents are less likely to have to take several jobs to pay for diapers and baby food than in the past or to rely on aid. If they go to college, per one study, women who delay kids gain 12 percent more in earnings per year of delay after completing their BAs, fattening their family's resources across their lifetimes.[23] For instance, if a young woman, let's call her Viola, graduates at 22 and then waits nine years to start her family at age 31.2 (the average age when female college grads had their first child in 2024), she'd make more than double the salary across her career than if she'd had her first child right after graduating.[24]

Those funds would also give her a different status in her relationships. In my interviews with later mothers, many told me they'd seen their own moms stuck in bad marriages they couldn't afford to leave because they didn't have sufficient marketable skills to support themselves and their children on their own. Their observant daughters delayed marriage and kids to the point where they could leave if they needed to. As a result, the power balance in their marriages differed from that in their parents' marriages from the start because it wasn't based in financial dependency. Dads also had it better, these women felt, because their wives' earnings meant that they weren't burdened with all the financial responsibility and spent more time with their kids.

Although news stories about a drop in total births may sound like a rise in people choosing against families, when that drop occurs among

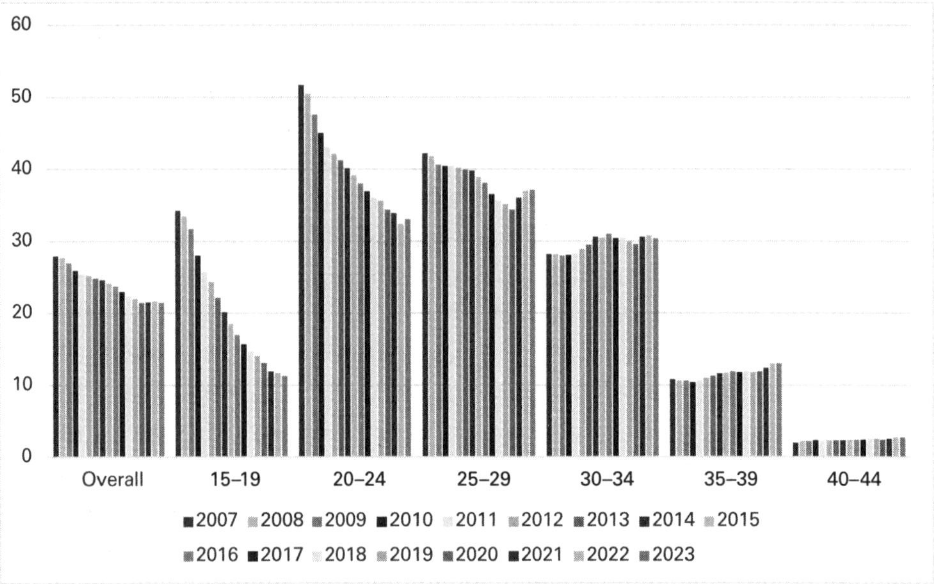

Figure 2.5 US first birth rates by age of mother, 2007–2023. Births per 1,000 women, aged 15–44, by age band. Data source: CDC Birth Data, via the WONDER database, at https://wonder.cdc.gov.

younger women, it often signals the beginning of a delay cycle called the "tempo effect"[25]—meaning not that Viola will have no kids, just that she's waiting a beat to begin. The average US family with children in 2023 had two.[26] Whether Viola starts a family later and how many children she has will depend on factors such as economic climate, her potential partner, if they encounter infertility, childcare availability and cost, pandemics, climate change effects, and whether she likes kids. Any children she has later will likely arrive into more settled and better-funded circumstances than if she'd had them when she was younger (though averages tell little about how particular situations will play out).[27]

Figure 2.5 tracks the ages when American women had a first child, from 2007 to 2023—documenting major declines among women starting their families in their teens and twenties, followed several years later by upward trends among women in their thirties and forties. These delay patterns gesture at a tempo effect, but as yet the decline in new young moms (second and third columns from left) is not balanced by an equal rise in new later mothers (columns further right).

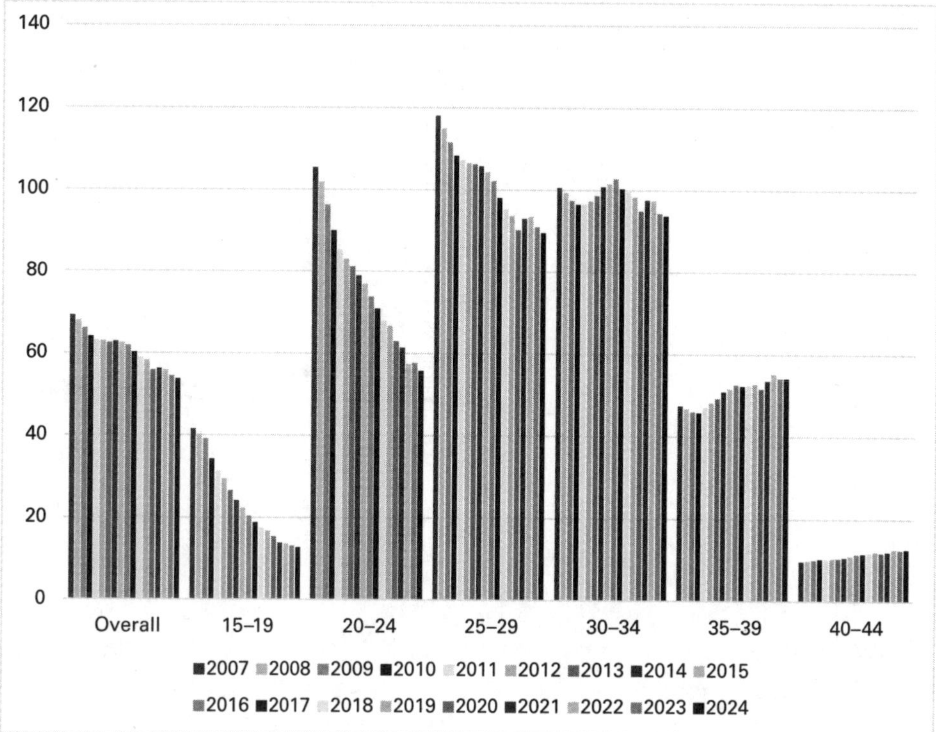

Figure 2.6a US fertility rates by age of mother, 2007–2024—columns. Births per 1,000 women, aged 15–44, by age band. Data source: CDC Birth Data, via the WONDER database, at https://wonder.cdc.gov.

Declines among young women in 2008 (the start of the Great Recession) and after began to be followed thirteen years later (2021) by small rises in first births among women in older age groups. If women who've established at work feel economically and personally ready to start families later, we could see increasing overall fertility rates even though rates continue low among younger women; but other inhibitory factors may also impact long-term trends downward. While overall the GFR continued to decline in 2023 and 2024, the data aren't available at press time on whether the 2023 rise in first-birth rates among women aged twenty to twenty-four continued in 2024.

Figure 2.6a illustrates how all births play out across age bands, not just first births. Those who start their families earlier may then have kids at varying intervals over decades.

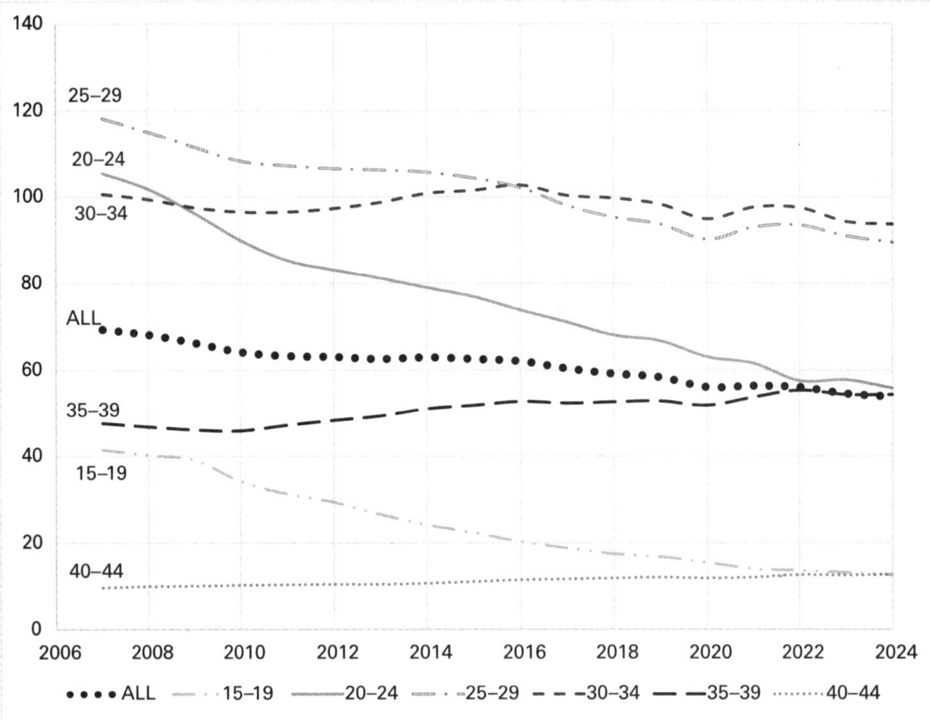

Figure 2.6b US fertility rates by age of mother, 2007–2024—lines. Births per 1,000 women, aged 15–44, by age band. Data source: CDC Birth Data, via the WONDER database, at https://wonder.cdc.gov.

Figure 2.6b uses the same data set but formats it to track converging fertility rates for women aged 20–24 and 35–39; and crossing rates for both 25–29 and 30–34 (in 2016) and 15–19 and 40–44 (in 2024).

DOBBS'S EFFECT ON FERTILITY THROUGH 2024

While fertility trends since 2007 responded to multiple factors, the introduction of state abortion bans, starting in 2021 in Texas and then, post-Dobbs, in fluctuating numbers of additional states added another set of complications. Pre-Dobbs in 2021 and 2022 (Dobbs in June 2022 did not much affect births in that year), national fertility rates fell among US women overall and among women aged fifteen to twenty-four, but rose or were steady among women aged twenty-five and higher. But in 2023, at least partly in response to the Dobbs decision, rates fell both overall and in all age groups except for a slight rise among women aged twenty to twenty-four. Overall rates fell in all states—with and without bans, for a decline of 2.6 percent in 2023. But examined by sector, fertility rates fell only 2 percent in the ban sector, while they fell 3 percent in the ban-free sector, indicating substantial difference in outcomes in the two zones.[28] In 2024, the decline continued, though at a slower pace at 1.3 percent overall. Rates rose by varying amounts in thirteen states (including seven in the ban sector and six in the ban-free, indicating that a variety of factors were in play, yet to be analyzed).

The 2023–2024 declines suggest that many women and their partners adjusted their fertility behavior in recognition of the altered options for family planning. These adjustments included the multiple factors cited earlier (including travel to access abortions in other states or through self-managed abortions at home; increased vigilance around contraception; permanent contraception through tubal ligation and vasectomy). Additionally, some will have refrained from sex; some moved out of ban states; some who intended to become pregnant chose not to, fearing doctors would not render aid if needed; and some women died while pregnant when doctors failed to assist with pregnancy complications.[29] But while fertility fell, some women in ban states were nonetheless forced to bear children they weren't ready for. Whether the 2023 and 2024 rates would have fallen less, more, or risen in different age bands had there been no bans is not visible in the data.

With so many new factors in play, the fertility scene is not comparable to that of past years, and it will continue to shift as the laws, resources, and economics across states and the nation morph further.

DECLINING GLOBAL FERTILITY

These complexities are all part of the background to contemporary discussions of fertility in the United States, and many of them are also active worldwide. As noted, the TFRs in most developed countries have fallen markedly recently. The tempo effect plays in—so there may be future rises in births to later mothers, but the likelihood is great that they will not equal the initial declines, as some people prefer staying childfree.

National policy decisions around affordable childcare, climate change remediation, and gender equity will affect outcomes.

Figure 2.7 provides a snapshot of the shift in TFRs for a representative range of countries around the globe (1950–2023). The U.N. estimates the global TFR at 2.2 live births per woman in 2024, down from 4.8 in 1950.[30]

Some nations that have had low rates for a while (including Japan, Italy, Germany, and South Korea) differ from those where they've declined more recently, in being more notably sexist (few men share childcare and policies block women with families from careers). This suggests that making national policy *more* sexist (by reducing women's reproductive rights, access to good jobs, etc.) might further decrease national fertility, even if the intent is opposite.

From 1989 to 2009, the United States stayed steady around a TFR prediction of 2.1 lifetime births per woman (known as "replacement level"). However, since then the TFR has declined—to 1.59 in 2024, spurring concern and much pronatalist discourse here. That rate parallels those of New Zealand, France, Australia, and Turkey, though it's still higher than those of ninety other nations, including in descending order Denmark, Argentina, Russia, Canada, Japan, China, and South Korea (at 0.75).

Nations that have more experience with population issues (including those where devastating wars on their territory meant that civilians died along with soldiers) have had policies in place to encourage more births for some time. Chief among them have been family-support infrastructures (including various constellations of childcare, family allowances, and baby bonuses), which aim to encourage procreation by making child-rearing less expensive and/or allowing women to combine careers and kids. The US failure to do likewise makes us an outlier among developed nations and has had the effect, as feminist economist Nancy Folbre and feminist labor and reproductive rights activist Jenny Brown have noted, of disincentivizing childbearing, since women's careers and wages suffer when they commit to child-rearing without childcare support.[31]

But recent declines in the TFRs of countries around the world that do provide substantial care indicate that other factors play in as well—including issues of gender inequity, climate, war, and other looming dangers. The option introduced by expanded longevity to reschedule such life events as child-rearing for later in life through delayed family formation

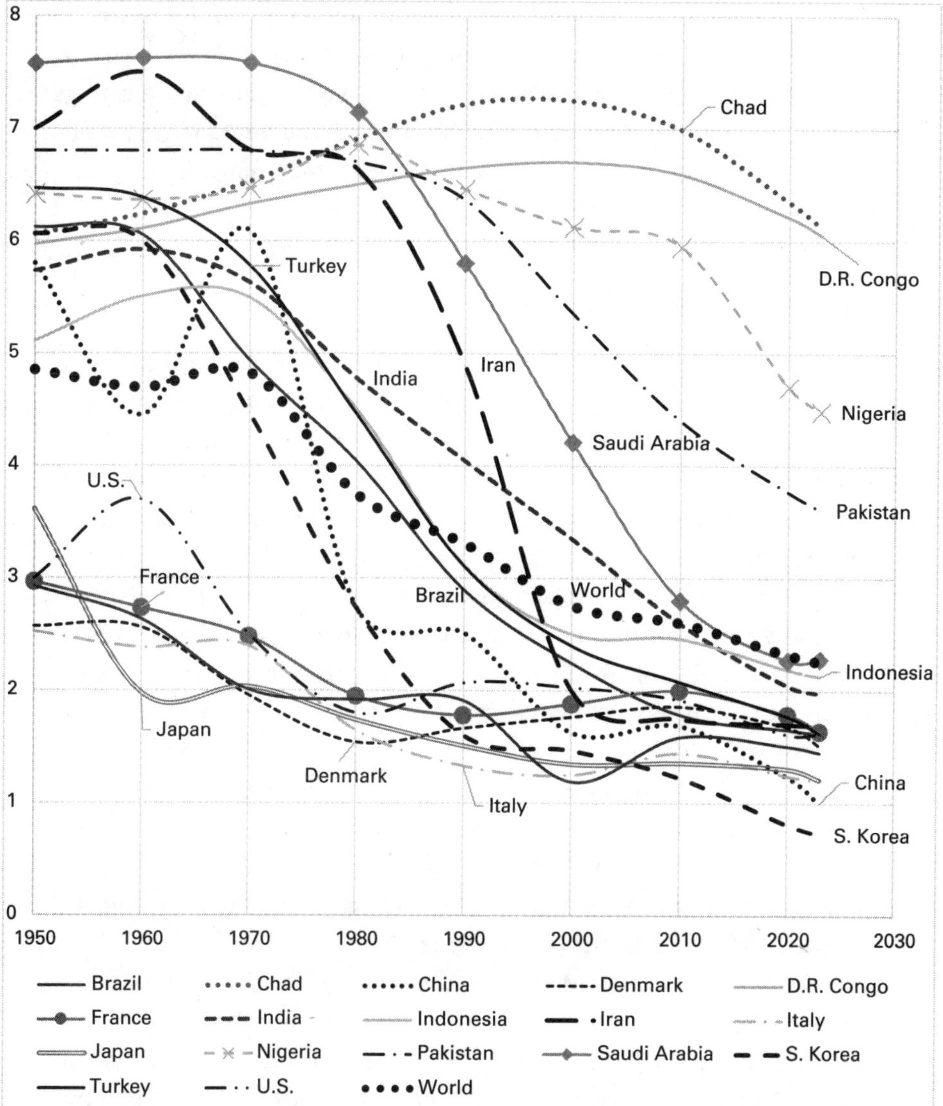

Figure 2.7 Global total fertility rates for selected nations, 1950–2023. Data source: Saloni Dattani, Lucas Rodés-Guirao, and Max Roser Roser, "Fertility Rate," Our World in Data, 2025.

also plays in for some (as it did in my family). Reflection on this nexus of concerns is essential to addressing the pragmatic workforce concerns of the future and, more positively and constructively, to building a caring democracy in which families can thrive. Indeed, the hesitancies around childbearing expressed by young people suggest that imagining the second is essential to fixing the first.

THE NEW/OLD PRONATALISM

Such reflection has not characterized the pronatalist discourse that has proliferated among conservatives lately, which often rhymes with the anti-abortion policies that have redefined our nation since the 2022 Dobbs ruling: both aim to increase the number of births, planned and unplanned, and to reimpose on the young people of the nation an earlier form of fertility control—of the patriarchal kind.

The topic rose into media consciousness in 2024 with J. D. Vance's resurfaced interview (from 2021) about "childless cat ladies" who "don't really have a direct stake in [our country]."[32] In that recording, Vance invoked two female leaders of color and one white gay leader as examples of irresponsibly childless Americans: Vice President Kamala Harris, Representative Alexandria Ocasio-Cortez, and Transportation Secretary Pete Buttigieg. His examples' political focus indicated that he didn't just disapprove of people without kids; he specifically didn't want people from three groups in positions of authority making national policy: women, people of color, and LGBTQ+ individuals.

Vance's critique ignored current birth-timing and family formation realities: Harris (a stepmom) began to co-parent at forty-six, Buttigieg and his partner adopted twins in 2022 when he was forty, and Alexandria Ocasio-Cortez (thirty-one in 2021) might yet choose to have children (or not, up to her). Vance and his wife (both Yale law grads) started their family at twenty-nine and twenty-seven, respectively. Delaying parenthood has enabled women's movement into policymaking roles like those of Harris and Ocasio-Cortez. Blocking from such roles all who've delayed or refrained from biological procreation would leave very few women with the education and experience to serve in those roles, harming both them and their constituents.

Vance's views reinforce those expressed by tech billionaire Elon Musk, columnist Ross Douthat, and marriage advocate Brad Wilcox, all right-wing white men. Likewise, the Heritage Foundation's Project 2025 holds that children need "the nurturing of a mother and the play and protection of a father" and urges that the government "prioritize funding for home-based childcare, not universal day care" and eliminate Head Start and other childcare funding.[33] Though candidate Donald Trump disavowed knowledge of Project 2025, in his second term its lead author became director of the US Office of Management and Budget, and the Project's regulation-and-service slashing, personnel purging, and actively patriarchal agenda steers the administration's policy at press time.

While the anti-abortion movement hasn't presented as specifically pronatalist, more births are an implied outcome.[34] Instead, that movement has focused its rhetoric on bringing all fertilized human eggs to term. But its lack of support for families after babies arrive, and its threats against contraception, imply different aims: to increase births and thereby grow two low-wage workforces—impoverished parents who take any low-wage paid job to feed their kids, and unpaid women pushed into dependency at home, where they function, as Silvia Federici noted, as servants (also a workforce dynamic) without civic voice. That's the tradition we inherit and that tradwife influencers laud.

Oddly, though conservatives urge young people to have more kids, they also support expanded fossil fuel drilling and departure from the Paris Accord, actions that ensure that the world such children inhabit will be much less favorable to health and thriving than what it could be if they acted oppositely. But that pattern is consistent with denying abortion access while also cutting services for children.

While their major motivation may be reaffirming patriarchal roles, conservative pronatalists also play on public concern that if fertility rates continue declining, there soon won't be enough working people to serve the growing population of long-lived retirees or, longer term, to continue the species. Contradictorily, their solution—sending women home to raise the workforce of the future—reduces the already-small workforce of the present (and the future too, if the women-at-home model persists).

Nonconservatives also worry about what falling fertility rates could mean for our economy and also, down the line, for our species, but they also recognize the need to think the way forward without abandoning progress toward democratic change. Demographers like Vegard Skirbekk (author of *Decline and Prosper!*), Catherine Bowen, and David Miles find the interaction of the confluent demographic changes in fertility and longevity to be economically and socially positive, as we'll explore in the chapters to come.[35]

Clearly, a model that allows people of all genders to both work and raise families would best serve present and future. While many men as well as women welcome that opportunity, pronatalists' relish for the deferences and discounts created by the patriarchal fertility model suggests their subset do not.

Rather than attempting to force women into early births, leaders can both address people's concerns around family formation and build a fair, welcoming immigration system. Addressing family concerns would require building a care infrastructure so both parents can combine family and career, committing to prompt climate action, and incentivizing dads to fully share care. Visibly advancing these goals would be an important step in itself. Though it's unlikely that a demonstrated national willingness to invest in families would immediately cause every young person to want one, more couples on the fence in nations like the United States that have taken an "it's your family, so it's your problem" approach to date would be at least reassured that the prospect could be positive and that their children would have a chance to thrive. But first and most important will be engaging young people in actively planning the future that they will have to live with, rather than reinforcing the knee-jerk patterns that brought us to the current catastrophe.

3

REPRODUCING POVERTY VERSUS PLANNING TO THRIVE

At the Crossroads

One thing's sure and nothing's surer
The rich get richer and the poor get . . . children!
—F. Scott Fitzgerald, *The Great Gatsby* (1925)

Woman has, through her reproductive ability, founded and perpetuated the tyrannies of the Earth. Whether it was the tyranny of a monarchy, an oligarchy or a republic, the one indispensable factor of its existence was, as it is now, hordes of human beings—human beings so plentiful as to be cheap, and so cheap that ignorance was their natural lot.
—Margaret Sanger, *Woman and the New Race* (1920)

Just as reliable birth control (RBC) has had many knock-on effects, so the previous lack of it had consequences that shaped the economy we inherited. The continuous stream of births to young couples was key to the old economic model, and in this chapter we'll examine its operations and effects and explore how they've altered.

Usually, births are discussed as producing the next generation of workers, but equally importantly, they have also produced current-generation workers: the suddenly focused set of committed parent-earners pressed into jobs in order to feed children, who often remain in those jobs for life. In the United States in 2023, 42 percent of households lived under the level the United Way calls ALICE (Assets Limited, Income Constrained, Employed)—including 13 percent under the (extremely low) Federal Poverty Level and 29 percent still struggling to afford basic expenses.[1]

Historically, the firstborn child introduced this focus, and additional births then increased the earning commitment—of both father and mother. Dad might be in the paid workforce with mom supporting him and the child through care work at home, or both parents might be in the paid workforce with childcare (either paid or unpaid, from grandparents or others). Either way, both parents were working hard, benefiting employers and society. As we've seen, the worker-multiplier effect of unplanned births delivers three workers to market (or two if the father exits): the parents who must support the child, and the future worker/child (also a consumer in infancy, and thus a jobs creator).[2]

This dynamic has not been much explored by economic theorists, apparently because they assumed that inevitably such births, many of them unintended (though predictable), would supply both a steady workforce at all class levels and a pool of consumers, ongoingly.[3]

Whether consciously or not—as Margaret Sanger, the key exception among such theorists, recognized—employers of workers at all income levels have counted on births (planned or unplanned) to reproduce their future workforce and to concentrate their current workers' focus on pleasing their bosses and keeping their jobs. Employers of low-wage workers in particular have counted on unplanned pregnancies to generate and motivate a desperate staff. As the song from *The Great Gatsby* affirmed, "One thing's sure and nothing's surer / The rich get richer and the poor get—children." Swapping out the "and" in the second line for "because" further clarifies the point.

TEEN TRANSFORMATION

But lately that dynamic has been changing. The 22.4 percent fall in the US fertility rate between 2007 and 2024 includes a dramatic teen component: births to teen moms (and dads) fell by *69.6 percent* (from 41.5 births per 1,000 teens aged 15–19 to 12.6); see figure 3.1.[4] Mississippi's rate, though still the nation's highest in 2024, fell from 70.1 to 22.8 births per 1,000 in that span (68.3 percent); while New Hampshire, the nation's lowest, fell from 19.3 to 4.6 (77 percent). This teen decline links to the 30 percent fall in births to unmarried women from 2007 through 2023 (from 51.8 to 36.4 births per 1,000 unmarried women aged fifteen to forty-four) while births to married women, who are also, not coincidentally, older, remain higher—at 81.6 per 1,000 in 2023 (having fluctuated in the 80–89 range since 1995).[5] Key to this decline have been ongoing improvements

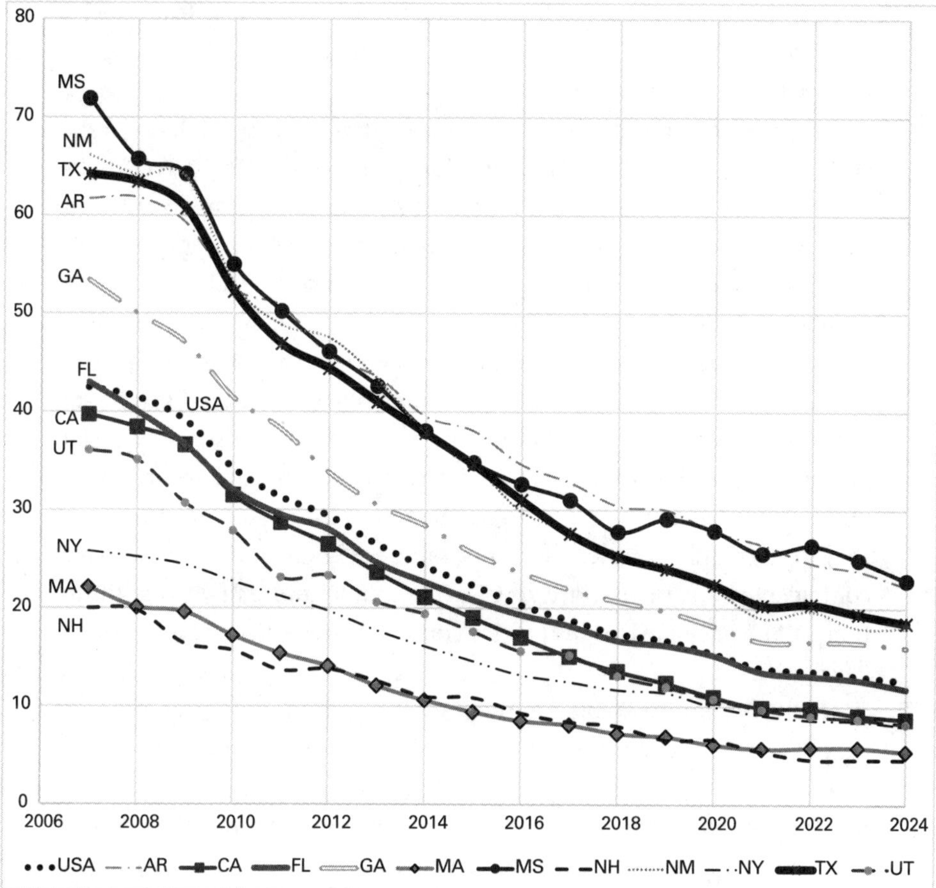

Figure 3.1 Teen fertility rates for the United States and selected states, 2007–2024. Births per 1,000 women, aged 15–19. Data source: CDC Birth Data, via the WONDER database, at https://wonder.cdc.gov, and CDC, "National and State Patterns of Teen Births in the United States, 1940–2013," *National Vital Statistics Report* 63, no. 4 (August 20, 2014).

in contraception—along with economic pressures, climate fears, social isolation around COVID, and expanded screen time (the latter two especially relevant among teens).[6]

The teen decline also reflects the fact that same-sex relationships are now more common: a 2024 Gallup poll found that LGBTQ+ self-identification had grown from 3 percent among baby boomers (now in their sixties and seventies) to 23.1 percent among Gen Z (now in their teens and twenties).[7] Whether or not this indicates a change in the number of people who feel attracted to people of the same sex, this data can't tell us, but it does show that more people in younger groups feel comfortable stating an LGBTQ+ sexual preference, are more likely to be out, and are less likely to be pushed into straight relationships by social pressures. As we'll explore in more detail in chapter 7, this means fewer births, planned or unplanned, to people forced into hetero relationships they wouldn't have chosen. But while same-sex encounters are effectively contraceptive, planned births to LGBTQ+ couples using in vitro fertilization (IVF) have increased in the new context of widespread acceptance of gay families.

Of course, until reliable family planning arrived, there was no concept of "unplanned" births—just the predictability that if a woman had hetero sex, she could become pregnant. Although the proportion of planned births increased after the arrival of hormonal birth control in 1960, unplanned pregnancies remained common—given the inconsistent access to health care in the United States and the limited availability of reproductive information in schools. By 1987, 57 percent of US births were still "unintended," defined as having "not been wanted at the time conception occurred, irrespective of whether or not contraception was being used."[8] By 2011, the proportion had fallen to 46 percent.[9] Recent fertility rate declines suggest that the proportion of unplanned births has fallen substantially further.

As the age at which women give first birth or adopt has increased, the rate of child poverty has markedly declined—from 27.9 percent in 1993 to 17.5 percent in 2007 and 11.6 percent in 2019 (pre-COVID), due to the combination of expanded safety net benefits[10] and reduced births to younger people (who are less able to support kids than they would be later). The pandemic Child Tax Credit enabled a big but brief drop to

4.4 percent in 2021, but when that was revoked, the rate rebounded, to 10.8 and 10.6 percent in 2022 and 2023, respectively.[11] This is a complex set of factors to analyze, but the absolute number of children born into poverty has fallen for three reasons at once: (1) increased benefits have lifted many out of poverty; (2) fewer births overall mean that the lower percentage in poverty is also of a smaller number of children; and (3) because fewer new parents are teens with limited earning capacity, the number and percentage in poverty is further reduced.

Relatedly, as fewer people start families young, fewer of them feel pressed to take jobs they don't want—so the numbers of job openings, including low-wage openings, have risen. As of August 2025, the labor market is tight in some industries, with 7.2 million job openings and 7.2 million Americans looking for work (many of them not in the right location or vocation to fill the openings).

Currently there's much confusion around employment trends (both supply and demand), since big changes are occurring on many fronts simultaneously, including artificial intelligence (AI), which is expected to spur job cuts; deportations (actual and threatened, already creating worker shortages in some industries); boomer retirements; DOGE and other federal job cuts; visa changes; lingering COVID effects; economic slowdowns; and more.

Fertility also plays a role. As we'll see in chapter 9, fertility declines since 2007 mean the incoming native workforce will be shrinking from 2026 through at least 2042, as fewer eighteen-year-olds age up into the workforce (a group further reduced because more of them are going to college). Many of these factors put new pressures on low-wage employers. Abortion bans aim to lessen those pressures by reintroducing high levels of desperation, leading new parents to take low-wage jobs, while also, contradictorily, aiming to push at least some young mothers out of the workforce (we'll return to this contradiction).

Unintended pregnancies and births can happen to women across fertile age bands and at all income levels, but when they occur among teens, they can have a negative effect on long-term career plans, given that teen moms and sometimes dads may be diverted from completing their educations and those who join the ranks of low-wage workers as teen parents are often stuck in similar jobs across lifetimes.

As the teen fertility rate plummeted after 2007, reported six-year high school graduation rates rose between 2006 and 2016 after years of remaining static, from 85 to 93 percent overall.[12] Although high school data are sketchy and not divided by gender, birth certificates are more reliable. Whereas in 2007 26.9 percent of first-time mothers had a BA or more, in 2024 that number jumped to 41.9 percent (a 56 percent rise), while those with less than a high school degree dropped from 20.7 to 9 percent (a fall of 57 percent).[13] The jump is partly due to fewer teen births, but it also reflects the fact that male and female college graduation rates both rose notably between 2007 and 2024—from 28 to 37 percent (+32 percent) and from 34 to 47 percent (+38 percent), respectively.[14] These changes are positive for the young people involved, their families, and society.

But they're not so viewed by all. In 2024, three attorneys general (of Missouri, Idaho, and Kansas) filed suit against the FDA for making Mifepristone (an ingredient in medication abortion) widely available, claiming that abortion undermines the state's interest in the progeny of its "teenaged" residents by causing a loss in "potential population or potential population increase" as well as "diminishment of political representation" and "loss of federal funds."[15] In response, Barbra Streisand tweeted, "This is what the forced birth movement wants . . . women as breeders!" (See chapter 8 on how fertility has historically been manipulated by states for exactly these benefits.) As more low-wage positions go unfilled due to diminished worker desperation, legislators in states like Arkansas are addressing the situation by weakening child labor protections to expand the set of potential low-wage workers.[16]

The increased education options created by reduced early fertility may have played roles in such recent advances as rising household income levels (up markedly since 2008), increased access to state-level health benefits (citizen demand has cut to ten the states that block access to expanded Medicaid [eighteen in 2015]), lowered child poverty rates (as noted above), and in some greater success of unions.[17]

Those advances challenge not just employers who count on parental desperation to bring in profits but also state legislators dedicated to attracting businesses across state lines with promises of a cheap (aka desperate) workforce and low taxes—which require low state investment in social services. Of course, that's exactly the opposite of the family-support infrastructure model advocated here and desired by people who are considering whether or not to have children. The fall in teen births, with its concurrent lowering of the level of worker desperation levels, also undoes the state-level ripple effects of unplanned fertility on the workforce.

It makes sense that the new workforce muscle of young people who are not parents also plays a big role in the recent conservative push to ban abortion. In 2024, Idaho Republican Senator Chuck Winder made news by connecting abortion rights to shortages of cheap labor, saying, "We complain that we don't have enough service workers, we don't have enough of this, we don't have enough people to do this. Well, I think there's a reason: It's not just low birth rate, it is the number of abortions that have occurred." The implications of this position did not escape Idaho Democratic Rep. Lauren Necochea, who replied, "I'm very surprised to hear Senator Winder say that forced pregnancy is a way to solve our workforce woes."[18]

Because Winder's remark references current policy, it may suggest he's worried about future workforce. But the present-tense discussion of resolving the "workforce woes" that he and his anti-abortion peers in legislatures across the nation (and their billionaire funders) anticipate from abortion bans isn't just more babies who'll work later but also more desperate parent workers to fill workforce gaps now. Likewise, bans that push more women into unplanned pregnancies could diminish the rate of increase of female policymakers (like Necochea) and thus undercut the effectiveness of their advocacy for expanded family-support infrastructure. Since such infrastructure challenges patriarchal patterns, it's unsurprising that conservatives would try to block it. As Jenny Brown has noted, until opportunities for family-support infrastructure benefits are increased, lower birth rates are effectively being used as a bargaining tool by the younger generation, not always intentionally but effectively.[19] Abortion bans can be viewed as union-busting efforts.

FERTILITY AND THE SOUTHERN ECONOMIC DEVELOPMENT MODEL

It's also unsurprising that the states that have enacted abortion bans are precisely those with the highest rates of impoverished people, disproportionately Black and Hispanic but also including many white families (see the appendix). Those high poverty rates link directly to policy decisions to restrict education, health care, and other social benefits to large portions of their populations as part of what economic sociologist Chandra Childers calls the "Southern economic development model" (SEDM), which has functioned since slavery times in that region to extract labor from workers as cheaply as possible by linking racism and economic exploitation.[20] As we'll see in chapter 8, low services enable low tax rates (and vice versa), creating the "business-friendly" environment used to attract companies to these states. But the quiet side of the business-friendly model means that due to the state's underinvestment in human capital through education, health care, and other services, there are also many underresourced laborers available for hire for very little, further lowering business costs. High rates of childbirth, in a context of low support for families, ensure that the desperation model binds parents to the grindstone to support these babies.

Finding ways to coerce free or discounted labor—including reproductive labor—is a hallmark of our actually quite vicious economic history. These include the expropriation of land and discounting of labor from Indigenous people, from enslaved Africans and postbellum African Americans, and from Hispanics (with and without documents), as well as the discounted labor of women at home and in paid positions and of immigrants of all races pushed into low-wage work on arrival. Among the most egregious were the white enslavers who raped the women they exploited as laborers in order to produce and sell their combined genetic offspring (i.e., their own children) as goods—a particularly perverse form of expropriation, while also taking sexual advantage.[21] All the tales of the inevitability of love for one's own gene pool fall apart with this example, as do all characterizations of the Black and white racial groups as distinct in the United States (since everyone is related). Enslavers manipulated mothers' emotional connection to their children as a means of ensuring their care work for those children along with the immense burden of field and other work they carried, also making it less likely that they would flee.[22]

After slavery ended, unplanned (but predictable) births continued a variation on that economic strategy by guaranteeing an adult workforce of underresourced, both racialized and classed groups (African Americans,

Hispanic Americans, and lower-class whites) through the glue of parenthood, especially motherhood—ensuring that many teens leave school early seeking jobs to support their children while also making it very likely that those underresourced kids will supply the next generation of cheap laborers.[23]

Of the ten states with the highest teen fertility rates in 2024, nine have full abortion bans, nine have among the nation's ten highest poverty rates, six were members of the Confederacy and three others were Confederacy adjacent, seven have the lowest possible minimum wage, and four have not expanded Medicaid. Mississippi, the state with the highest teen birth rate, also generated the Dobbs case. Those non-Southern states that have also put bans in place emulate the SEDM model. The ten states with the lowest teen fertility rates, on the other hand, have quite different characteristics (see the appendix).

The overlap of ban states and the Old South, and the division of the nation into two sectors where citizens have differing rights and status, is not coincidental. While all women in ban states are negatively affected, women of color carry a disproportionate share of the burdens of extra fertility and the poverty often linked to it.

Although sentimentalized rhetoric about the unborn does serve the ancillary purpose of activating many conservatives to vote in primaries, the purpose to increase unplanned fertility (more babies!) for the economic advantage of those in power has always also been operative in efforts to ban abortion and, I suggest, a major motivator of the support of the anti-abortion cause by conservative legislators, despite widespread opposition among their constituents. Whether or not most conservative voters consciously connect the dots between anti-abortion policies, unplanned births,[24] and a low-wage workforce, if they endorse a conservative religious agenda of uncontrolled births and compulsory heterosexuality, they effectively endorse the patriarchal socioeconomic system. Everyone in the South knows from experience that fertility, poverty, and a desperate workforce are linked and that historically it has been counterproductive to name the strategy aloud—either because admitting to that benefit undermines it (if you see yourself as benefiting) or because you risk repercussions (if you don't).

As many have noted, the fact that anti-abortion campaigners have never linked their campaign with attempts to help the children who result (most of them poor) undercuts claims of concern for the welfare of children, and when those campaigners also condemn contraception, as has occurred increasingly of late,[25] the intent of the anti-abortion movement to increase the number of births becomes clear.

The pronatalism embedded in the anti-abortion message overlaps with the overtly pronatalist "family" agenda espoused by Vance, Musk, Douthat, et al.[26] They encourage the women in their audiences to have many kids, stay home, and make sure there are enough people in the next generation to carry forward "our" culture, meaning white. But these policies affect women of all colors, whose babies will serve the various labor functions of the classes they are born into.

Notably, pronatalist advocates are almost entirely white men, advising women as a group to have more kids and leave the workforce, because they know best. Similar dynamics inform anti-abortion activism. Although there are certainly women involved in the pro-life movement, men (at 41 percent) identified as pro-choice in Gallup's 2025 poll at a rate 20 percentage points lower than women (at 61 percent). (But 13 percent of men and women both felt that abortion should be illegal in all circumstances, while 22 percent of men thought it should be legal under any circumstances, and 62 percent thought only under certain circumstances, versus 38/49 for women.)[27] Per the Pew Research Group, in 2022 62 percent of Americans said that abortion should be legal in all (29 percent) or most (33 percent) cases, and 36 percent said it should be illegal in all (8 percent) or most (28 percent) cases.[28]

Likewise, in the state legislatures that have enacted abortion bans, the overwhelming number of votes in favor were cast by men. The twenty bans in place one year post-Dobbs were voted in by 1,347 conservative men (1,292 of them Republican), with only 225 conservative women (214 Republican) joining in support. Women (50.7 percent of the population) cast 14.3 percent of the total 1,572 votes in support of bans, while men (49.3 percent of population) cast 85.7 percent.[29] Women have made progress in representation in recent years and now comprise a bit less than one-third of all state legislators (with proportions and party affiliations varying across states).[30]

All but 11 of the 394 Democratic women in ban-state legislatures in 2022–2023 voted against the laws (97 percent), along with 176 of the 390 Republican women (45 percent), meaning that the large majority of women in those legislatures (559 to 225—71 percent of the total 784) voted against them.

No question of whether male citizens had standing to vote on female citizens' ability to make decisions about their bodies was addressed in the Dobbs ruling or in any ban legislation, though insofar as bans will push many young women off educational paths, they work directly to block women from civic participation and so might be seen as prejudicial to their exercise of their rights to direct representation. When viewed from this angle, it becomes clear that the views that the right espouses mean to recreate the "traditional" environment of uncontrolled fertility that historically was used to ensure the low-wage labor of workers of both sexes and the uncompensated labor of women at home, to the advantage of the small cadre of wealthy and largely male employers who benefit from that exploitative labor model, and their advocates.

This is a "tradition" with few beneficiaries; though, in a form of patriarchal Stockholm syndrome, many victims, male and female, feel aligned with their captors for the limited benefits they do receive. The birth control revolution's challenge to this model has spurred those beneficiaries' increasing efforts to clamp down—through court stacking, voter suppression, and legislative gerrymandering to enforce the bans—a no-holds barred battle for power based in fertility manipulation.

ANTI-ABORTION IS PRO-POVERTY

As we've seen, the dependency of an infant on the care of its mother and other care providers has historically been manipulated to refuse care and status to the caregivers. Instead, the burden of doing all of society's dreck work for "free" has been imposed on women, while those who exploit that care labor lay waste to the environment and traumatize huge portions of the community with poverty, violence, and other harms. Abortion bans exacerbate these effects.

That's because, as the ten-year "Turnaway Study" documented, and as common sense makes clear, anti-abortion is pro-poverty.[31] Women denied abortions (due to state time limits) were notably more likely to live in poverty with their children (61 percent versus 45 percent) in the years after the unintended birth than were women who obtained abortions when they sought them but who were otherwise similar. The numbers also indicate that a large percentage of women who experience unplanned pregnancies are already poor (highlighting issues with contraception access). Many who choose abortions do so because they already have children and having more would lower the resources and time available to those already in the family.

That dynamic seemed operative in 2022 births in Texas after the state's 2021 abortion ban. In analyzing the data, I found that those primarily affected by the ban were Hispanic women aged twenty-five and over—precisely those most likely to have kids at home so they wouldn't be able to travel for abortion care.[32] In 2023, post-Dobbs, fertility rates fell in all groups in Texas, but, as noted, while some people became more vigilant about accessing contraception or abortion through various means, doubtless some families couldn't access care due to the bans, and some unplanned children were born into difficulty. Young people forced to carry unwanted pregnancies to term suffer when graduations are derailed and when they're locked into lifetimes of low-wage jobs by parenthood. But society loses too, as fewer skilled workers are available, women's perspectives are excluded from policy decisions, and female citizens feel devalued. Women and their families who earn less also spend less, reducing GDP.

Recalling the SEDM discussed earlier, it becomes clear that this impoverishment is intentional. Uncontrolled fertility among a population with no family-support infrastructure promotes a lower-skilled workforce, affecting all Americans. If Dobbs stands, in our world of interstate corporations where employees (and their children) can suddenly be assigned to states they weren't counting on living in, all American young women will again be unable to plan their paths as reliably as young men, since you never know, she might be having a baby instead of starting her freshman year at college, and who knows how focused she'll be able to be on learning after that. Some will be able to leave their state for an abortion if needed, but others will not. Currently, many ban-state women can access mediation abortions in their own homes, but ongoing anti-Mifepristone suits aim to close down that option.

Reversing the progress of the past century, women's status will decline nationally if fewer women are eligible to move into leadership roles, cutting the expansion of critical mass in business and government and depriving business and society of their skills and insights. Everyone will lose as the progress forwarded by women's rise in civic standing is undermined.

Anti-abortion legislation also directly harms women by raising the level of DV. Unplanned pregnancy and poverty often spur violence, separately and together, and abortion-ban states are already seeing rising levels of both. As one woman in a Texas DV shelter recounted, due to the abortion ban "I have to have my abuser's baby and now regret it every day."[33] The birth of what will now be her second child makes it all the more likely that she and her kids will have no choice but to return to the abuser for lack of better housing options—a common reason that victims stay. The amount of harm likely to result from the pressures of unplanned additional children, in a context where DV is already high, is enormous.

Together, increased violence, a likely rise in unsafe abortions, and doctors' fears about intervening in problematic pregnancies mean many more women are likely to die unnecessarily. This will only add to the already high rates of maternal mortality and morbidity in the United States. Rates are more than twice as high among Black women as among others, but they've risen in all groups, and per recent study, that rise is largely due to increased levels of preexisting ill-health (signified by comorbidities such as diabetes and hypertension) among mothers, itself fostered by factors such as lack of access to Medicaid health care before pregnancy in the ten states that have refused ACA expansion, limited access to healthy food for many, and the many stresses of poverty.[34] Although maternal mortality and morbidity can affect women in all socioeconomic classes (as evidenced by the death of Olympian Tori Bowie and the postpartum complications faced by Serena Williams), families living in poverty are affected disproportionally, and orphaned children in poverty have a greater likelihood of foster care.

STATUS CHANGE

Dobbs set in motion a decline in women's citizenship status—their voices unheard at the antique table set by the five in the majority on that decision, all of them unelected active proponents of a patriarchal religion. While in 2025 only 13 percent of Americans polled supported a total abortion ban (down from 20 percent in 2020),[35] women will now pay an effective fertility tax (bearing unwanted children and experiencing a huge decline in social and civic status) that men don't face. Men will bear some consequences too—including likely a lot less sex, since women without sure recourse will be way less interested. What will it do to the self-concept of American girls to learn that they—or if they're not currently in a ban state, their friends in the "other half" of the increasingly non-United States—could once again be forced to bear the child of any man who attacks her? That America's "commitment" to gender fairness is hogwash? What will that do to the self-concept of American boys?

Fortunately, the forty-nine years of expanded equity under Roe spawned millions of Americans over multiple generations uninterested in going back, as has been demonstrated by the many successful referenda on protecting abortion rights in both ban and ban-free states. With the threat of a national ban now looming, those who believe women are full citizens still have the opportunity to make it so, if, recognizing that resistance is fertile, they use their clout to organize allies in business and civic life, challenge the judicial and federal systems that allow the sacrifice of female citizens' rights by states, and bring out the vote for candidates who support preserving all women's ability to make their own reproductive choices, in all elections over the next few years.[36]

Accomplishing that will require organizing to effectively combat their very well-prepared opposition at this tipping point—by raising their voices and using their clout while they still have it. In doing so, they may preserve democracy for everyone in the nation and engender positive change for the long term.

4

REASSIGNING GENDERED WORK AND PAY

Contested Ground

A man may work from sun to sun, but a woman's work is never done.
—Adage

By denying housework a wage and [calling it] an act of love, capital has . . . got a hell of a lot of work almost for free, and it has made sure that women . . . seek that work as the best thing in life. . . . At the same time, it has . . . trapped [the male worker] . . . by giving him a servant.
—Silvia Federici, "Wages Against Housework" (1974)

Terminology-wise, standard definitions tell us that *sex* is determined by a person's biology, while *gender* is the "behavioral, cultural, or psychological traits typically associated with [their] sex" (Merriam Webster). The term *sexuality* covers an individual's sexual partner choice. Although they're different, sex, gender, and sexuality (SGS) overlap and interact. There's an enormous amount of change underway in what's understood and socially acceptable in all three of these areas, but in this book we're focusing on the ways those changes intersect with fertility dynamics, especially as they affect economics and workforce.

This chapter explores the way gender dynamics have operated within patriarchal economies to control reproduction and the human capital resources (aka people) that result, as well as to create labor discounts (for employers and male householders) through limiting who can compete for and access which jobs and at what pay levels. Then we'll explore how those dynamics have shifted in the context of birth control and expanded longevity.

Over the years, the gender category has come to be recognized as the most inherently unstable of the SGS trio. Back in 1935, anthropologist

Margaret Mead documented that gender roles vary across cultures and change over time within individual societies, indicating that they are not "natural" as is often claimed but are learned through growing up within a given culture and moment.[1]

Earlier, I asked you to think of gender in terms a bit different from the standard dictionary version cited above. Instead of as a set of inherent human qualities, we can think of it as a *work-assignment system,* which has historically operated to dictate the kinds of work people who were identified as either male or female at birth are allowed or required to do, as well as the pay and status linked to that work. The behaviors, clothing, and affects tied to gender (i.e., the view that it's "feminine" to be sensitive and "masculine" to be tough) are less the substance of gender in themselves than they are qualifications for the gendered jobs and status assigned them. In other words, it's not because women are caring that they do care work; instead, it's because women have been assigned care work that they're trained to be caring in our culture. In other cultures, men are known for their caring "natures" and skills.

For the past six thousand years of what we can call the Patriarchal Age, in many parts of the globe, a sex/gender hierarchy has been a keystone of our evolving economic systems, though the degree to which women participated in civic life and in decision-making has varied by period and locale.[2] Within this age, some phases have been more flexible, so women have not always been entirely excluded from civic life, as feminist historians have documented. For example, women in medieval Europe often shared status as householders with their male partners, their work on farm and in markets was respected, and female healers, midwives, and wise women dispensed skilled health care, including assistance with childbearing and with abortions, offering women a say in when and if they gave birth.

But in the transition into the Renaissance, as Silvia Federici documents, things got substantially worse for European women, as serfs were pushed off their land and into cities as part of the "primitive accumulation" of the land, labor, and materials needed to build modern capitalism. In that process, hundreds of thousands of women characterized by their persecutors as witches (meaning "disobedient" women with a sense of their own value and capacities) were murdered across Europe. As Federici describes, "the witch-hunt was, at least in part, an attempt to criminalize birth control and place the female body, the uterus, at the service of population increase and the production and accumulation of labor-power."[3] Women's challenge to the incoming power structure was silenced, and their labor was again narrowed to care tasks, degraded to a form of household servitude, and denied the dignity of recognition as work—viewed as mere instinctual activity, deserving of no compensation.

Instead, as feminist economists outlined in the 1970s and 1980s, in the modern wage-based labor system, especially as it's evolved since the industrial revolution, the payment a man received from his employer included some payment for his housewife's labor to "reproduce" him—to ready him for work each day. Although it was his duty and to his benefit to support her for all the work she did, the whole wage belonged to him. In addition, part of his pay packet effectively included higher social status linked to his gender—a form of compensation in itself (only partially a result of the higher wage), whereas her lack of monetary compensation brought with it a lower social status that was viewed as linked to her gender (enabling his higher status through comparison) and requiring her deference toward him.

Such extra status and pay shape the intrinsically hierarchical operations of labor discounting linked to identity factors in capitalism by which you are paid less because labor of people in your group is marked as less valuable and vice versa. In the past two hundred years, however, things have changed significantly; particularly in the past sixty years, women and other long-discounted groups have expanded their ability to work and earn and in the process raised their civic status. As I write, we're in the midst of an effort to turn back the clock on that change, but that effort ignores the structural shifts that spurred the change that will be hard to override.[4]

CARE AS A GENDERED WORK ASSIGNMENT

In patriarchal cultures around the globe, women are taught that their essential contribution is the biological bearing and nursing of babies—and then by extension (since they're home anyway), that this work should also include rearing those children through adulthood and caring for all other family members too. Although one might imagine that since women suffer through the process of bearing the young, men should raise them, that hasn't been the pattern. Instead, women, individually and as a group, have been assigned the hugely time-consuming task of raising and maintaining society's workforce—without cash payment. For billions of people, the combination of childbearing and associated family care work has been a lifelong job, with tasks including cooking, cleaning, weaving, sewing, teaching, shopping, providing sex on demand, entertaining, sympathizing, organizing schedules, nursing the ill, tending the infirm, and (depending on context) kitchen gardening, dairy work, crafts, and other duties as assigned. Although people of either sex can do all of it except breastfeeding (less of an issue with infant formula), all of this essential care work has been gendered feminine when done at home for free.

Linked to their child-rearing tasks have been requirements that from girlhood women learn and exhibit the affects associated with care (being tender, attentive, cooperative, good humored, pleasant, reliable) and those linked to dependency (being submissive, obliging, sexually attractive). Boys, on the other hand, are expected to learn and exhibit affects associated with mastery, so though they are expected to be civil, it hasn't been required that they seek to make others comfortable; instead, masculine affects include directing others and being tough, not being particularly concerned with their looks, and sometimes being harsh or even violent as "needed." As a result, men are viewed as generally more competent and authoritative than women (as documented by transgender scientists Ben Barres and Joan Roughgarden, who each experienced different judgments of the same work when they presented it from different sides of the gender line).[5] In reality, all humans have capacity in both affect sets, but women are judged if they don't present as consistently obliging and men if they are perceived as too obliging.

Even today, girls are schooled to develop feminine skills—itself a proof that they're not "natural." But the characterization of women's work as instinctive and thus not deserving of pay has meant that gender has been viewed as a labor category only tangentially, mystified as an indicator not of labor relations required by the economic system but of an individual's personal essence, which pushes men and women to identify with and buy into the assigned roles. As a result of this mystification, the products of women's care labor—including most notably the children themselves (who have many kinds of value, including but not limited to economic)—haven't been counted in standard measures of economic value production, as Marilyn Waring and others have documented.[6]

Although the reigning gender narrative long held that women belonged at home, all along some women have worked outside their homes in addition, particularly those in lower class positions whose families needed more income or who were solo or self-supporting. In the United States, that group includes women of all backgrounds but disproportionately women of color and immigrants due to the intersectionality of pay discounts, which deepen as the number of discounted categories involved increases (race/ethnicity, gender, class, sexuality, nativity, among others). Generally, women's paid work has involved care tasks similar to those done at home, and the fact that those tasks are done for free at home has also contributed to their low valuation when done by women outside the home. Men doing jobs involving comparable levels of skill earn more: for instance, janitors (long a male-only job) earn more than cleaning women (the job title includes the gender). But even within job titles bias reigns, so now when women can be janitors, male janitors still often make more than female janitors, and when called to account for why, the difference is generally attributed to gendered ideas of competence or strength.[7]

In addition to lower monetary compensation, female workers may pay a special tax of harassment—itself an offshoot of their low pay.[8] Because these workers are often paid little and they've until recently had few public advocates, predatory male supervisors have long felt free to demand sex to ensure that women get the shifts they're desperate for in order to support themselves and their families. If those lady janitors happen to be undocumented workers, that makes them all the more vulnerable.

"Men's work," on the other hand, isn't generally called that because that would be redundant: what men do is viewed as "real work," gendered masculine, and just called work, as opposed to women's work, which is viewed as a form of self-realization (despite the acknowledgment in the adage that labor is involved). Men's work can comprise anything that isn't characterized as care work (like manual labor, military service, engineering, and computing)—though, as Joan Tronto has noted, much of that work also involves important elements of care for the community.

When men's work does involve care work as standardly defined (like male janitorial work or surgery), sometimes in an administrative role (like school principal), it's better paid.

Marxist theorist Leopoldina Fortunati, part of the Wages for Housework movement with Federici, describes the male/female relationship under capitalism "not as one of individuals but rather a relation of production, an exchange which takes place between women and capital, mediated by men."[9] In hetero-paired households of recent day, as in ages past, the wife reproduces several forms of value:

- the children themselves (the workers of the future)—a form of capital production not fully accounted for by economists since it includes both a child's physical body and its innate capacities as well as what's called "human capital" today, meaning the educational investment made by family and society in the child (see chapter 8 for discussion of the economic role of mere existence, in census counts)
- the daily "reproduction" of the adult (male) laborer for his job—achieved through feeding him, comforting and entertaining him, clothing him, and providing a "meaning" that "makes it all worthwhile"

Some of the value of such reproduction of paid workers is captured in the couple's lifetime earnings, as is some of a third form of value—her daily self-reproduction (essential to the group), which undergirds the others but is largely invisible.

Whereas a housewife's care work has immense use value, it has no exchange value on its own (since if women aren't paid, they can't directly exchange the fruits of their labor for goods and services). Marx took that as inevitable and viewed housework as having therefore effectively no value. The lack of cash, along with the 24/7 on-call service required for the endless care tasks, means women have had neither influence nor time to expend on policy advocacy, and employers have gotten and still get a big discount for the cooperative, able workers deposited at their doors by women and families.

GENDER, CASTE, AND LABOR DISCOUNTS

Several mechanisms have enforced this gendered work system over millennia—the principal one being uncontrolled fertility, which in the absence of a family-support system has long locked women into care work and dependency at home.

Another mechanism is the enforcement of an effective gender caste system. Castes are identity hierarchies: they're similar to class but differ in that some aspect of the identity of individuals is used to prohibit or limit their movement out of an economically and socially compromised or benefited position. In America, as Isabel Wilkerson has shown—drawing on Martin Luther King Jr.'s analyses, race bias against Black people has functioned similarly to the Indian caste system. In all cases, caste manipulates pools of competition to create labor discounts among the lower castes and labor bonuses among the upper castes. Once a group is put at an initial power disadvantage, they are characterized by their antagonists as being intrinsically less worthy, and their sphere of work is restricted to a realm that those in power either don't want to operate in (so they seek to ensure that others must) or don't want to pay full value for. This realm may comprise even the most intrinsically valuable and essential tasks—as I suggest is the case with gendered care work—so assigning these tasks as the only option to a large group of workers guarantees they're done cheaply.[10] Ancillary benefits to the upper caste—like a steady flow of next-gen laborers, easy access to sex, and a class of people to feel superior to—all ensure it will be enforced all the more fiercely.

Law and custom have been developed to create and enforce an artificially constrained large pool of female workers (excess supply) who compete with one another in the marriage or housework markets for that limited set of jobs (paid through barter, with occasional cash benefits). Even though there are many openings available within this job category, the pool of applicants is larger (if you don't take the offer, someone else will), which furthers the desperation (very Jane Austen).

In addition to saving employers money, this system also protects those in the higher-status group from competition for the jobs they do want because the pool of competitors is smaller than it would have been had the lower-caste people been allowed to apply. These jobs will also be better paid, both because the upper caste (men) can negotiate among more job options—playing off employers against one another—and because, as noted above, the employers are paying part of the value of the caregiver's work to the male householder instead of to her, so his higher salary includes that bonus. If the housewife were paid her share directly, the husband would make less. As in any rigged game, the system is fixed to advantage management.

Over the past few decades, diversity, equity, and inclusion efforts in the US job market have attempted to undo castes of gender and race, as well as of sexuality and dis/ability. In some measure they have succeeded in mitigating the protected status of men, whites, straight people, and those without visible disabilities. Addressing the intersecting caste systems through DEI has allowed direct competition for jobs that previously would have gone to a white man, even though others outside the pool of privilege might be more competent. Like affirmative action, DEI may also break ties in favor of the historically disadvantaged candidate, aiming both to bring more perspectives into a business (an economic gain) and to create a critical mass of equitable representation that is likely to be more open to recognizing value in diverse candidates going forward (also a gain).

The backlash against DEI that we've seen of late responds to both of these dynamics (expansion of competition and affirmative tiebreaking), seeking to reinstall an SEI (sameness, exclusion, and inequity) system, long known in the South as the good old boy network.

Caste exploitation redounds to the personal benefit of those in the upper caste subset, but that is offset both by the harm to those forced into the lower caste and paid little or nothing and because the economy overall loses. The labor of the lower caste registers at a lower value to the wider economy than it would have if those forced into limited job options had been allowed to compete equally in the full economy. Society suffers the cost of their unrealized potential—including lost economic energy, lost invention, and lost taxes—and is less prosperous overall.[11]

DEGENDERING JOBS AND PAY

While social stratification enforces all castes, childbearing adds a physical enforcer to gendered caste, pushing many women out of paid labor competition and into dependency early on. But as reliable birth control has transformed birth timing, and women as a group are not sidelined early, the barriers around gendered work types have lowered. It's now more economically feasible and culturally acceptable for both parents to combine caring for kids with contributing to family support, though not all do.

But because it's embedded in all societal systems, changing a longstanding caste system takes time. Over three decades, growing numbers of women have been advancing up the ladders of work and realigning the gender caste system, largely by integrating into the world of better-paid jobs. In so doing, they gradually expand the set of gendered qualities associated with women to include some formerly viewed only as masculine (like competence, authority, and, occasionally, forcefulness). But along the way, they encounter a double bind, as women leaders are considered "too tough" if they adopt the demanding attitude that can signify male competence and "too soft" if they seem "too" nurturing. Likewise, the gendered tasks assigned to men have shifted to include more care work, but so far that's mostly care done at home, not for pay. Qualities gendered masculine are also expanding to include emotional attentiveness and parenting. And it's increasingly recognized that all genders can be both competent and incompetent.

If this evolution continues, instead of being viewed as a low or unpaid instinctive behavior of all women, care work could become a specialization open to workers suited by temperament (innate, learned, or both) rather than by sex or gender (returning to Mead's analysis), and the gendered wage discount would evaporate. We can predict that if pay rates for care work increase relative to other jobs, more men will begin to see those jobs as desirable. For many, those jobs' history as low-status "women's work" will likely still taint them, but eventually they may be recoded as nonbinary. If rigid dichotomies between masculine and feminine behavior fade, all people could develop an equal likelihood of a temperament for care work, if children regularly cared for by both fathers and mothers came to see those roles as valued positions open to people of all genders, as Nancy Chodorow argued.[12]

But currently, as female caregivers have moved into the paid workforce, leaving the site of their longstanding unpaid household labor, the blocking of competition through gender has continued. Over the last forty years, feminist economists have identified multiple tactics by which gendered work guardrails are reinforced, including continued blocking of access to well-paid jobs; unequal pay for the same job; and noncomparable pay for jobs that involve similar skills, skill levels, or effort levels to jobs filled by men but are paid less specifically because a woman does it. These situations are rectifiable through tracking comparable worth and adjusting the salaries where the jobs are essentially the same[13] or involve similar skill levels (as with janitors and cleaning women, or tailors and seamstresses), or where a woman's job involves equal or higher skill levels and value but has been paid less (as with truck drivers and nurses, or mechanics and secretaries).

Sociologist Ruth Milkman documented similar tactics at differentiating pay in Detroit during World War II, when automakers offered women lower wages than their male counterparts (though much better than what they had been making in their prior jobs, so they didn't complain initially). Milkman understood management to have imposed gender divisions in the paid workplace to serve multiple ends: The sex-typing of paid jobs reinforces skills used in women's unwaged household labor, thus ensuring the continuation of their restorative care work from which the husband's employer benefits. The association of women's work with their unpaid labor at home also brings down the valuation of their paid labor. And by guiding men to derive a sense of status from making more than women, employers promote disunity, so the genders don't band together to fight for better conditions for all.[14]

In response to such analyses, some instances of these discrepancies have been addressed, but many still function. These exclusions are not necessarily consciously enforced by individuals, who may not intend to be part of a wider network of bias, though often they are aware and do so intend, as people continue to push their advantage where they find it in the absence of sufficient community support infrastructure.[15]

Here's an example of such advantage pushing that I encountered a while back in Houston, the energy capital of the United States. Houston houses over two thousand oil and gas (O&G)-related companies and a similar number in other energy types (including renewables). That environment directly affects gender dynamics here, as the O&G industry is among the most male dominated (84.5 percent male, globally).[16] Many O&G employees in Houston are highly paid execs, skewing the proportion of men and women in town with their own money compared to other cities. But there are women in the industry, some of whom fill me in occasionally on women's progress.

One described an increase in the number of female vice presidents, and I asked when she thought there'd be CEOs. She smiled and clarified (and I paraphrase), "The VPs are good, but most of them won't rise further. The men a bit above them in the pipeline mentor them not because they think they'll lead, but to cut the competition in half." They know a woman won't get the top job because the gendering of work there wouldn't allow it. The strategy allowed for some indicators of improvement (the few VPs), but they were not signs of real change; they were a distraction used to conceal a further tightening of the set of eligible big earners.

Whoa, that depressed me! Since then the numbers of women in O&G overall have barely budged (an O&G employment equity report found no progress between 2017 and 2021), though there are now a few female CEOs, meaning that either some shift has occurred or some other sleight of hand is being perpetrated, perhaps also involving token exceptions, which counter critiques of sexism from without but end up "proving the rule." All to be determined.

As noted, all caste systems limit competition for what are defined as the better-paid jobs to the group in power. Over the past century, we've seen versions of this effect when men resist the "feminization" of a work realm historically marked as masculine in order to preserve their wage levels—which can only be better if they're better than someone else's—a pay hierarchy that functions through the gendering of competence as masculine. But the O&G leadership pipeline example involves not just an effort to maintain the same limits on competition and to block women's ability to compete, but also (given that men have always also competed against each other within their caste) an effort to use the presence of women in the pipeline to narrow the limits further to an even smaller subset of men than formerly (in both cases overwhelmingly white).

Nonetheless, some change has occurred in most fields, and the kinds of jobs women hold have expanded (see figure 4.1). Among the best-paid professions, women have made varying levels of progress, advancing to 35 percent of the whole group in 2021 from 13 percent in 1980 (though still low in O&G).

Although inherited gender roles still differentiate many of us in terms of aspirations, affects, and opportunities, the sharp distinctions between

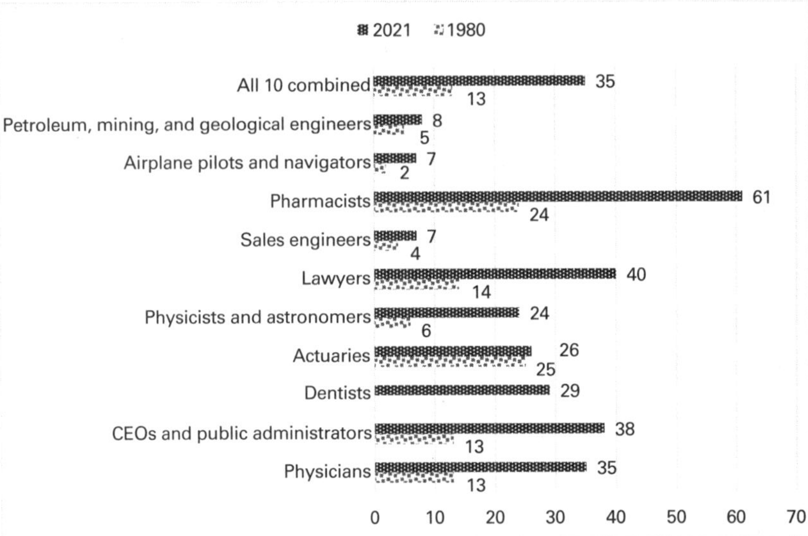

Figure 4.1 Women's presence in the ten highest-paying occupations in the United States, 1980–2021. Data source: Kiley Hurst and Richard Fry, "Women Have Gained Ground in the Nation's Highest-Paying Occupations, But Still Lag Behind Men," Pew Research Center, November 2, 2023.

genders have been muted community-wide as work assignments have shifted. More women run businesses; some do physically demanding jobs, requiring more toughness and less tolerance of time-wasting; and more men do care work and actively nurture. As fewer women are dependent, gender definitions based in dependency (deference, lack of complaint about sexual harassment) or power over (masculine harshness and freedom to harass) have shifted toward a center of common civility and respect. There are many exceptions: reactive hypermasculinity and hyperfemininity flourish too—in speech, behavior, and body as costume (aided by exaggerated muscles, implants, and fitness regimes), and in monetary forms, as gendered wage and wealth inequities. But the scene is different from 1920, when suffrage was enacted.

As we've progressed in de-binarizing work assignments, women's wages have trended up, in fits and starts. Nationally, they've risen overall as a percentage of men's wages from 1960 to 2024, but fell in the last year, as table 4.1 shows.

Table 4.1 US women's wages relative to men's, over time, 1960–2024

	1960	1970	1980	1990	2000	2010	2020	2024
Percentage	60.7	59.4	60.2	71.6	73.7	76.9	83.0	80.9
Loss/Gain		–1.3	0.8	11.4	2.1	3.2	6.1	–2.1

Data sources: US Census Bureau, "Income, Poverty, and Health Insurance Coverage: 2016," September 2017, https://census.gov; Megan Wisniewski, "What Is the Gender Wage Gap in Your State?," March 1, 2022, https://census.gov; and Melissa Kollar and Zach Scherer, "Income in the United States: 2024, Introduction," September 9, 2025, https://census.gov.

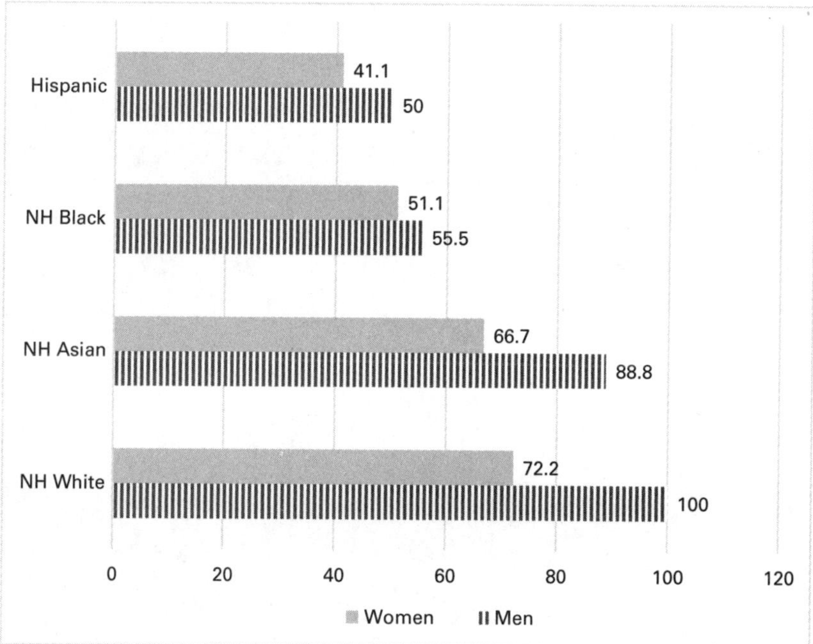

Figure 4.2 Harris County, Texas, median annual earnings in cents to the dollar paid to full-time workers, by gender and race/ethnicity, relative to those of the highest earners in the region, full-time working non-Hispanic white men (2023). Data source: Steven Ruggles, Sarah Flood, Matthew Sobek, Daniel Backman, Grace Cooper, Julia A. Rivera Drew, Stephanie Richards, Renae Rogers, Jonathan Schroeder, and Kari C. W. Williams, *IPUMS USA: Version 16.0 [dataset]* (Minneapolis, MN: IPUMS, 2025), https://doi.org/10.18128/D010.V16.0. Data from the U.S. Census Bureau, American Community Survey (ACS) 2023.

Although wage advances have allowed increasing numbers of women to become financially independent, gendered disparities continue and are especially disabling at the lowest pay levels, and in areas with more gender-biased industries. Figure 4.2 breaks out the gendered pay gap by race/ethnicity in Houston/Harris County, where the statistics are starker than nationally due to the confluence of O&G industry bias, the SEDM model, and the state's heavy reliance on undocumented immigrant workers. The figure also reveals a pattern of enormous disparity among men by race/ethnicity that also varies by region. All of these disparities require redress in order to build a functional democracy.

5

OVERTURNING WOMEN'S RIGHTS

Injudicious

There is no such thing as a baby—meaning that if you set out to describe a baby, you will find that you are describing a baby and someone. A baby cannot exist alone but is essentially part of a relationship.
—D. W. Winnicott, *The Child, the Family and the Outside World* (1964)

In making the claim in the epigraph, pioneering child psychologist Winnicott points to the comparatively premature birth of all humans. As a result, we're the species with the longest childhood. Expelled from the womb at the point when they can breathe and continue to grow in the external world but before they can walk, talk, or care for themselves, human babies only survive the first decade or so of life through a kind of social amniotic fluid of caregiving, often called love.

As we know, the resources available to families vary widely in the United States: many babies are born into poverty, which often leads to hunger and violence in the household. As a result, many babies are traumatized from the start despite their parents' best intentions. Although the nation pretends to value equal education for all, in reality states invest very differently and rarely sufficiently to the needs of all or even most students, and school systems distribute resources variously across neighborhoods. As discussed in chapter 1, creating desperation in new parents around supplying sufficient food to keep their kids alive, leading them to take low-wage, undesirable jobs, is an operating principle of capitalist economic systems. And the children of such parents are then set up by a lack of supports to continue the donation of their discounted labor to the wider capitalist system.

It's against this background reality that the current discussion of abortion rights occurs, though the sentimentalized appeal made by anti-abortion campaigners seeks to repress what's at stake. Likewise, the effects of babies on women's ability to participate in civic life and in the economy are occluded. The dyadic aspect of the human story that Winnicott foregrounds is omitted in discussions of fertility control and motherhood by those who privilege embryos' "rights" over those of the women they develop within and who will be expected to care for and support them for years, even if the circumstances a child would be born into are inhospitable to its thriving. Just as babies are shaped by the relationship with their caregivers, so caregivers are shaped by their relationships with babies.

As the realized member of the potential dyad whose skills in providing for their young will be relied upon in bringing them to maturity, women's judgments about when is the right time to welcome their progeny trump those of others, whose interests are often not those of either the child or the parent. Instead, as recent events have shown, the loudest defenders of the "unborn" are often those who seek to exploit them as voter bait and, down the line, as cheap labor.

In the best cases, love binds families through rituals of care and a sense of paying forward; it keeps parents vigilant on their children's behalf and functions as a contract that society expects them to fulfill. That contract is reinforced through physiological means (oxytocin hits for nursing mothers and other pleasures in interactions with children); a personal sense of connection (such as love and pride); social approval (good parents get applause, bad ones are [sometimes] shamed); and labor exchange—for millennia, children supplied labor that helped the family flourish, and they may still be expected to help their parents as they age. The love effect is often the major "compensation" offered women as part of what's characterized as their instinctive caregiving. As Silvia Federici put it, "They say it is love. We say it is unwaged work."[1]

But sometimes childbirth has quite negative effects—both for those pushed to care for babies they can't afford to feed, don't want, or don't feel ready for and for the babies born into those circumstances. Historically, those negative effects have included bringing children into situations of hunger, abuse, and other kinds of misery; increasing the poverty of older children and parents; denying women as a group access to participation in civic decision-making; erasing women's ability to earn and build separate lives on their terms; rerouting young fathers' ability to move forward on career paths or life courses they'd hoped for; ensuring that the better-supported children who would have been born later are never welcomed; and blocking society's access to the insights of half its population.

Across time and around the globe, women of all ages have had to responsibly gauge the consequences of a pregnancy for the family as a whole, considering many factors, including the family's economic situation, the social context, the readiness of the mother to focus on a child, and her own health—if she doesn't survive the pregnancy, who will care for this child and any older siblings? Where they've judged it not beneficial, many women across history have aborted pregnancies they didn't feel prepared for, often with the help of female healers or midwives (the women killed in Europe's witch hunts).

Only in a world where women's value as citizens and essential members of their community was debased, and their role reduced to reproduction of an exploitable workforce, would the insight of the people best able to judge the likelihood that a child, its family, and its community would thrive be disregarded. An effort to degrade the standing of women similar to that of the witch burnings is underway today.

ECONOMIC AND WORKPLACE EFFECTS OF DOBBS

The relative consistency of women's access to reliable birth control (RBC) in most states between the Roe and Dobbs decisions in 1973 and 2022 played a key role in the expansion of women's civic and workforce participation across the nation. When Roe was the law of the land, a woman promoted in a corporation with offices in multiple parts of the country felt reasonably sure she'd have the same rights in those different regions should she be transferred there—and her rights under Roe shaped her rights within each regional office, allowing her to keep climbing the ladder from one town to another, the same as her male counterparts.

But if Dobbs stands for long, women in ban states will increasingly have a very different status from women in ban-free states and from their male colleagues. In states with abortion bans, the most intimate decisions about their families and reproductive lives, and all the work and civic consequences that will follow from those decisions, will be controlled by conservative male legislators and their sponsors, whose recognition of the rights of women as citizens doesn't extend to including exceptions for rape or for nonviable pregnancies into their legislation.

Such an attitude of disrespect for women, at the highest levels of many state legislatures and judiciaries, cannot help but affect the way women are viewed and treated in other aspects of life in ban states. In 2025, we've already seen that contraception is next on the conservative hit list. If that succeeds, it will not be a return to the world before birth control—it's very different to actively deny women access to self-determination through known means than to live in a world where contraception and safe abortion were unheard of.

Employers to date have said or done little to combat the reduction of the rights of their employees in ban states, reluctant to alienate customers on either side. But employers, especially corporate employers, do have clout, and over time their female employees will feel betrayed if their bosses refuse to use it to support their reproductive rights. Some employees, male and female, will refuse to move to ban states when posted there if they feel that the move could put them or their children at risk, or they may leave unsupportive companies. Both are bases for corporate concern. But unless there is a big public pressure to do so, many businesses will also not want to abandon profit generation in ban states, which could create internal rifts.

Alternatively, or even simultaneously, employers—unable to predict whether female workers will have to step out due to unplanned births—may return to viewing all women as unreliable workers whom they should hesitate to invest in with raises and promotions because "she might get pregnant." That was often the case before the increasing reliability of birth control radically transformed women's workforce participation. If employer investments in female workers fall, fewer women will move up, and momentum toward change will dissipate. That would be especially likely if there were a national ban but would also obtain in a nation split into ban and ban-free sectors, which might quickly evolve into two separate socioeconomic systems, reminiscent of pre–Civil War days.

The economic fallout of efforts to push women out of business and leadership roles is hard to imagine in specifics given the many unknowns. But if successful, it's clear they'd have enormously negative effects overall in terms of workforce losses, reductions in GDP as many earners exit, loss of both insight and perspective, and loss of the American story about its investment in equality and democracy. Even naming those outcomes makes clear how important it is to avoid that path.

PATRIARCHAL LEGAL VIEWS

Accomplishing that turnaround will require legal efforts as well as a political pendulum swing, as the recent changes have come through both avenues. As noted, by returning to the states the decision on whether a woman can make her own reproductive choices, the Dobbs decision has demoted women's "rights" to revocable privileges in those states where abortion remains legal (for the time being). This differentiates them from their male "peers" and marks them as secondary citizens. In states where the local group of men in power have decided that women have no authority over their own futures, their "rights" have become what might accurately be considered a full-on "wrong," or absence of rights. If Dobbs stands, American women as a group will have a lesser status than before.

This reduced status is reinforced by what legal scholar Melissa Murray has characterized as a "jurisprudence of masculinity" in the Supreme Court's rulings in three cases in June 2022, including Dobbs.[2] In Dobbs, the court clearly finds "women's bodies . . . particularly susceptible and well-suited to public regulation" by states and not federally protected. But in *New York State Rifle & Pistol Ass'n, Inc. v. Bruen* and *Kennedy v. Bremerton School District,* Murray demonstrates that the Supreme Court "insulates men's bodies from the imposition of state regulation," protecting men's federal rights to guns and to prayer in public schools. In ruling on the two cases on men's rights, the court found constitutional basis for protecting these rights although they had previously been denied, but overturned Roe's longstanding precedent recognizing a constitutional right of privacy and referred the women's rights case to the states, subjecting women to varying judgments in each.

Murray contextualizes this referral, which occurs eleven years after the Supreme Court's *Shelby County v. Holder* ruling invalidated the Voting Rights Act preclearance formula and enabled the gerrymandering that guaranteed that many states would be able to pass abortion bans in 2022, even though majorities of voters in those states opposed them. In so doing, the justices effectively used the state legislatures as an arm of the court. At a point at which the anti-choice court majority was itself unable to reasonably ban abortion at the national level, given the precedent and public sentiment, they referred it to states primed to impose bans as part of a gerrymandered expression of a distorted "will of the people." These judgments seem to pervert the rule of law to corrupt ends.

These rulings occur as part of the wider effort to reassert patriarchal control and, as I've argued, to reactivate the multiple workforce effects of unplanned fertility that have been put on pause by RBC. That these bans are not the people's will has been demonstrated through the many referenda where majorities supported protecting abortion rights.

A similarly patriarchal dynamic informs the fetal personhood campaign in conservative legal discourse of late, which also aims to diminish women's rights. It makes a radical argument against the citizenship status of women, asserting an effective "right to be hosted" for fetuses, which builds on an implied religious claim about souls that ignores the views of those who don't subscribe to that claim and the views of the women forced into "hosting." This campaign disregards both the fact that the huge majority of fetuses are biologically nonviable when aborted and the impact of fetuses on the lives of the people whose bodies they develop within and upon whom most will depend for sustenance and support if and when they are born.

By attributing rights to fetuses as a new class of "persons"—rights that depend on overriding women's decision-making authority over their own bodies—this campaign operates as a political effort to undo the advances women have made in the past two hundred years into active participation in the polity, a form of disenfranchisement that reassigns them to the "civil death" under which women suffered before contraception under patriarchy. If recognized, the fetal personhood claim would reactivate the vicious cycle in which unplanned births effectively exclude many women from civic life so that they are less likely to move into policymaking roles in numbers sufficient to assert their rights as full citizens and to overturn laws that harm them as a group. That includes laws that enforce fetal personhood or fail to provide a care infrastructure to allow women to fully participate. And in itself, fetal personhood laws return us to days before the Nineteenth Amendment, when women's personhood was legally occluded through the denial of the rights of citizenship.

Legal scholar Julie Suk suggests that Dobbs could be challenged on the basis of either the Thirteenth Amendment's ban on involuntary servitude (when a woman who wants an abortion is forced to serve a state's claim of interest in forcing her to bear) or the Fifth Amendment's Takings Clause, which would obligate the state to compensate her for the use of her womb for public purposes (leading to the surrender of the child at birth to the state).[3] But the whole framework in which the misogynistic decisions were made to date could be challenged, with those who implemented them forced to recuse for conflict of interest.

The Dobbs decision and the subsequent wave of abortion bans are endorsed largely by individuals who are advocates of patriarchal religions, a fact that has been too little examined. But it makes a difference if justices aim to impose their religious views on others and thus that the current majority of six conservative Catholics have not recused themselves in cases where their judgments are informed by those views, which reinforce the workings of the economy of desperation and exploitation rather than democracy.

The justices have made it clear that they seek to turn back change, literally. Many of the state bans that were reaffirmed after Dobbs originated more than one hundred years ago, before women had a vote in shaping them. This pattern echoes the "originalist" bent of many court members who insist that the Constitution only authorized laws that were already in place in 1782, a patriarchal time. That originalist doctrine has gone unchallenged even though its premise is grossly self-serving and preposterously based in a view that time does not pass and learning and cultural change do not occur. It ignores the fact that a democratic republic was itself a revolutionary idea at the time.

Although abortion bans are presented by their advocates as efforts to save the lives of fetuses, this claim rings hollow given the lack of support those same advocates offer to children once born, especially those born into poverty. Instead, these bans (a malicious pseudo-care) limit the capacity for thriving of members of families of all classes in an effort to ensure the existence of an impoverished class of low-wage workers, glued to their jobs by parenthood they did not choose. Reliable birth control, on the other hand, short-circuits the historical role of desperation parenting in funneling many into low-wage work.

In ban states, women's rights to make decisions about their own lives and bodies and those of their family are now sacrificed daily to a sentimentalized fantasy constituency of the unborn, which the anti-abortion advocates claim to protect—but only up to the point when they arrive in the world and require services, like health care, childcare, clean water, and a sustainable climate. That's the scenario that anti-abortion activists ask us all to pretend we believe, in deference toward others' religion, even when they include revoking the rights of actual citizens—the 51 percent of Americans born with a uterus.

While the "rights" of fetuses to develop in the womb and to be born are urged by fetal personhood advocates, the rights of female citizens to structure their lives outside or in addition to the realm of childbearing are ignored. Women make fertility decisions based on their own knowledge of the context in which a pregnancy occurs—which affects the pregnant woman, the potential child, and others who would be responsible or affected. The pro-choice phrase "Trust Women" recognizes women's ability to use a complex awareness of the situated needs of all family members, in the near and longer term, to anticipate and respond to those needs. On that basis they can make the best choices for their family, including when not to add to it. This benefits the wider community as well.

On the other hand, the argument that women will be unaffected by being forced to carry and bear children they don't want to bring into the world because they can then be given up for adoption is blatantly false, whether or not they then go on to raise them (and most people do raise the children they bear). Lives are often greatly affected on many levels by the process of carrying a growing fetus to term.[4]

Recent moves in states (including Indiana, South Carolina, North Dakota, Oklahoma, and Texas) to declare fertilized eggs "persons" and to punish abortions as homicide would further criminalize women while leaving unanswered questions about who in the community the proponents of such bills understand to be responsible for the care of the thousands of unwanted babies who might result. The lack of care or planning for this is clear, and a first wave of ban babies have already ended up in dumpsters, presumably because the women who carried them were unprepared or in dangerous circumstances.[5]

In opposition to the views put forward for fetal personhood, the alternative view, operative under Roe, holds that while fetuses are potential people and potential citizens, they aren't there yet. This view too involves multifaceted understanding, since prospective parents may think of a wanted baby as a member of the family as soon as they learn it's developing; but women who don't want or aren't ready for a baby think and feel very differently, and that feeling and intention shapes the experience of the pregnancy and the rest of their lives.

The understanding that it was a woman's private choice whether or not to bear a child was US law from 1973 to 2022; not illegal in any state before 1821 and only illegal in all states from 1910 to 1972—contra the claims of "originalists" that abortion was always forbidden before Roe. That understanding is still law in the thirty-one states where abortion remains legal. The "My Body, My Choice" slogan underlines the reality that fetuses are not separate beings but part of the body of the pregnant woman until they are born.

Unlike fetuses, however, women are both fully realized people and—at least nominally—certified citizens. The fact that until recently these actual constituents have had no voice in shaping the rules they live under has, however, limited their status. To begin to achieve full voice and status, they've needed protection from . . . the unborn. When that protection is removed without their consent, their status as citizens is undermined.

The ability to delay first births until a woman feels personally and financially ready has worked as a class elevator for many women and their families. Forcing people to bear children they don't feel prepared for, often into straitened circumstances, means that the better-supported children who they could have borne later if they were allowed to wait are never welcomed into the world and the economy. That next generation of happy, wanted children whose parents are prepared to help them flourish are the unborn we should be worried about.

The positive changes of the past century were all put at risk by Dobbs, which seeks in its "originalism" to return us to eighteenth-century America. The slavery-based, female-excluding "democracy" back then was one step on the road to real democracy. The Constitution provided tools for realizing full equality, which Americans have used since, moving the arc of the moral universe toward justice, as Dr. Martin Luther King Jr. described, while expanding productivity. Opposite the claims of the "moralists" who seek to ban abortion—first in states and then coast-to-coast—national abortion access has proven to be a key part of that moral universe, supporting the equality of all Americans.

Although abortion access is widely discussed as an individual rights issue, nullifying Roe is already having major negative social and economic impacts on America, as the opportunities of families to flourish—as well as women's health, citizenship status, and lives—are sacrificed by conservatives committed to the patriarchal model, including the current Supreme Court majority (largely Catholic) and the Christian nationalists (largely Protestant) behind the Heritage Foundation's Project 2025.

We often hesitate to discuss others' religious choices in a nation based on principles of religious freedom and separation of church and state, but as that separation is eroded increasingly, it cannot be avoided that a religious agenda drives these influential groups and that patriarchy and gendered control of resources are at the core of both. The view that women's insights about what is best for their families don't matter, and that instead the view of conservative Christian churches and their proponents (many of them billionaire capitalists too) should matter, rhymes with the absence from the Christian divine family (composed of a father, a son, and a genderless ghost) of any female authority.[6]

Most Americans' goal—to expand democracy and extend the benefits of thriving to all members of the group—differs markedly from the goal of the patriarchal capitalists: to maintain the inherited system and hold power and resources for themselves, while claiming to mean well by all. While discussions of mutual thriving are derogated as "socialist" and "un-American," Joan Tronto's description of a "caring democracy" more precisely names the concept that keeps many of us committed to moving the American project forward.

6

ACCOUNTING FOR HARM

The Economics of Gendered Violence and Coerced Sex

I have to have my abuser's baby and now regret it every day.
—Texas DV shelter resident, post-2021 abortion ban

Although women have entered noncare fields in greater numbers, sometimes for decent pay, there remains firmly in place a realm of labor paid in a different currency that remains "traditionally" gendered. That currency—of vulnerability and harm—operates on the dark side of the gendered economy, a nexus rarely discussed by economists, and includes both sex commerce (clearly a form of labor) and violence. While "punching bag" may not sound like a job, for many that is the reality. The beneficiaries of the dark economy, like the employers who count on desperate parent workers, also profit from women's poverty, dearth of employment options, and, again, from their need to feed kids.

High rates of sex trafficking and violence against women continue due to their still-low representation in government and business policymaking roles and the still-limited economic options of many. These may push women into sex commerce (which also puts many at a heightened risk of pregnancy in an environment in which abortion may not be available) and/or situations of dependency that include domestic violence (DV). The $15 billion-plus porn industry also depends on the availability of sex workers, whose objectified images then influence the way both the consumers of pornography and society overall see and value women.[1] Although they are rarely addressed in discussions of women's economic progress, these outcomes are also part of the gendered economy and linked to fertility.

THE ECONOMICS OF VIOLENCE AND THE VIOLENCE OF ECONOMICS

Economic dependency fundamentally shapes relationships, both personal and societal, as we've seen. Dependency creates vulnerability—which, unless that dependency is fully mutual, also involves an implied threat of withdrawal of support, mistreatment, or violence. Although a sense of love or decency—backed by fear of social censure—often bars such responses, abuse is common, especially when a woman has nowhere else to go. Our narratives haven't much explored how society's treatment of women constitutes a form of abuse or how a society where women were equally represented in decision-making might differ. But submissiveness enforced by fear would play a smaller part in defining femininity.

In some couples, dependency involves violence. Overwhelmingly, that's violence by men against women, though sometimes women fight back or even first, and same-sex couples may also be violent—according to who's vulnerable. While DV and its subset intimate partner violence (IPV) may occur in any income band, it happens most where men feel both put upon and enabled by society: in situations of poverty and patriarchal dominance. Federici holds that men with the least economic privilege often exercise gender privilege most harshly: "The poorer the family the higher the enslavement of the woman. . . . We find the most unsophisticated machismo in the working-class family: the more blows the man gets at work the more his wife must be trained to absorb them. . . . The more the man . . . is bossed around, the more he bosses around."[2] Recent revelations around the Jeffrey Epstein/Ghislaine Maxwell sex trafficking network, which included many wealthy men and leaders from the United States and around the globe, indicate the widespread engagement with these practices and that it's not just poor men who enjoy exercising power over vulnerable women.[3]

Although some well-to-do women are also abused, it is overwhelmingly poor women who come to DV shelters.[4] That's in part because better-off women often have other options, including access to money and friends with a spare room. Poorer women have fewer options, so they stay in abuse longer to avoid making their kids homeless. If they do find shelter for a while, when that access ends they may have to return to the abuser or the streets. Wage equity and a childcare infrastructure that allowed women to work and earn consistently could lower vulnerability and abuse.

For generations, such abuse was legal. Criminalizing it and creating more resources for women fleeing DV were huge steps toward reducing it. Since the 1994 enactment of the Violence Against Women Act (VAWA), DV rates have fallen by 67 percent, while rapes and sexual assault have declined by 56 percent.[5] But despite those enormous declines, rates remain high (indicating how bad things were previously). The recent rise in gun access through permit-less carry laws in some states links to rising rates of IPV homicide, nonfatal shootings, and literal domestic terrorism—where, as one young woman in a shelter recounted, an abuser may hold a gun to his girlfriend's head at home daily "for fun."[6]

If you've never been in or near a violent relationship, it's hard to comprehend what it's like or how many people are or have been. But bring up the issue in almost any group, and you'll hear stories. The steady calls to DV shelters document the ongoing harm being done. In one interview I did with a shelter resident during COVID, she told of being locked in her apartment with her abuser and hearing her neighbors being beaten too: "It's like, everybody was having the same issues. And that was even more traumatizing. I would sometimes hear—'cause there was one couple that lived right next door to me, and he would tell his wife that, 'It's a pandemic; the cops aren't coming.' And that, that's heartbreaking to hear."

Others offered related descriptions:

> "My children's father lost his job . . . being at home, the aggressions were more constant . . . [the pandemic] did affect [the situation] by a lot because . . . [before] I only had to put up with it in the afternoon or on weekends, but when the pandemic hit it was every day, at all hours."
>
> "I wasn't allowed to work . . . if I left I'm not gonna have a job, I don't have any money and how am I gonna, you know, take care of my kids? So it became me staying there because, you know, number one, I was scared to leave because I knew how violent he can get. And number two because of the financial situation I was in with him, and he controlled every aspect of that . . . he knew that I was fully dependent on that."

Whatever their social rank, women who depend on their spouse—for support, status, and other needs—are at risk. Addressing the inequities in women's wages would lessen violence by raising both the individual woman's and the family income, lessening the pressures on everyone, and making an abuser less likely to harm and a survivor less likely to stay if he does.

Lately, these issues have received more attention. Rachel Louise Snyder's extraordinary 2019 book documenting society's active failure to collect and share DV data that could save lives raised awareness.[7] In 2024, Cristina Rivera Garza's memoir about her sister's DV murder (aka femicide) in Mexico won the Pulitzer Prize, signaling expanded openness to discussing DV.[8] Between 2015 and 2023, more than 7,000 women were killed in Mexico in similar assaults in a context of no follow-up or consequences. In the United States (with a much larger population), between 2001 and 2012, 6,410 men killed women with a gun,[9] a figure that doesn't include femicides by other means (such as choking and beating)—again, the scarcity of data signals need for more attention and funding. Per the UN, globally, more than 500,000 women were killed by an intimate partner or family member in 2017 alone. Of course, many more women suffer nonfatal abuse daily at the hands of intimate partners and other family members. But until society follows up with consistent punishment for abusers and with infrastructure that allows survivors to support themselves and their kids, many victims cannot protest.

The economic cost of IPV homicides is hard to track but can include state expenditures for police work, trials, incarceration, fostering surviving children, and the lost lifetime wages of the woman and her incarcerated spouse, as well as the effect of the trauma on the earnings and expenditures of surviving children and on those of the wider community. Likewise, trauma and lost wages accrue to victims of nonfatal violence.

But in addition to such monetizable harms, a psychic economy is in play—of traumatizing risk to women and of perceived benefit of violence to abusers. The right to harm others operates as a form of sub-rosa compensation within patriarchy, as a kind of payback pleasure for abusers, as a means of passing on harms done them by others.

As Carol Gilligan has outlined, a capacity for violence is among the qualities that boys are taught to value in themselves within patriarchy, as part of the gendered work assigned them—in war, sports, the streets, and some jobs. She suggests that quality is fostered in part by the violence done to boys when they are denied access to the caring aspects of themselves in their upbringing.[10] Feminist theorist bell hooks characterizes patriarchy as "the single most life-threatening social disease assaulting the male body and spirit in our nation."[11] Although many men refrain from violence, by raising young men with a sense that masculinity is the opposite of caring, we increase the likelihood of harm. Including care in the approved skill set of boys would lower the levels of violence, improving the lives of all involved. Although many DV advocates focus on aiding the immediate victims at their doors, everyone in the gender system needs help.

SEXUAL ASSAULT AND THE DOBBS DECISION

Of course, domestic abuse isn't the only violence women experience. Many are also raped and sexually assaulted, by attackers known and unknown. The 2024 case of Gisèle Pelicot in France involved both. Pelicot (seventy-two years old at the time of the trial) was drugged and then raped over ten years by at least fifty men that her husband met in an online chatroom entitled "without her knowledge," inviting them in by turns to have sex with her while she lay unconscious in their bed. Dominique Picot, the husband, filmed these encounters, providing the prosecution with incontrovertible evidence. Because she was asleep (often snoring), she didn't know what was happening. The crime was discovered when the husband's computer was reviewed after he was arrested for up-skirt filming in a shop. All fifty-one served prison time, but many observers felt the sentences (between three and twenty years) too light.

The story, and the large number of men who participated, was seen by many women to represent a huge failure of solidarity between what seemed to be everyday male citizens and the women in their lives. As Pelicot told the court, "I wanted all woman victims of rape . . . to say: Mrs. Pelicot [spoke out], we can do it too. When you're raped there is shame, and it's not for us to have shame, it's for them."[12]

While the particulars of that case were shocking, sexual assault is not. In January 2024, the nightly news in Houston led with three stories:

- the funeral of an eleven-year-old girl who'd been abducted, raped, hit on the head, tied to a rock and thrown in a river by her father's friend

- the rescue of a twelve-year-old girl who'd been abducted and held for a week by a twenty-seven-year-old man
- the revelation that the Houston Police Department had failed to investigate 4,017 sexual assault reports since 2016 due to lack of personnel

Apart from perhaps the last item, such reports are not unusual in any US city.

As with DV, our culture doesn't like much detail on rapes—because they're depressing and because they shine the light too clearly on the harm suffered in our society that likes to think well of itself. But simultaneously, we make fictionalized versions of such attacks the subject of our nightly entertainment on the many police-themed TV shows America puts itself to sleep by. "A woman is killed" is the standard premise, but the question that follows is always "whodunnit?"—never "why are all these women being murdered and raped, on screen and in life, and what can we do to stop it?"

The VAWA led to some progress on sexual assault. But the more recent degradation of women's status following the Dobbs decision may increase such assaults, including attacks with intent to impregnate. Most of the post-Dobbs abortion bans include no exceptions for rape or incest. In a 2021 interview, J. D. Vance referred to rape as an "inconvenience" that doesn't counter the "right" of the fetus to be brought to term,[13] a view without insight into the many harms such outcomes create.

All people born with a uterus who are between roughly twelve and forty-four years old are at risk of becoming pregnant against their will, and among those who do, many choose to abort. But even in ban states with exceptions for rape or incest, access to abortion is very limited due to short reporting windows and other barriers. Based on past numbers, a 2024 study estimated that for the eighteen months after the Dobbs decision (July 1, 2022–January 1, 2024), in the then fourteen states with active total abortion bans there were 519,981 survivors of completed rape, and of those, 64,565 experienced rape-related pregnancies (roughly 12 percent).[14] Some of the victims may have accessed an abortion, but doubtless quite a few gave birth against their wishes. And the pattern continues.

Rapes and sexual assaults by people who victims depend on for housing and financial support often go unreported. They're often not one-time occurrences: some women suffer repeated assaults and sometimes repeated pregnancies. The pattern of ensuring pregnancy when a woman doesn't agree by denying contraception, often to ensure she'll stay, is called "reproductive coercion." One woman I interviewed in a Houston shelter in 2021 described her experience:

A: He made me have kids . . . all my kids are a year apart . . . once I was healed, he would make sure he would knock me up again. . . . After this last baby . . . I lied and told him that . . . I needed to go see a doctor . . . because he was already talking about having another . . . and I got the shot that lasts three months. . . . But he did force himself [on me] to, you know, get me pregnant.

B: . . . why was he doing that do you think?

A: Control. I asked him . . . "Why do you feel like you have to always have me pregnant?" And he would make jokes. . . . "I'm going to keep you knocked up because I don't want nobody looking at you." . . . He figured . . . who was going to want a woman with four kids, three babies?

This kind of rape does not show up in court.

SEX AS WORK

Also not much discussed as part of the wider economy, sex work informs the status of both women and men in patriarchy and in the economy, whether or not they participate. Generally, the term signifies sex for pay, but relationship sex when it's a duty may also be work. While sex is experienced as personal and ideally gives pleasure, that personal investment serves to embed us in the larger systems that depend on the reproduction of workers. As Fortunati explains it, "the male/female relationship . . . appears to be a personal relationship but is, in reality, a relation of production."[15] She differentiates between male/female relationships before and within capitalism as being in the first case an exchange of labor between women and men and in the second case an exchange of women (and their labor) between men. This happens within marriages, where a woman's labor is not waged but advantages the waged male she cares for and also his employer, as we've seen. And it occurs in commercial sex, where most prostitutes work for subsistence and a pimp takes the profit.

RELATIONSHIP SEX

Sex is part of the economy of marriages (and other partnerships) and also operates as a form of compensation—for both partners in the best case. It's something men in particular have historically felt entitled to claim in exchange for the room and board women received, including when wives have been unwilling (marital rape only became a crime in the early 1980s).[16] Not talking about the role of sex in our economy keeps problems with it unaddressed. Recognizing sex as a form of work expands understanding of the economics of gender.

The core species work of reproduction requires hetero sex, so in that respect the labor of baby production can be said to involve sex. Nowadays, the joining of gametes involved can be accomplished in a test tube, but for most couples who become parents, it's still done in person. Most marriages and nonmarital partnerships involve sex for pleasure as well as procreation, and since hormonal birth control became available, couples can have as much sex as they desire without risk of more children than sought. Pleasuring one another may be seen as recreational, but it may also be part of the overall job of both partners, to keep the other happy and mentally healthy—and may sometimes involve going along even if you're not fully into it. Best case, you don't see it as work, most of the time. But in reality, many people stuck with partners they don't trust or like but can't afford to leave do experience sex as an unpleasant experience and a form of forced labor.

SEX COMMERCE

Outside of personal, nonpecuniary sexual relationships (and despite their increased availability post–reliable birth control), there remains high demand among men for paid sex. Brothels are plentiful in wealthy neighborhoods, indicating interest and available cash. But commercial sex work occurs in neighborhoods in all income levels. Much of it is forced, coerced, or "chosen" by women with limited options. Like paid domestic labor, sex work is a monetized form of an aspect of the care work that women have historically done in exchange for their room and board. Like housework, commercial sex is highly gendered and open to all women, including trans women. Male sex workers are often homosexual and/or feminized, though not always. One study estimates there are forty-two million female and ten million male prostitutes worldwide.[17]

Like domestic labor, sex work involves an artificially constrained pool of largely female workers: the two fields long constituted the major viable options for women to support themselves and their children. Within marriage, women's work involves sex, but in the case of prostitution, the buyer has no responsibility to please or otherwise compensate the woman or to rear any children who might result. One report reviewed twenty-five studies of pregnancy incidence and outcomes among sex workers, finding high levels of both impregnation and abortion. Although 85 percent aborted in one study,[18] the remaining 15 percent is a substantial cohort of children born into difficult circumstances, likely to further the poverty and desperation of the mother; bans will increase the percentage.

As anarchist Emma Goldman framed it in 1910, "Nowhere is woman treated according to the merit of her work, but rather as a sex. It is therefore almost inevitable that she should pay for her right to exist . . . with sex favors. Thus it is merely a question of degree whether she sells herself to one man, in or out of marriage, or to many men. Whether our reformers admit it or not, the economic and social inferiority of woman is responsible for prostitution."[19]

While Goldman viewed both marriage and sex commerce as prostitution enforced by a patriarchal economy that requires that women pay with sex for their "right to exist," nowadays, birth control has made nonmarital sex socially acceptable, and a wider range of jobs are open to some women. But for many, wages remain low and job options few.

While in the twenty-first century there's been much discussion of the rights of individuals to choose to sell sex, those who defend that right generally argue that women should be able to take their best paid job option—rather than making the case for giving women more options. Some advocate for legalization, which could lead to better terms (including health inspections, health insurance, a guaranteed minimum wage, and less risk of violence), as has happened in New Zealand, parts of Nevada, and Holland. That raises the price to consumers, requires policing of unregulated competitors, and makes customers trackable, to all of which many powerful people object. Hence the limited change.

Although we often hear of "willing" sex workers who set the terms of their employment and pay, they are estimated to be about 2 percent of all sex workers. While some of them may be in it as a career, most willing workers are there for the usual reason: to feed their families as best they can. The remaining 98 percent have no other option or are coerced or forced. Many have no choice about where or how many times a day they have sex or whether they are paid at all beyond subsistence.

That this system of global exploitation continues to operate freely despite prohibitions suggests some government collusion, even if only in the failure to pursue. Many sex workers are poor or otherwise precarious women. They may also be trafficked for domestic or agricultural work, and so forth. Sexual favors may also be enforced by bosses on nonsex jobs in exchange for shifts, another form of currency. As with DV, the need to support children often holds women in these roles—another economic ripple effect of fertility.[20]

The National Organization of Men Against Sexism (NOMAS) finds that 16 percent of men in the United States regularly purchase sex, but such numbers are imprecise and rates vary globally.[21] Whether demand fuels supply or vice versa, essential to the industry's flourishing is the fact that although it's illegal, johns see few consequences. Women who sell sex are criminalized and often punished, however, indicating systemic bias. Sex work isn't lucrative for most and doesn't offer avenues into positions of influence where women might expand their job options. Instead, they face objectification, low status, and limitation to jobs linked to serving men personally. This reinforces some men's investment in the status quo gender hierarchy.

So what's the purpose of this behavior for the johns? It's hard to disentangle the sexual release these encounters provide from their exploitative context—which is the attractor? Orgasm doesn't require a partner, but human contact adds pleasure, especially if you're lonely. Is the interaction made sexy by the woman's pretense of interest (if offered), or is it her desperation—confirming her low status—that provides even poor men with the pleasure of feeling superior? Or the sense of solidarity among men, as the group that runs things? What studies there are show that several of these factors are in play, and the others are also plausible.[22]

While women's wages may not be kept low on purpose to maintain the sex industry, the easy availability of trafficked sex for hire results from those low wages. Estimates of the profits earned annually by the global sex trade range from $150 billion to $245 billion, based on limited documentation. One study reports that pimps in Southern California average $670,000 per year, though it is likely shared with coworkers in the "pimp sector" (cited as "drivers, guards, procurers, seasoners, madams, brothel owners, complicit landlords, investors, lawyers and bribed officials").[23] But the sex workers themselves aren't mentioned. Yet again, many get rich from exploiting low-status women. This vampiric dynamic can only be challenged within a democratic economy of care that provides women with more options to make a decent wage and that doesn't let them disappear from their neighborhoods without outcry.

Coerced sex commerce, DV, and sexual assault all have economic basis, springing from the twin factors of women's relative poverty and lack of civic status. All should be tallied in the loss column in national economic ledgers.

7

EXPANDING SEX/GENDER/SEXUALITY

LGBTQ+ Workforce

Multiplication, that's the name of the game!
And each generation plays the same.
—Bobby Darin, "Multiplication" (1961)

Is "the body" or "the sexed body" the firm foundation on which gender and systems of compulsory sexuality operate? Or is "the body" itself shaped by political forces with strategic interests in keeping that body bounded and constituted by the markers of sex?
—Judith Butler, *Gender Trouble* (1990)

Charting one year after the Pill hit market, singer Bobby Darin's claim was already wrong on arrival—and it's become increasingly so with each generation since. Today, human "multiplication" (aka reproduction) works in quite a few new ways, some involving technology changes and others reflecting shifts in the way people feel comfortable presenting themselves in terms of their physical sex, their gender (tied to tasks, appearance, and affects), and their sexuality, which includes but isn't limited to sexual orientation. These three sometimes shift separately, sometimes in combination.

But as with the movement of women into public life, the changes in the sex/gender/ sexuality (SGS) realm are large enough by now to have spurred backlash. Recently, we've witnessed a conservative attack on the LGBTQ+ community, most focused on stigmatizing and traumatizing transgender people. At his 2025 inauguration, the president attempted to reimpose old binaries by fiat, declaring that the federal government will only acknowledge the existence of two sexes: male and female, as defined at birth.

This despite the fact that 1.7 percent of people are born intersex (one out of every fifty-nine), and many others don't feel at home in the sex/gender combination assigned to their body at birth. Trans people exist, notwithstanding the executive order denying that one might have a sex/gender identity separate from one's sex at birth. Many seek to physically manifest the sex they identify with and to be recognized—by friends, family, and passersby—as who they are. They may identify with the "opposite" sex or gender, or as nonbinary, or yet differently, and they may choose to express that identity through transvestism, hormone therapy, surgery to alter genitalia and/or breasts, and/or other means.[1] As one Texas trans woman put it, "Sometimes I'm asked whether I've tried just not being trans. My answer is simple: Yes, for 40 years. For 40 years, I did everything I could to mortify this seemingly innate sense of self. The thing people don't understand is that, when I came out, I didn't start trying to be something I wasn't. I stopped trying."[2]

The many attacks on this small, vulnerable group—which in 2025 included scrubbing federal websites of all mention of their existence—aim to reimpose a retro world of compulsory heterosexuality, where women were secondary citizens and gay Americans hid in the shadows. But as with women's advances, it's too late to push the LGBTQ+ change genie back without a fight. Here too we're at a tipping point.

This chapter explores the flux in SGS categories and identifications and the effort to stem that flux—as they relate to fertility and its interactive workforce, economic, reproductive, and social ripple effects in our moment. Whole libraries remain to be written.

Sex, gender, and sexuality overlap under patriarchy, around linked M/F binaries that attempt to define all bodies as male or female, tie those bodies to the affects stereotyped as masculine or feminine, and enforce opposite-sex sexual orientation. All three binaries have been variously inaccurate for many. Increasingly, as social and workforce realities have evolved and people have more agency in defining themselves, increasing numbers have publicly rejected their assignment to one or more of these realms, and sometimes they reject the binary altogether, viewing standardized gender roles, sexual desires, and physical manifestation as deeply informed by social strictures.

This has been most visibly reflected in rejection of rules around compulsory heterosexuality (*comp-het,* for short) over the more than fifty years since the Compton's Cafeteria riot in San Francisco (1966) and the Stonewall riots in New York City (1969) as well as the ensuing legal breakthroughs (including the legalization of same-sex marriage in 2015). Those events spurred surges in formerly closeted individuals identifying publicly as LGBTQ+ and expanded acceptance. More (though not all) now feel comfortable bringing their full selves and insights to work and to their communities, along the way creating new markets to cater to their newly overt identities, as greater acceptance means many now have better jobs and more to spend.

Previously, however, America's history of stigmatizing homosexuality meant that many people who might have identified as LGBTQ+ were pushed into the closet, either not sharing that they were queer or not exploring forbidden desires. As acceptance has risen, the list of recognized sexuality markers—gay, straight, bi, queer, ace, pansexual, or "write in your own term"—has multiplied.

Per a 2025 Gallup poll, LGBTQ+ self-identification has also grown over the years—to a current 9.3 percent of US adults—and across generations (figure 7.1), with numbers progressing from 1.8 percent of the Silent Generation to 3 percent of baby boomers, 5.1 percent of Gen X, 14.2 percent of millennials, and 23.1 percent of Gen Z. The last two comprise 26.3 million Americans of childbearing age (10.3 million and 16 million, respectively).

Dividing the group who identify as LGBT+ by letter gives us 14.6 percent lesbian, 21.1 percent gay, 56.3 percent bisexual, 13.9 percent transgender (not a sexuality marker per se), and 6.4 percent "+" (including pansexual, asexual, queer, or other LGBTQ+)—with some overlap. There are generational differences in these statistics too: among LGBTQ+ folks, those who identify as bisexual increased from 11 percent in the Silent Generation to 19 percent of baby boomers, 44 percent of Gen X, 52 percent of millennials, and 59 percent of Gen Z. Of all respondents to the survey on sexual orientation, those who identified as women were more likely to also identify as LGBTQ+ (10 percent versus 6 percent of men), and they were the majority of those identifying as bisexual.[3]

Conservatives attribute the rise in LGBTQ+ identification to "grooming" that leads people to identify as queer who wouldn't otherwise. But

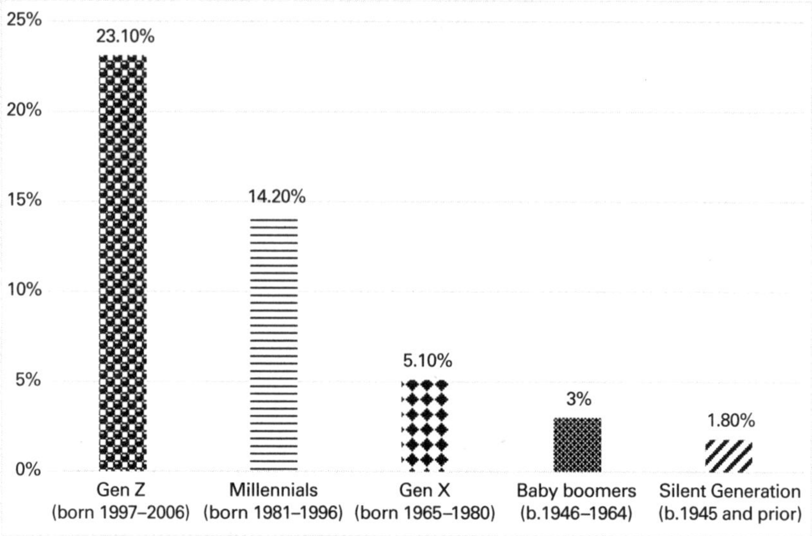

Figure 7.1 US adults' self-identification as LGBTQ+, by generation, 2024. Data source: Jeffrey M. Jones, "LGBTQ+ Identification in U.S. Rises to 9.3%," Gallup Poll, February 20, 2025.

the anti-gay legislation suggests that conservatives fear merely stating the possibility of options other than hetero ("saying *gay*")—since that presents those options as "speakable" and even respectable, meaning more people who would have closeted in the past now don't. Most Americans don't see gay rights as a problem, but as in many right-wing political campaigns, the "issue" is pushed by influencers seeking to gin up concern (especially among older voters).[4]

The "danger" to patriarchy lies in the relaxation of centuries of lifelong training (real "grooming") that has pushed boys and girls into specific roles, backed up by economic and social carrots, as well as by the stick of punitive violence at home or in the streets for not toeing the hetero line. If many now abandon the comp-het model to thrive in their chosen identities, conservatives fear they'll move the culture in directions that don't align with exploitative capitalism.

The large percentage of young people identifying as bisexual indicates that the gay/straight dichotomy itself isn't operative for most in this group, including those identified as straight, who also recognize this binary as unfixed. In the short period since the 1960s riots, much has been learned about people's desires that was repressed in the past. In trans lawyer Chase Strangio's view, "systems like the gender binary . . . make no sense . . . serve to oppress us, and . . . limit the beauty we can build in the world."[5]

Notably however, coming out is still risky in many sectors, signaling the precarity this population has lived under all along; so an anonymous Gallup poll is among the best sources of information we have on a major portion of our society. Since historically many have felt pressured into hetero relationships and/or hesitated to identify themselves publicly, Gallup's older generation numbers no doubt reflect substantial self-censoring/closeting. The current anti-gay effort intends to push people back into the closet.

Nonetheless, the recent big percentage rise indicates that the number has always been greater than recognized. Our inadequate measures of LGBTQ+ data stem from the complexity of documenting populations put at risk of violence, job penalties, and stigma, if they share too much. People won't share data you could use against them, and responsible researchers don't gather it in hazardous forms. But without some understanding of who's present and what they're experiencing, communities can't provide their members with the services needed. So methods like anonymous polls and tracking trends through service providers called on when things go south are helpful.

LGBTQ+ FAMILIES

The gay pride movement and the Supreme Court's 2015 *Obergefell v. Hodges* decision, legalizing same-sex marriage, have opened the way to an expansion of out gay families. Just before that, a 2013 Pew Research survey found that 35 percent of LGBTQ+ adults were parents, including grown children (some from prior straight relationships), compared with 74 percent of all adults.[6] In same-sex couples, 43.3 percent of children are adopted or stepchildren, compared to 10.5 percent in opposite-sex couples (2019 data).[7] Apart from direct parenting, childless adults of all stripes have long served as alloparents to their nieces and nephews.

But post-Obergefell, the scene has been changing, and the 2019 LGBTQ+ Family Building Survey found that 48 percent of LGBTQ+ millennials were "actively planning to grow their families" with a first or later child, compared to 55 percent of non-LGBTQ+ millennials—a small gap. And an additional 15 percent of LGBTQ+ millennials were considering a family later.[8] Apparently, acceptance expands family formation.

While LGBTQ+ families have long existed, they've been increasing since access to IVF and adoption expanded, starting in the 1980s.[9] The embrace of those methods, along with wider positive media representation of gay people (including personalities like RuPaul, Ellen DeGeneres, Elton John, Wanda Sykes, Ricky Martin, Laverne Cox, Leo Sheng, Jim Parsons, Jodie Foster, Neil Patrick Harris, and Billy Porter), has led many straight Americans to recognize gay people as similar to themselves. That feeling of connection, backed up by legal action (around equal access to fertility treatments, workplace benefits, freedom from harassment, and ability to adopt), the removal (in 1973) of homosexuality from the American Psychiatric Association's list of disorders, and the increasing likelihood that people would know and love out gay people in their own family or community, laid the path to the same-sex marriage ruling.

Per the American Community Survey, as of 2023 there are 1.3 million self-reported same-sex couple households in the United States, including 774,600 married couples (60 percent); 17.3 percent of the married couples and 9.5 percent of the unmarried include children (versus 37.6 percent of married and 33.8 percent of unmarried opposite-sex couples). The 17.3 percent includes three times as many lesbian couples as gay male couples.[10]

While the number of LGBTQ+ people planning families has risen, unplanned pregnancies will be relatively few (though young people identifying as bisexual or gender fluid may be less prepared to contracept if they move unexpectedly into an opposite-sex relationship, potentially raising rates).[11] Ultimately, large numbers of young people in same-sex relationships means a reduction in both unplanned births and desperate parents in poverty. That will affect the total number of children but may not greatly impact the number of parents long-term. The high proportion of intentional parents may be part of the finding in multiple studies that not only do children in LGBTQ+ families do as well as their counterparts in straight families, but they often do better.[12]

While many welcome the normalization of gay families, there's debate in the community on whether people are pushed into heteronormative lives in order to be accepted. Certainly, some LGBTQ+ people do not want kids or families or to be involved in the reproduction of patriarchal culture. But while in the past it may have, today this doesn't differentiate them from many of their heterosexual peers.

SEXUAL IDENTITY AND ECONOMICS

Internationally, heterosexuality has long been enforced through threats of socioeconomic outcasting for those who reveal themselves LGBTQ+. Gay teens thrown out of their family home with nowhere to turn have often supported themselves through sex work or other low-paid options, and face violence and other harsh treatment, daily. Those who are more supported and move into middle-class jobs may still face lack of acceptance at work (75 percent report at least one negative interaction in the past year), leading to people being closeted there (40 percent per one study), even if they're out elsewhere.[13]

At work, family context affects financials. Pre-Obergefell, LGBTQ+ couples' lack of option to marry meant they also had no access to the tax, health, and other benefits that marriage offers.[14] And as with women, gay men may feel excluded from hetero male social circles at work, which may affect careers. Even today, "family men" are rewarded with more raises and promotions[15]—because dads with kids to support are assumed to be more committed workers (a middle-class variant on the desperate workforce effect)—and since gay men are less likely to have kids, childless gay men lose out in that calculus.

The family effect works oppositely for women of all sexualities, however. Women make less on average because it's assumed they might have kids and that if they do, they're likely to be primary caregivers and have to step out sometimes, given the lack of a US family-support infrastructure. Lesbian households get a double rate cut since both partners may be seen as potential caregivers.

Despite these personal financial limitations, LGBTQ+ people have nonetheless been major economic contributors—across the board and in creative fields in particular—where their less gender-limited perspectives add insight and often spur invention. Positioned as outsiders, able to think against the grain, and often committed to caring for others in light of their direct experience of harm, their perspectives expand the pool of ideas. Conversely, making LBGTQ people feel unwelcome, so that they can't bring their full selves to work, reduces that benefit.

Some data are available on LGBTQ+ earnings from the Census and the American Community Survey (ACS), which allow us to compare data for partnered and married same-sex couples with data for partnered and married hetero couples. (Data for single LGBTQ+ people aren't available.) Drawing on 2019 and 2021 ACS data, Engin et al. find that gay married men make roughly 8 percent *less* on average than hetero married men, controlling for children and other factors, and married lesbians make roughly 5 percent *more* than hetero married women.[16] This is in part due to the tendency of LGBTQ+ people to cross occupational gender boundaries more than hetero folks: gay males are more likely to break with their gendered work assignments and enter occupations traditionally considered female and paid less, and vice versa for lesbians.

Other studies have found that same-sex partners are concentrated in fields focused on creativity, psychology, and law/social work and are underrepresented in engineering and teaching;[17] that gay men in traditionally female fields are less likely to hold senior-level positions than straight men in these fields;[18] and that lesbians achieve more senior-level positions in traditionally male fields than straight women, though they still make less than men there.[19]

CHILDHOOD LESSONS

Although we think of the disciplines of economics and psychology as separate, finances may also shape identity. In the infancy of psychoanalysis, Freud theorized that all people were *omnisexual* at birth, taking pleasure in all bodily sensations and able to bond with and feel attracted to people of either sex. He detailed a process by which people are then directed into exclusive heterosexuality within hetero nuclear families—through perceived threats of potential loss of love or even physical dismemberment if children's desires don't comply with the "mature" human norm. Freud viewed heterosexuality as that norm, but he didn't explore the extent to which the threats he described were coercive. Nor did he examine how economics and social imperatives might inform object choice.

But in his day, girls were raised conscious that they had to marry a man to be supported and that well-paid jobs were not options for them—the fertility/dependency nexus. Insofar as he discussed alternatives to heterosexuality, Freud saw them as failures to mature properly. But "maturity" in that light equates to conformity with or acquiescence to socioeconomic norms under patriarchy, and "immaturity" looks more like sustained hope that those norms might be negotiated.

If women are not dependent on men, then the economic rationales for women's attraction to men as earners lessen. This is the complaint of contemporary "involuntary celibates" (incels)—men who would have had more marital options in the preliberation days. Now men (like women) actually have to make themselves attractive to find a partner. The economic shift needn't alter any individual person's sexuality, but as the increase in LGBTQ+ identification affirms, it opens up more options for those people who might have chosen a same-sex partner or no partner or felt fine waiting longer to find the right partner if there weren't the economic (or the related social) pressure.

If, as I've argued, gender is largely about assigning tasks and wage levels, then the shifting dynamics of work are in and of themselves transgender. These shifts may put a woman (gay or straight) in what was formerly a man's job or vice versa, but more basically they open up questions about what men and women are, if they are no longer defined as those who do "men's work" versus those who do "women's work." Not that we are anywhere near erasing those assignments, but the gender blur opens up questions about what might replace old ways while also creating anxieties among those most invested in them.

Adopting the caregiving role also aligns with prescribed affects, as discussed, and these lessons are instilled early. Feminist theorist bell hooks illustrated the importance of men's performance of hetero manliness and women's performance of hetero submission through a childhood story: when she won a marbles game over her brother, her dad beat her—for what she there learned was a gender crime, and he forbade her playing again.[20] Her less aggressive brother wasn't beaten for the inverse crime—of losing and not caring about winning—but the lesson hit home that they both should care about enforcing standard gender divisions. For most children raised in a hetero home or within a patriarchal world, that lesson is conveyed early on and internalized into a lifetime of self-policing. That was exemplified for me by a student's account that he couldn't walk his girlfriend's miniature dog when she was away because it looked too femme. No word on how the dog handled that. Relatedly, a Fox News host declared in July 2024, regarding a "White Dudes" fundraiser for Kamala Harris, that "when a man votes for a woman, he actually transitions into a woman."[21] "Is that right?" asked his female co-host.

SEXUALITY, HISTORY, PATRIARCHY

But such rigid boundaries aren't needed for procreation, which requires only that male and female gametes sometimes join up, not that humans have heterosexual encounters exclusively, nor that they invest in any particular gender identity. We can assume that prehistoric hunter-gatherers had multiple sexual encounters or relationships, in series or in parallel—not so different from today; and given their frequency in known history, we can assume some of those were same-sex. If patriarchal gender/sexuality rules emerged with the development of a steady food supply and the accumulation of wealth, prepatriarchal communities may well have involved a de facto bisexuality for all.

Post-Neolithic, the regulation of sexuality within patriarchy has varied across time. Historian John Boswell has documented widespread acceptance of gay people in Rome, Greece, and the early Middle Ages in Europe, as well as the growth of intolerance in the thirteenth and fourteenth centuries, a departure from the norm to that point. He notes that levels of intolerance soared with the rise of "corporate states," which instituted many new laws—all focused on enforcing conformity and obedience to new economic rules. Prohibitions proliferated against not just gays but also Jews, Muslims, and heretics; lepers; women with knowledge and power (labeled witches); sorcerers; and so forth, all based on creating "widespread fears of alien and disruptive social elements, fears which could easily be focused on vulnerable or little-understood minority groups."[22] All were early versions of the political hate hustles seen today, which seek to distract public attention from some grift, power grab, or other shady action of the distractor (like reallocating common lands to the wealthy, as was happening back then) through manufactured outrage.

Since the late Middle Ages, restrictions on LGBTQ+ love have recurred more and less fiercely around the globe, with various rationales. Concerns about *birthrates* are sometimes cited, but gay sex needn't preclude reproduction and hasn't historically: many bisexual people with both same- and opposite-sex partners have had children, as have many who prefer same-sex relations but also have a hetero marriage—either because that was required or specifically for purposes of reproduction. More recently, lesbian couples have used IVF to conceive with donor sperm, while some gay couples have used both IVF and surrogates (both requiring funds). Many same-sex couples adopt—also a contribution to the health and strength of the community by directly aiding vulnerable infants in foster care.

Another rationale condemns homosexuality as *unnatural*—even though many species engage in homosexual acts and, conversely, even though many human behaviors are vaunted precisely as valuable because we claim to be unlike other species. It's sometimes characterized as *dangerous*—perhaps for its implied risk to reproduction or just because it's viewed as potentially contagious (i.e., popular).

But the core spur for condemnations of homosexuality is that heterosexuality *sustains the structures of modern patriarchy*. Those structures require that men support one another's privilege by actively asserting both the dominance of men over women in their daily interactions (including sexual), and through continuing women's dependency on men (via hetero marriage and childbearing), to guarantee women's free labor at home and model separate male and female work realms. Although not generally a conscious intent for people picking their love interest, it is nonetheless the effect of going with the flow in a patriarchal society.

Men who choose a same-sex partner are understood as betraying the brotherhood, and those who style themselves *femme* affirm the value of women and their work, undermining the case for its low compensation. Whereas femme men reject both their assigned gender role and the concept of such assignments, women who present as *butch* or otherwise independent similarly signal their rejection of both assigned gender roles and dependence on men. Per Foucault, "homosexuality was constituted from the moment it was characterized . . . less by a type of sexual relations than by a certain quality of sexual sensibility, a certain way of inverting the masculine and the feminine in oneself . . . and a kind of interior androgyny, a hermaphrodism of the soul."[23]

Recognition of such blurring by LGBTQ+ people also opens the possibility of blurring among people who think of themselves as heterosexuals, putting the whole binary at risk. Hence the clampdowns we see in the form of various attacks, especially on men perceived to be gay. In our moment, trans women are often attacked by their own sexual partners, who project their self-blame outward, through violence against the person who called their prohibited feelings forth.[24]

TRANS-FORMATION

Christine Jorgensen made news in 1952 as one of the first Americans to successfully undergo gender affirmation surgery, but she had to go to Denmark for treatment. It wasn't until 2008 that the American Medical Association recognized denial of treatment for gender dysphoria as discriminatory and recommended that health insurance cover it. Rates of suicidal ideation, suicide attempts, and completed suicide are high among people with what doctors call "body dysmorphic disorder," meaning that their sense of identity does not align with the sex assigned them at birth.[25] For many, the option to transition has been lifesaving.

The Williams Institute at UCLA estimated in 2022 that the trans population constituted 0.6 percent of the US population aged thirteen and over, with about 1.3 million adults (eighteen and over) and 300,000 youth (thirteen to seventeen) so identifying publicly. As with public LGBTQ+ identification overall, out trans identification has increased recently, with 1.4 percent of youth aged thirteen to seventeen publicly identifying as transgender, 1.3 percent of those eighteen to twenty-four, 0.5 percent of adults aged twenty-five to sixty-four, and 0.3 percent of those sixty-five and older.[26] Per the 2025 Gallup poll cited earlier, 1.3 percent of US adults overall identified as trans.[27] As the option becomes more known and accepted, more people feel comfortable claiming that identity. These numbers indicate growing dissatisfaction with the way standard gender options limit who a person may be or present as in our society. Only with time will we register how many people have felt misaligned in their assigned genders all along. And, of course, the definitions of what gender means will continue to shift, along with how people feel comfortable expressing themselves.

Gender transitions may involve diverse levels of intervention, linked to preference and bank accounts. Physical change through hormones or surgery or both can be costly, and some who'd like to physically transition don't have the option due to lack of funds or insurance. Others don't want physical intervention, preferring to cross-dress or engage in alternative gender behaviors, variously defined. With time, more choices will evolve to reflect new technologies and new understandings.

All forms of transness challenge stable ideas of all elements of SGS. For example, even though individual choices to transition to another recognized sex and/or gender may be perceived to affirm the established category they transition to, insofar as that transition is known or evident (vs. passing) it destabilizes the new identity category even as it embraces it. In a shifting scene, the terms change steadily. Relatedly, when a person in a hetero relationship transitions, that person and their partner are often perceived to suddenly enter a homosexual relationship, destabilizing ideas of sexuality.[28] Likewise with gay couples, who may be viewed as newly straight when one transitions. But they still love the same people.

Those who embrace nonbinary status (through behaviors/affects, clothing/presentation, and/or physical interventions) add a different kind of destabilization. The introduction of the nonbinary option into common discourse and corporate dropdowns affirms the possibility that people needn't choose between traditionally masculine and feminine traits, though they may if they like.

Destabilizing effects are also accomplished when people shift their identity over time, again acknowledging that identity need not be fixed to any one socially constructed set of attributes, skills, or capacities, and that we all contain multitudes. These aspects can be newly expressed, in a world where people don't have to play a prescribed role to be valued, in social or economic terms.

GENDER-AFFIRMING CARE BANS

Conservatives have responded to the increasing take-up of options to intervene physically to change sex and/or gender by banning puberty blockers and hormone therapy (aka GAC) for minors. In Texas, this has also involved accusing parents of child abuse if they assist their minor children in accessing such care (though, quite oppositely, they offer support to *avoid* trauma).

Legislators claim to mean to force minors to wait until they are adult in order to make decisions that may impact their long-term fertility and that they might regret in the future, which might seem reasonable to the uninformed, but these laws are often the opposite of helpful. The Texas bill prohibits doctors from "performing mastectomies or surgeries that would sterilize a minor or remove otherwise healthy tissue or body parts and from prescribing drugs that would induce transient or permanent infertility."[29] But medications to suppress puberty do not cause infertility; they delay puberty (and thus the onset of fertility) and are still legal in Texas for use for girls with early onset menstrual periods, suggesting that legislators know they're not harmful. If you go off puberty blockers, puberty resumes, unchecked.

For adolescent patients whose identity does not align with the body they're born into, puberty blockers provide relief and more time to decide the way forward, while avoiding physical changes they don't want and that will require much more intervention to override, post-puberty. Insurance data document that such medications are not used profligately, with less than 0.1 percent of US adolescents receiving gender-affirming medications between 2018 and 2022, none under twelve years of age, and that gender-affirming surgeries were rare in that population.[30] Should they decide to move to hormone therapy once they're adults, they'd go through the puberty related to the sex they identify with, avoiding the need for some surgeries as well as wrong-body trauma.

When and if trans minors who achieve majority do move on from puberty blockers to take estrogen or testosterone—which may impair fertility in some cases—or to undertake surgeries, they are counseled to consider their fertility-preserving options, including egg and sperm freezing.[31] People with ovaries may still conceive if they go off testosterone or lower their dosage. Although the numbers are not tracked precisely, one study found there were 1,907 births to people born biologically female but who identified as men between 2014 and 2018, and doubtless many more have been born since then because the number of trans men has risen.[32]

People born male will not produce sperm if they go on estrogen, and the return of that ability is possible but not guaranteed if they go off. As it happens, advances in technology (discussed below) suggest it may not be long before sperm can be produced as needed by other means. But again, intentional births to men with uteruses or women with penises are not the kind of fertility anti-trans legislators seek.

Although they're framed as efforts to sustain young people's ability to have biological children when they're older for their benefit, these bans, like all the anti-gay bans, operate to reinforce patriarchal gender norms. Although the GAC bans don't directly affect people over the age of eighteen, they have reduced the overall availability of trans health care in ban states, as many doctors have departed for states where they can provide full services. Consequently, adult trans people in ban states may also have hard times accessing medical services.[33]

Among adult trans people undergoing surgeries, less than 1 percent express regret over permanent surgeries to align their bodies with their sense of self (versus an average of 14 percent regret among cisgender patients who had mastectomies for cancer).[34] We can recall the "interests of the state" in "population increase" noted in the Missouri anti-Mifepristone case and question states' claims that they're seeking to help young people. Instead, legislatures seem to seek to increase the likelihood of births (especially unplanned) to people denied GAC and pushed into hetero relationships, while manufacturing voter outrage.

TRANS SPORTS

During the 2024 election, conservative ads focused on the unfairness of having high school and college athletes born male allowed to play on female teams. The question of how often this is actually an issue was not addressed in the ads, but the National Collegiate Athletic Association (NCAA) president testified in Congress in 2024 that out of 510,000 NCAA athletes, fewer than ten were trans.[35] This is another example of political use of what is largely a non-issue to stigmatize transgender people within a wider anti-LGBTQ+ effort. Although ongoing discussion of how best to categorize trans athletes in local, state, and international competitions is needed, that's no reason to limit the rights of trans people generally.

Among potential methods of handling sports so that everyone can compete on a level field are assigning all people to teams based on their testosterone level (a method already in use in international sports); handicapping in applicable sports (like swimming and track) based on height, musculature, or other physical advantages gained pretransition (this would also adjust for unusual physical advantages not linked to transitioning); creating separate nonbinary leagues in which trans men and women can both compete (especially as numbers rise) along with others who identify as nonbinary; and other solutions to be developed.[36]

As the number of trans-identified people has grown, so has homophobic defense of patriarchal privilege. While anti-gender-affirming-care laws are aimed at LGBTQ+ folks, they're part of a wider effort to restrict the rights of everyone—gay or straight—who transgresses the rigid gender boundaries that reinforce the patriarchal economy, by asserting value in care labor and rejecting the operative gender hierarchy. Anti-trans bills mean to police and enforce old divisions of SGS—attempting to detour the radical flux now underway across all individuals in our culture, not just among trans folks—the bellwethers.

GAMETOGENESIS

As everybody's SGS identity expressions have been shifting, big scientific advances are also shifting the rules by which sex, sexuality, and fertility interact. The increasing numbers of adults seeking to form families who encounter infertility (whether caused by age, hormone therapy, environmental pollution, or other factors) spurred researchers to explore whether their pluripotent stem cells might assist them to generate new and viable gametes (eggs and sperm).

That led to the discovery that cells taken from a mouse of one sex could be stimulated to produce the gametes associated with the other sex.[37] This means that a male's cells could produce eggs bearing his

DNA, and a female's cells could produce sperm bearing hers—because all embryos have the capacity to develop in either direction before they differentiate by sex, and each human's DNA holds code for both options (at core, we are all trans). This process, called *in vitro gametogenesis* (IVG), was developed to generate new sperm cells for men with low count and viable egg cells for women without them. But its additional uses for gay couples and for people of all ages was immediately noted, as were possibilities for designer babies.

Per one expert, "IVG . . . would render the biological clock irrelevant, helping anyone of any age have a genetically related baby—same for anyone single, gay, trans. . . . [Indeed,] IVG could make traditional baby-making antiquated for everyone."[38] Those involved noted that society-wide discussions and much ethical and legal reflection and guardrails would be crucial.

Both revolutionary and controversial, operational IVG would mean that *two sexes were no longer required to create human babies*—totally transforming ideas of human fertility, gender, and the society based thereon (though this point has been elided in the media stories about the developing technology). Some predictable ripple effects include the following:

- Same-sex female couples could have babies more easily than same-sex male couples, with two wombs available.
- All children of lesbian couples would be female (XX), while the embryos created for male (XY) couples would be one-third female and two-thirds male (XY). (YY matches could not survive, since the X chromosome holds key directions for early development.)
- Older couples could have their own genetic children.
- People might steal cells from passersby and have their children unbeknownst, requiring a new legal infrastructure to avoid paternity/maternity claims.
- Gender roles would shift notably if male primary caregivers became common.
- Many women might be pushed into surrogacy work (for male couples), with attendant risks of racialization and underpayment.[39]
- Embryo selection combined with gene editing could lead to "designer" people, with no limit on the possible gametes produced for experiment.

- That could also reduce genetic disorders, potentially increasing the group lifespan and leading to unpredictable evolutionary changes.
- There would be different access to these resources based on income or nationality.

Such technology, a step toward fulfilling second-wave feminist philosopher Shulamith Firestone's dream of ending enforced family formation through reproductive technology combined with communal child-rearing, opens the way for many transformative scenarios and much debate.

EXPANDING FUTURE

The dynamics of SGS are swiftly changing on many fronts in our moment. Clampdowns on LGBTQ+ love (as with abortion access) might raise birth rates in some sectors, but they risk harms and substantial ripple-effect population losses in other ways, including increased out-migration from ban states, as well as declines in interstate in-migration, as our recent study predicted, and recent statistics confirm (see chapter 8).[40] Such shifts would affect workforce and skilled talent attraction to ban states, and those could be further affected if impacted businesses begin to take stands in support of their LGBTQ+ and female employees, to maintain the skilled staff needed to stay in business.

Recent changes on the fertility front for LGBTQ+ Americans, as for others, are enormous and ongoing, and they directly intersect with economics in multiple ways. The efforts to push LGBTQ+ Americans back into the closet and into comp-het fertility patterns are the opposite of an effort to care and help thrive. Among its first acts, the 2025 administration issued several executive orders regarding transgender people: reassigning those in the federal correctional system to the prison associated with their biological sex at birth (currently enjoined), initiating separation proceedings for thousands of service members and blocking trans recruits (a policy one judge described as not based on lack of military readiness but instead "soaked with animus and dripping with pretext"), and allowing only indication of sex at birth on passports. These were followed by further restrictions and acts of disrespect.

By the time this book comes out, more harms may have been done to this community, but they will have occurred alongside many fertile acts of resistance and coalition. Again, while anti-trans and anti-gay policies and laws are directed specifically at LGBTQ+ folks, they're part of the wider effort to restrict the rights of all who challenge the patriarchal economy.

Those who identify with any of these linked fights for workforce and civic equity can best advance their goals by rejecting divide-and-conquer strategies and cooperating to build a caring democracy. Such a system would reject the huge human capital, insight, and energy losses created by the traumas of outcasting and instead invest in growing an economy of mutual thriving through care, as we'll see in chapter 10. But first a case study of care-less-ness.

8

CARING LESS

Texas: A Case Study

You've heard of Paris, Texas? Welcome to Vichy, Texas.
—Quip

It's time to revive my old proposal that Texas be made into a national laboratory for bad government. Having a bad idea in your state? Come to Texas and see how it works out in practice.
—Molly Ivins, "Texas: Laboratory for Lunacy" (1997)

"As I would not be a slave, so I would not be a master. This expresses my idea of Democracy."
—Rep. Barbara Jordan (D-TX), 1976 Democratic National Convention Keynote, citing Abraham Lincoln (1864)

Texas is a famously large state, with a major role in the American story—including its fertility/gender/sexuality story: 10 percent of US births occur here annually, and the state has been a legal innovator on the fertility front, though not always intentionally. The 1973 *Roe v. Wade* abortion rights case began in Texas (Wade was the Dallas district attorney) as did the 2003 *Lawrence v. Texas* case (based in Houston), which ended the criminalization of nonprocreative sex acts (aka sodomy) between consenting adults (both straight and gay). Both cases involved people suing against state policies they opposed, but those bringing suit were Texans too, and their work generated national progressive policy from which all Americans have benefited. Transgender rights also had a source in Houston—where Phyllis Frye (the grandmother of the transgender movement) organized six International Conferences on Transgender Law and Employment Policy, between 1992 and 1997, laying the groundwork for trans rights and creating networks of activism.[1] Later, Houston's second woman mayor and the first lesbian leader of a major city, Annise Parker, appointed Frye as the nation's first transgender judge.[2]

These advances occurred in Texas against a background of business-focused conservatism, supporting the growth of the oil and gas (O&G), aeronautics/space travel, clean energy, medical, and agriculture industries. Perhaps activists could be more active here specifically because their backbones were steeled in a furnace of repression. Recently, Texas conservatism has adopted a directly intrusive fertility-policy focus in response to the declines in teen and other fertility rates and their progressive ripple effects for women and families. As we'll see, the state has stepped up efforts to limit and punish departures from "traditional" gender, sexuality, and fertility patterns and to reimpose a patriarchal economic and social model that serves the interests of a small set of actors with money to influence politicians.

But first, a bit of background. The largest state in the lower forty-eight, full of resources the rest of the nation depends on (especially energy), blessed and cursed with Gulf Coast weather, and the only state to have been, briefly, a separate country,[3] Texas amplifies its own mythology as a maverick forging its own way, not subject to others' rules. There's a lot to love here: big sky, astounding landscape, the many friendly people, the weather from October to May, the unique history, and what seals the deal for many—it's cheap. The state's population is diverse: as of 2023 it was 40.2 percent Hispanic, 39.8 percent non-Hispanic white, 13.6 percent Black, 6 percent Asian, with a foreign-born population of 17.2 percent, from countries around the globe.[4] This mixture makes for a lively, multilingual cultural scene in the major cities, with great food and lots of hopeful people working hard to get ahead.

But the beauty and energy inhabit a framework of great suffering:

- 13.4 percent of the population lives under the official poverty line ($30,000 per family of four, versus 11 percent nationwide)—that's 4.1 million people (twenty-three states have fewer).
- 42 percent of households earn under $50,000 per year—also in reality a poverty wage (versus 31 percent nationwide).
- 6.8 percent of the population is undocumented (2.1 million as of January 2025) and at risk.

- 16.7 percent of residents have no health insurance (5.2 million)—the highest proportion in the nation because the state (like nine others) won't expand Medicaid.[5]

When things are bad in Texas, it affects many people. For the extremely impoverished people who *are* Medicaid eligible, the paperwork is complex and requires frequent redos. So people are often sick.

The refusal of Medicaid reinforces a long history of actively refusing to provide needed services to large swaths of its own people, including

- livable wages (the minimum legal wage is $7.25, the lowest allowed for documented workers and undocumented may get less),
- decent educational options (the state is 47th in education investment per student),
- child well-being (Texas ranks 44th),
- and environmental protections (50th in toxic air and water).[6]

These refusals are not accidental—they're an active policy of care-lessness, for profit. That too is a form of labor manipulation, pushing young people further into desperation via refusals of basic support.

But the story here is not solely negative: cities and counties counter by building small-scale supportive infrastructure that offers some regional resources, some of it quite innovative. And many individuals and organizations do care about others enormously: their energy and commitment sustain the state every day, caring for the ill and unhoused and feeding the hungry through direct services. Likewise, political and community groups work hard to change oppressive systems. But charity is insufficient to the need for consistent basic services for all—as rights, not handouts—and efforts at systemic change have been largely unsuccessful. All of this work wears down the do-gooders, many of them women, who often work their own jobs as well as the family and community care jobs they add on.[7]

The state also uses both large quantities of undocumented labor and a school-to-prison pipeline to keep people tied to low-wage jobs and unlikely to challenge the system. The lack of state investment in education limits job options and pushes many into crime and then incarceration (the state has the most prisoners by far).[8] As nationally, Black offenders often face more severe charges than white offenders, and are less likely to be able to meet bail.[9] Although not counted as part of the business economy, prisoners are discounted laborers, working for little or nothing, providing state services (like wildfire fighting), and producing goods at prison farms or in prison factories where their labor is rented out.[10] Once released, parole limits their voting and civic participation, so the prison pipeline is also a form of voter suppression.

In limiting services for its poor, Texas embraces the "business-friendly" Southern economic development model (SEDM) outlined in chapter 3, coercing labor discounts that serve as perks to in-migrating businesses and their staff, as do other incentives, including no personal and corporate income taxes, corporate tax credits, lack of regulation on pollution, easy permitting, and low cost of living. Businesses that take the lure happily pay the lower "going" rate in SEDM environments, though they may evince highly principled HR views and pay employees more in other states.

While high earners can pay for what services they need out of pocket if they're not supplied by their employer, the lack of an income tax means many social services are not available to those who can't pay themselves. Those with funds can access world-class medical centers, but others without insurance avoid care until they're near death, so doctors here see advanced stages of illness unusual in developed nations. Levels of violence linked to poverty and related stresses are high, but services to address these are few: the Texas foster care system is one of the worst in the nation, and DV shelters have insufficient beds and high turn-away rates.[11]

All of this feeds a vicious cycle, as desperate people with families must take the low wages on offer. Low-income Texans contribute to the state's "low cost of living"—adding to the business draw at a high price to themselves. The state's mythmaking about its own cowboy loner history feeds pride among some voters in being unwilling to take help from others. Those who aren't loners and recognize they'd benefit from a state service infrastructure are often blocked from voting to express their views, and when they do manage it, the gerrymandered legislative map blocks their effect.[12]

The state's low rate of investment in education and health creates a shortage of educated workers needed to run the businesses attracted to Texas, meaning that many administrators, professionals, and skilled laborers have to be hired in from more care-*full* states that do make such investments.[13] While businesses and wealthy individuals benefit from the lack of income tax, for those who make less, the lack of income tax is largely offset by higher than average property taxes[14] and a high sales tax (8.25 percent versus the national average of 7.3 percent).[15] Unlike income taxes, sales taxes are regressive, disproportionately affecting the poor, who pay a bigger portion of their income for the limited services.

ANTI-ABORTION, ANTI-LGBTQ+

Texas's large population (second after California) has historically been maintained through a combination of a high native fertility rate and high in-migration. But here as nationally, the fertility rate has fallen markedly of late, in all age groups. So it's no accident that recently the state has pushed two new groups into active hardship—women and the LGBTQ+ community—through its leadership role on conservative policies banning access to abortion and GAC and denying support to LGBTQ+ communities. These policies aim to raise fertility and increase hardship, while also bringing out conservative voters and pleasing billionaire donors (including Christian nationalists) invested in the patriarchal family model for personal and business reasons (which often overlap).

Texas introduced a six-week abortion ban under Roe in 2021, a move that was followed post-Dobbs by a total abortion ban in 2022, and in 2023 by a ban on GAC for LGBTQ+ minors. Rather than embracing the opportunity to include more skilled women and men in the workforce that reliable birth control offers, these policies aim to move the clock back to the "traditional" patriarchal model of unplanned births, while forcing women to provide the care work that the state won't on the "it's your family, it's your problem" logic, and passing that discount along to business.

As of summer 2025, the Texas abortion ban has ensured that pregnant people receive diminished emergency care—those who present hemorrhaging at emergency rooms have been sent home to self-manage—risking death by sepsis, heart failure, or blood loss;[16] women carrying fetuses with fatal anomalies have been forced to carry to term; and women with dead fetuses have had to wait for weeks to miscarry because doctors fear the state won't support their diagnosis and will imprison them if they provide the normal dilation and curettage treatment.[17] In May 2025 the state passed a "Life of the Mother" bill to clarify in which medical emergencies doctors can perform abortions, so some of these harms may be avoided in the future if doctors feel secure enough to carry them out, but underlying health risks are not among them.[18]

The abortion ban provides a rare instance of better-off Texans facing the hardship that ordinary Texans have to negotiate daily. The fact that medical emergencies must be addressed immediately means that women can't reliably be whisked off to hospitals in other states; the harm done here became more visible when well-to-do white couples with the status to be heard began complaining. Those suffering include not just pregnant people—everyone who sees a gynecologist is seeing services reduced, as many established OB/GYNs have left ban states, where they can't use best practices for patient care, and few OB/GYN residents are incoming because the training there wouldn't fully prepare them for their profession.[19] Apart from physical complications, the ban also means that unwanted births will increase the financial and care burdens in families that would have chosen to abort a pregnancy they couldn't afford.

Simultaneous with the abortion bans, the bans on the recognition of LGBTQ+ lives in schools (Don't Say Gay), on library books that represent gay lives, and on GAC for minors are chilling the lives of LGBTQ+ adults and kids nationally. Texas's expanded GAC bans threaten prison terms for parents who help their kids access care, causing some families to relocate. Many without that option have remained, hoping to help improve things.

Studies confirm the predictably bad effect on the mental health of LGBTQ+ youth of such legislation, including youth in ban-free states who fear its spread.[20] While some legislators may see an LGBTQ+ exodus as desirable, the negative effects on the workforce and on the morale of Texans whose family and friends are pushed out are also huge.

As in all states with rights restrictions on women or LGBTQ+ residents, Texas employers will lose the skills and insights of both those who migrate out and the many potential job migrants who don't apply.[21] Between 2022 and 2025, per the US Census Bureau, net domestic migration to Texas was reduced by 70 percent (from 609 per day to 184).[22] A study of postal change-of-address forms found that the net outflow of people from abortion-ban states (all of which are also GAC-ban states, since 2023) increased by 129,000 in the year following Dobbs, particularly among single young people—countering what had been a steady north-to-south migration flow.[23] Since educated people tend to be more mobile, this migration may further draw down the educated workforce in ban states. Zoom can help some businesses serve their ban-state clients long distance, but in industries requiring more hands-on efforts, upper-level employees required to work in ban zones may require hardship pay and short rotations. Although Texas boasts about high in-migration rates, once they arrive, many transplants aren't comfortable and move on, as happened with the majority of tech companies during the pandemic.[24]

A few businesses (many of them owned by women) have spoken up against the bans, arguing that they'll undermine business and other activities, and citing public disapproval of the policies, concern that health risks will deter people who want children from having them, and fear that pregnant attendees at conferences and sports events booked in ban states would risk negative health consequences in emergencies.[25] But so far, most companies have not objected publicly, perhaps because so far most corporate employees have been able to access abortion through medication or travel, if needed. Should that access diminish, corporations could reconsider their roles in the interstate business realm, which they've played both sides of for centuries.

UNDOCUMENTED IMMIGRATION

Total business expenditures on wages are brought even lower in Texas by the presence of roughly 2.1 million undocumented people, whom the leadership claims to dislike but on whom it depends, and whom it has welcomed for decades, turning a blind eye in exchange for lower wages and workers willing to do many labor-intensive jobs that citizen-workers won't. The dependency is beginning to be acknowledged by businesses here, as the federal administration deports growing numbers in 2025–2026.[26] These underpaid workers hiding in the shadows have long cemented the state's "low-cost" status (and its "abundance" reputation for quick housing construction). As with the artificially constrained pool of female workers forced into low- and no-wage care jobs, the many undocumented workers competing with one another further lower the wages paid for the hard jobs they have no option but to do. They also lower the wages offered to some documented workers, with whom they directly compete for some jobs. Despite talk of immigrant criminals, undocumented immigrants (who aim to avoid attention) commit fewer crimes than US-born citizens.[27]

To balance things and allow US-born workers to compete without penalty, a guest-worker program that brought in a like number of workers legally could fill many jobs. But those positions would earn higher wages than are currently paid to people without papers, and some benefits would have to be supplied (making Texas less lucrative for businesses). Such a program would also remove the fear element that prevents undocumented people from reporting unsafe working conditions or mistreatment. That fear and few options also make them exploitable for backbreaking farm labor, domestic services, sex work, construction work, and other forms of trafficking.[28] The easy availability of trafficked undocumented sex workers here also "benefits" those who use them and negatively affects gender dynamics in the state.

Historically, the anti-immigration discourse has been doubletalk: combining politicians' interest in bringing out voters by playing on their opposition to immigrants not "playing by the rules" with those politicians' equally strong interest in encouraging many undocumented immigrants to succeed in entering. Anti-immigrant political discourse also serves to distract attention from issues that affect voters more directly, such as lack of health care access, low wages, underfunded education, unpopular abortion bans, and how to improve immigration policy.[29]

Although for decades tough talk didn't block entry, it did push undocumented immigrants deeper into the shadows, increasing their exploitability. Between 2020 and 2024, the number seeking entry at the US Southern border rose, and all parties concluded that more regulation was needed. However, a bipartisan bill to increase border funding to process cases and expand border patrols was quashed in 2024 by candidate Trump, adding to the sense of political theatrics. If mass deportations actually occur in 2025 and after, the dog-that-caught-the-car effect will immediately raise prices in Texas (and nationally) and disaffect voters, a double loss for conservatives.

It will not only cost huge sums to carry out millions or even thousands of arrests, incarcerations and extraditions, but it will also vacate many of the over 9.7 million positions those workers currently fill nationally, at a time when the United States already has a low-wage labor shortage.[30] In Texas it would cut 9 percent of the active workforce, cut tax revenues (many undocumented workers pay taxes but get no benefits), and traumatize families and whole communities.

Rising labor costs in Texas would raise the price of its major commodity—energy—and that rise would ripple nationally. While those who profit directly from labor discounts and tax cuts in Texas live there, the indirect recipients of the cheap O&G that runs the American economic engine include the inhabitants of all the states that more virtuously invest in their own workers. So undoing the current immigration system without an alternative in place in Texas will affect all Americans.

CENSUS BABIES

Population manipulation is an old game that the South in particular never stopped playing but that others sometimes imitate, as we saw with Idaho politician Chuck Winder's comments and the Missouri Mifepristone suit. Along with the low-wage workforce, there are additional spinoff effects of enforced procreation. Those include things that ordinary people may not think much about, but politicians do—like expanding their state's Census body count. More bodies mean more federal funding since the more people in a state, the bigger the per capita federal block grants it receives. Those grants are allotted for basic state necessities like highways, public health, and education. But there is no requirement that all the people whose presence generated those payouts receive the benefit or even that the funds go to the purpose they're assigned for, especially if many people are dissuaded from voting.[31] Just how that money is distributed is largely controlled by state legislators, who may choose to use it to replace rather than augment state funding. Thus, Texas, for instance, spends only 4 percent of its population-based federal Temporary Assistance for Needy Families (TANF) grant for the basic assistance the grant was enacted to address (the lowest percentage of all states), and redistributes the rest to cover services that other states fund themselves, like child welfare (40 percent of TANF funds go to this) and pre-K (33 percent).[32] That frees the state to further cut taxes since now the feds are covering those basic state costs—so instead of helping those suffering TANF dollars fund tax breaks for the rich.[33]

Higher census numbers also generate expanded representation in Congress, giving the state more political power to shape federal policy and funding—yet another motive driving both competition for residents from other states and efforts to raise internal fertility rates. If increased population is your aim, abortion bans and lowered access to contraception can look like ways to meet those goals. This goal generally goes unstated because it's not a high-sounding moral argument like "saving the unborn." But since it would be a principal effect of a blanket ban, we can regard it as intended. In their zeal to try any argument that might stick, however, those filing the case against Mifepristone for Missouri said the quiet part out loud: that their purpose in seeking to limit access to abortion medication was to raise the teen birth rate in order to avoid the possible "diminishment of political representation" and the "loss of federal funds" associated with lower census numbers.[34]

MATERNAL HEALTH

Some might expect that a state ostensibly focused on conservative family values would emphasize maternal health, but not so. Since 2021, the abortion ban puts the health of female citizens last on the list of items their doctors should be concerned about, but for years before that, poor mothers' health was already directly endangered by the state.

In particular, the health of Black mothers has been badly affected by a nexus of failures of support—including lack of health care most obviously, but many other stresses exacerbate that lack. Women's health in a context of poverty is further deteriorated by the plethora of care tasks they're forced to take on in the absence of public services. These are much more numerous for poor women, who unlike people with money or insurance, can't hire someone else to do some or all. There's no time left over for exercise or shopping for and preparing healthy food. Lack of health care doesn't just spur whatever ailments a woman develops; it also worsens the health of her caregivers. In a state where 5.2 million people have no health insurance, much of the care of sick family members falls on moms and other women—who are often managing health conditions and illnesses themselves.[35]

Along with tending the sick, women in lower-income families are tasked with raising children, helping elders, emotionally supporting their stressed partners, and advocating for their communities while also often working paid jobs to help feed the family. Living in an underresourced area, where many of your neighbors express mental health and other traumas brought on by hardship, can also be traumatic. As others have noted, managing poverty is itself an extra job.

The federal government does offer states assistance with health care through the expanded Medicaid program, but while Texans all pay federal taxes, the state has refused the $5 billion-plus federal dollars per year that an expansion would return, dollars that would provide health care to the nearly 1.5 million Texans in the Medicaid gap. Those payments would go directly to hospitals in both urban and rural districts that under the current system have to supply unreimbursed emergency room services to the uninsured who have nowhere else to go (for services that would cost much less at a doctor's office). This system has led to many hospital closures, disserving whole regions. Although the failure to expand is generally attributed to state leadership valuing grandstanding against Obamacare above the health of their residents (a heartless move), it also serves their agenda of keeping poor Texans desperate.[36] The national administration's 2025 budget, with its deep cuts to public service funding including Medicaid and rises in health care premiums, learned directly from the SEDM model that Texas follows. As a friend in another state lamented in 2025 as cuts to services of all kinds were enacted nationally, "It's like we're all living in Texas now."

Lack of access to health care also negatively impacts maternal health even before a pregnancy starts since ill-health coming into pregnancy sets a woman up for further health difficulties during. In Texas, the rates of maternal morbidity are twice as high for Black mothers as for others and rates of maternal mortality are 2.5 to 3 times as high, reflecting the multiple comorbidities that many suffer prepregnancy.[37] Those are caused by lack of access to health care, by the stress on poor women without state support for family care tasks, and by the toxic offerings of the fast-food industry—the only dining option in many poor neighborhoods.

All of these pressures also create vulnerability to DV, which further harms maternal and mental health. As previously discussed, many women stay with abusers because they can't afford to house their kids on their own, and many abusers enforce additional births (reproductive coercion) on purpose to ensure moms can't leave. Deep cuts to housing assistance for DV survivors in 2026 will further erode survivors' ability to live independently.[38]

The Dobbs decision negatively affected the mental health of adult women in the fertility age band (eighteen to forty-four) in all ban states, a Johns Hopkins study found, likely linked for many to concerns about having to bring children into an already impoverished or otherwise unprepared situation, and the general loss of autonomy in decision-making around life-shaping events.[39] Women over forty-five and men of all ages did not show those symptoms, nor did women under forty-five in ban-free states.

POST-BAN FERTILITY

For decades, a steady teen fertility rate was ensured in Texas by offering very little information that would help teens avoid pregnancy, especially those from poor families—via abstinence-based and error-filled sex education courses to which parents have to actively opt in for their kids;[40] limited investment in education; limited access to clinics where birth control might be prescribed; and limited access to health care of all kinds. But the availability of LARCs and Plan B undermined that low-wage pipeline, and the decline in teen birth rates over the past few years was so great that the state put drastic action into play with a six-week abortion ban in 2021.

An abortion ban might be expected to counter the downward trend and increase both the fertility rate and the desperate parent worker rate. Initially, the Texas abortion ban seemed to be doing that—the rate rose by 2.04 percent overall in 2022, with Hispanic people most affected (seeing a rise of 5.1 percent), while the teen fertility rate rose slightly (0.39 percent), for the first time in fifteen years, also largely affecting Hispanic teens (who saw a 1.25 percent rise). But in 2023, post-Dobbs, the general fertility rate fell in Texas, as in all fifty states. As figure 8.1 shows, the

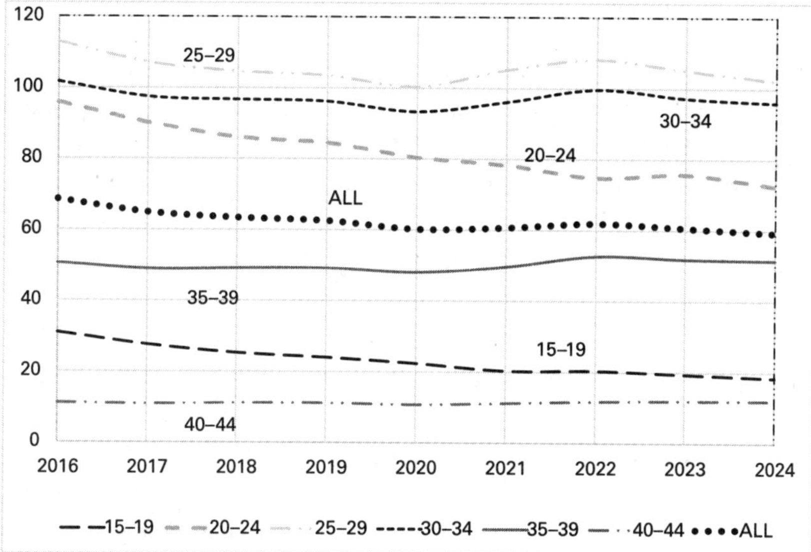

Figure 8.1 Fertility rates by age of mother, Texas, 2016–2024. Births per 1,000 women, aged 15–44, by age band. Data source: CDC Birth Data, WONDER database, at https://wonder.cdc.gov (accessed November 2025).

general rate fell 2.1 percent in 2023 and went down another 2.3 percent in 2024, to new lows, while the teen rate fell 4.71 percent in 2023 and went down another 5 percent in 2024.

The abortion ban has had mixed effects nationally to date—lowering fertility rates and bringing out majorities of pro-choice voters in some elections but not others. Similar dynamics operated in 2024 in Texas: falling fertility rates indicate continued use of abortion and contraception, but conservatives won across the state (suggesting issues both with who's voting and with gerrymandering, and that voters choose candidates based on more than one area of concern). More discussion will follow on all sides on how to address fertility rates, workforce demand, and women's rights in the state. Key to addressing the needs and preferences of the population, not those of gerrymandered political representatives (could they care less how Texans suffer?), will be replacing dog whistle sloganeering with real talk about what's at stake in these issues, and ensuring all eligible voters have ballot access.

TEXAS AS COLONY

To understand why a state would operate by commodifying its people rather than serving them, it's helpful to consider Texas not just as a state but also a kind of colony—because that's how it behaves.[41] Of course, exploiting the many for the benefit of elites is what all class systems do, but the fuller colony comparison arises for Texas because a large proportion of those benefiting from the exploited labor of the local residents live or come from elsewhere. Indeed, despite all the anti-immigration rhetoric we've heard from the state recently, Texas is totally dependent on immigration: from other nations (both with and without documents) and from other US states.

For comparison, think of India from 1757 to 1947.[42] The British colonizers rewarded Indian elites for cooperating in the exploitation of the rest of the population and imported hordes of Britons to administer business and civil systems. On one estimate, they extracted $45 trillion.[43] While a small portion of the population received educational and financial benefits, most locals went without.

Likewise, in Texas, a small elite with access to markets and a legal enforcement system runs the state, exploiting the labor of most of those born in Texas and immigrants—including skilled labor from other states. Initially, the chief sources of income were agriculture, cattle, and shipping. Since the drilling of the first gusher in 1901 and the development of extraction, refinement, and transport infrastructures, O&G has enabled huge profits for individuals while also enabling the United States as a whole to develop many industries based on these suddenly plentiful and affordable resources. Low labor costs increase that affordability.

Texas's history of refusal of service to its own is entwined with the history of federalism, which allows for differential rules across states. That system, built in 1786 to ensure that states' diverse interests could be served, allows for a different approach to the welfare of citizens than is taken by most developed nations, which generally provide consistent legal protections to all. The principal rights diversity among states in 1789 lay between free and slave states, and as we've seen, labor discounts still proliferate most in former slave states. Free labor in antebellum slave states, including Texas, was itself a resource from which all states benefited economically in the form of cheaper goods, even if they didn't themselves allow the practice.

To change the pattern of differential services would require rewriting some of the federalist rules, a project with limited support to date. However, the combination of potential backlash to recent anti-democratic overreach and climate pressure could create a crisis environment, allowing innovations previously blocked.

Perhaps the biggest example of the "care-less" history of Texas is that of the O&G industry's failure to acknowledge or seek to assuage the climate harm caused by fossil fuels. This huge failure of care has generated enormous profits here and enabled many others to profit across the United States and globally, on large and small scales. How to structure a system of compensation for the harms, while leveling the playing field going forward and focusing on repair, will require much thought and collaboration. On the positive side, there is an active and innovative green energy sector in Houston, the nation's energy capital, to move that forward.

After a quick exploration of the recent longevity-linked transformation of workforce dynamics in chapter 9, the closing chapters explore ways to frame the process of sustaining our fragile world, with care.

9

STAYING ALIVE

Expanding Longevity, Declining Fertility, Workforce

Human life expectancy has increased by some thirty years since the beginning of the twentieth century. We are living in new territory, drawing the maps that will give it meaning.

—Mary Catherine Bateson, *Composing a Further Life* (2010)

Across this book, we've noted multiple factors now affecting workforce simultaneously. Expanded longevity, which is transforming human experience almost as fundamentally as reliable birth control (RBC), also increases demand for labor and directly affects gendered work patterns.

Odd though it may seem, as fertility rates have fallen over the last two centuries—winnowing the numbers in each family and freeing women to take on other jobs—the overall population has been increasing. The earth's human inhabitants have quadrupled in the past one hundred years, from two billion in 1925 to eight billion in 2025, after doubling over the prior century.[1] That's due in important part to improved health around the globe, leading to longer lives and to more generations being present simultaneously (figure 9.1 portrays the effect in the United States).

In 1900 US life expectancy was 46.3 years for men and 48.3 years for women (including high rates of infant mortality and higher fertility rates); by 1980 it was 70.0 and 77.4, and in 2023 it was 75.8 and 81.1—an addition of roughly 30 years per person over the past 120-plus years. Such changes have ripple effects, which are increasing as boomers retire. While in 1900 4.1 percent of the population was age sixty-five and older, by 2023 it was 17.5 percent, forecast to be 20 percent by 2030 (figure 9.2). Previously, working-aged people met the labor needs of their own age

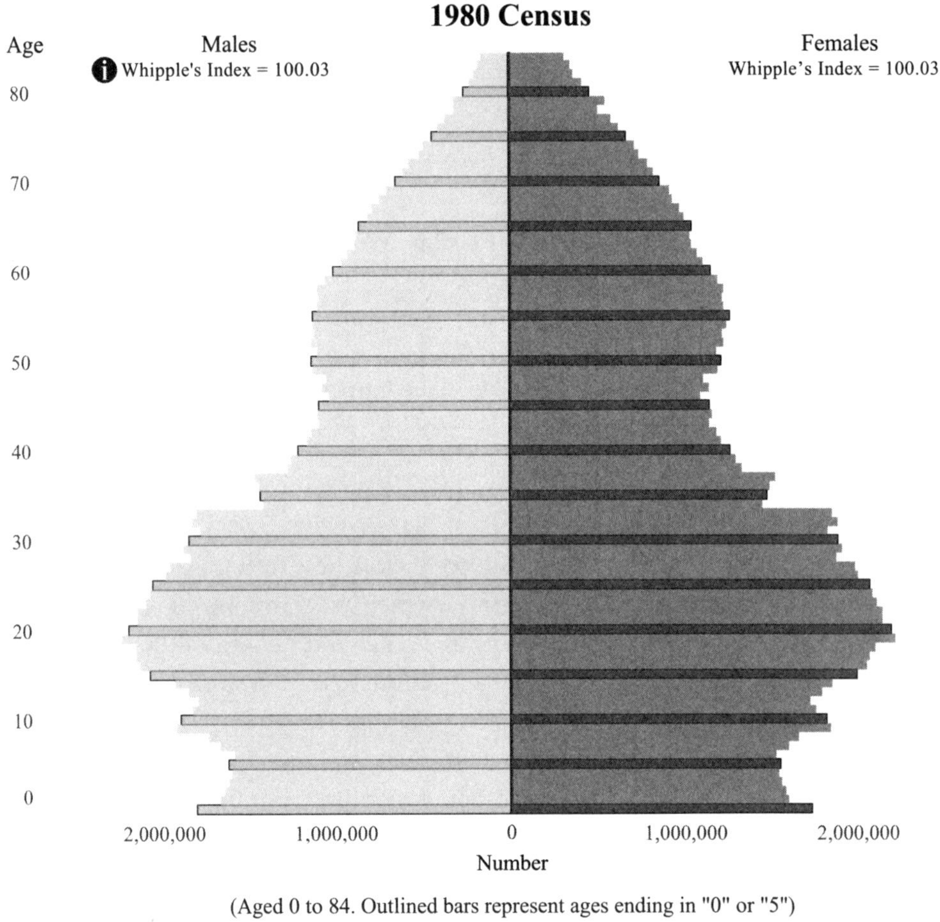

Figure 9.1 US age-sex pyramids, 1980 and 2020 censuses. Data source: "Age-Sex Pyramid for the United States, 1980 and 2020," US Census Bureau, May 25, 2023, accessed November 2025, https://www.census.gov/library/visualizations/interactive/age-sex-pyramid-for-the-united-states.html.

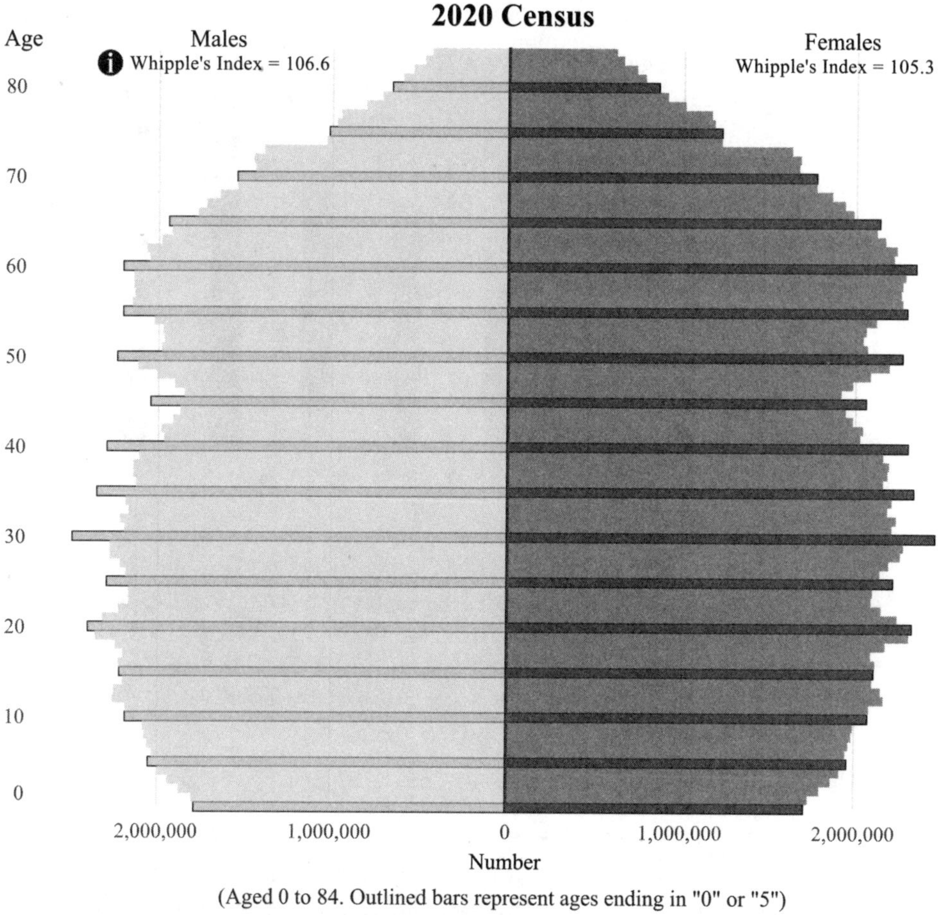

Figure 9.1 (continued)

group reciprocally as well as those of their dependent children and surviving elders. Each addition to the length of the average life that expands the number of nonreciprocating retirees adds demand for labor. While the longevity effect on the economy has been much discussed in terms of the Social Security shortfall looming, which could be addressed variously (see below), the labor effect has been less discussed. However, as more elders retire and then live longer and longer, the demand for additional workers to serve their needs in all realms—not just medical professionals but also tour guides, plumbers, couriers, salespeople, government workers, and so forth—will grow. Who will fill that demand?

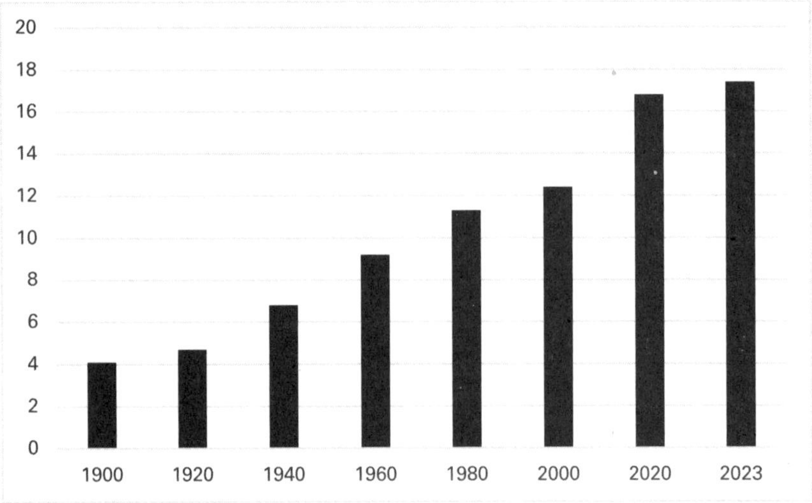

Figure 9.2 Percentage of the US population aged 65 and over. Data sources (all from the US Census Bureau): Wan He, Manisha Sengupta, Victoria A. Velkoff, and Kimberly A. DeBarros, *65+ in the United States: 2005* (December 2005), Table 2.1, "Total Population and Older Population by Age for the United States: 1900 to 2000," 9; Carrie A. Werner, *The Older Population: 2010* (November 2011); Zoe Caplan and Megan Rabe, *The Older Population: 2020* (May 25, 2023); *The Older Population: 2023* (January 2023).

THE DELAY GAP

On the way to answering that, a quick detour. While delaying first birth has positive economic effects for individual families, if large numbers do so at once over several years, it creates a near-term decline in available workers, which isn't addressed by pronatalist calls for more babies, who would enter the workforce eighteen to twenty-five years later.

Starting eighteen years after the recent fertility rate decline linked to delay began (in 2008), a gap in the number of young US-born adults flowing into the workforce will open, expanding annually. This means that beginning in 2026, and continuing until eighteen years after the overall fertility rate rises notably (at least through 2042), there will be a growing reduction in the influx of young workers (roughly a 9 percent decline in the influx over the first three years, rising to 22.4 percent over the first eighteen). For the first few years, that shrinking of the cohort of new workers entering the workforce coincides with increasing boomer retirements (though many are working past sixty-five).

Those two demographic transformations are colliding in our moment, with growing numbers of retirees raising demand for labor and falling numbers of new workers at both ends of the age spectrum shrinking supply. The threatened mass deportations would of course further cut workforce.

These dynamics require us to consider how to most efficiently identify and move additional workers into open jobs. The two readily available worker pools are *immigrants* (who would need to be reassured that they are welcome and will be treated decently) and *people now on the labor-force sidelines* who are present but not working or are working part time. The latter includes those not working due to lack of family care support (largely women) or discouragement (laid-off workers), as well as ex-prisoners.[2] Many will need training or retraining. To find the best matches in skills and temperament, efforts to override the effects of gender and caste systems that have blocked certain groups from job categories in which they could excel if allowed would help. More DEI, not less, is needed, within a context in which the full dynamics in play are discussed, concerns are addressed, and systems fair to all are enacted across realms.

A care infrastructure that allowed current home caregivers into the workforce for eight to ten hours per day would help families thrive, and, as we'll see in chapter 10, the economic, personal, and societal benefits would ripple throughout their communities. By contrast, the pronatalist effort to move women home to bear and rear kids for the workforce of the future accomplishes exactly the opposite of what's needed: it reduces current workforce still further and hugely cuts CGP; and if the pattern continues, it reduces future workforce too, while undermining democracy.

PAST PARALLEL

Prior to our moment, a similar dynamic played out in the 1960s through the 1990s, when falling fertility also intersected with rising longevity among retirees[3] and with strong boomer demand for goods and labor. The lowered number of births per family after 1960 due in important part to the Pill (the US TFR fell from 3.6 in 1960 to 2.0 in 1972, where it basically remained until 2010) of course included reductions in the total number of births, both male and female, which meant that eighteen to twenty-five years after 1960 (1978–1997), the influx of native young adult white men into the American business scene was diminishing.[4] Simultaneously, the demand for labor from the expanding group of elders and the strong boomer economy continued apace, opening the way for more efficient uses and distributions of working-age labor across identity groups (recall figure 2.4).

While there were many additional factors in play affecting labor demand and supply at different points, the simultaneous steady demand for workers combined with the reduced set of young white men born put pressure on the old-boy gender and race caste systems, which broke down partially, in the face of the need to fill the jobs. Men of color and all women could take positions with less likelihood of being seen as pushing out white men since there were more jobs open. Their wages then diversified markets and expanded demand. While this was a win for equity, it also responded to the demographic changes and the growing economy.

However, the full participation of those new groups was hobbled by the continued action of gender and race caste systems to still reserve a good proportion of the best jobs for white men (still viewed as more competent) and by the lack of family-support infrastructure. As we've seen, many women used RBC to delay the arrival of first births to create their own shadow benefits system and access better jobs. But many could not do that, leaving roughly 25 percent of women aged twenty-five to fifty-four still out of the workforce for thirty-five years after 1990.[5] DEI gradually allowed more competition for higher-level jobs, which has recently generated backlash. As in the O&G VP example, to the extent that caste still advantages the smaller pool of white men to access leadership roles, it narrows the talent available for sorting—a pattern that often results in weaker hires than would occur were the full pool considered. Nonetheless, the labor force participation of women twenty-five to fifty-four rose post-COVID to new levels, perhaps in response to growing demand (expressed as rising wages) and/or to lower births. More such workers will be needed to fill shortages going forward.

VOTING AND AGE EQUITY

Another one of the knock-on effects of the confluence of fertility decline and expanded longevity is an enormous shift of political power—away from the young and toward the expanded population of elders now present, who vote in much larger proportions, especially in primaries. In Texas, where the median age is 35.5, people aged 18 to 30 (20 percent of registered voters) comprised only 4 percent of primary voters in 2024, those over 50 (45 percent of registrants) comprised 80 percent of primary voters, and those 70 and older (14 percent) comprised 37 percent.[6] Conservative candidates have weaponized evidence of change from social patterns that elders grew up with as a way to spur their outrage (on issues they formerly ignored) and ensure their votes.

This means that candidates who'll make state-level rules around fertility, gender, and climate are selected by voters raised in very different cultural moments who don't comprehend and won't personally face the consequences of the policies they're imposing on their children's and grandchildren's generations. In the United States in 2024, people under thirty made up 14 percent of voters in the general election, those aged thirty to forty-four made up 24 percent, and those forty-five and older made up 63 percent.[7] The people who will be affected longest, those under eighteen, have no voice at all in these decisions. Expanded longevity exacerbates the skewed viewpoint representation that results from the long historical pattern of low voting rates among younger people.

Just as we can question whether male legislators have standing to regulate the bodily autonomy of female citizens, we can ask whether all age groups should have equal standing on decisions that could drastically affect younger generations. Should elders have a full vote on these, or could votes on some issues be weighted or separated out for a vote by those whose fate depends on them? Public debates on this question are overdue.

The issue is further complicated by the coming delay gap, which also means a decline in the number of eligible young voters. During that period, representation of the interests of their age group will be even further unbalanced.

The experience of trans people in particular has been played upon to spur outrage by conservatives. Trans and nonbinary identities may be less recognizable to elders because these are new options in gender and body expression in mainstream American culture, and elders are less likely to be in touch with youth, who comprise most of those identifying as trans now.

It's essential for elders to listen to youth insights and concerns around the harms that old gender roles have imposed and not seek to recreate the world of their childhoods through legislation that punishes those who break old patterns. Likewise with climate change, when elder (and other) voters are encouraged to not believe the science but to stick with the energy sources of the past, it only exacerbates the great harm already done.

The discussion of the socioeconomic impact of expanded longevity continues in chapter 10, as part of the exploration of options for growing the thrive through care.

10

GROWING THE THRIVE

The Collaborative Economy of Care

What makes us free, actually, is our capacity to care and make commitments to what we care about. . . . It requires action rather than consumption. It requires engagement with others.
—Joan Tronto, *Caring Democracy* (2013)

A very different concept of social and economic policies from those on display in the United States as this book goes to press animates the care-*full*, democratic world that many Americans envision—of, by, and for the people. Those three prepositions encapsulate the care agenda: it's generated of the people, run by them, for their mutual thriving. All the people, not privileged subsets. As women have surged into civic roles over the past thirty-plus years, a mandate for an affordable care infrastructure has emerged, which can help all members of society thrive by providing needed services, allowing all to contribute, and admitting all to full civic status. Our moment is challenged to supply the care that can support our progress toward that real democracy, for the people.

Analyzing the interface of fertility and labor, as we've done to this point, expands understanding of how our full economy (paid and unpaid) has operated, of the essential role of care, of the harms done by care-lessness, and of the roles long played by identity and caste in assigning tasks, pay, and power. Investing in a care infrastructure will spur significant economic growth through expanding care markets, which will generate jobs, purchases, taxes, and overall economic and social value (positive externalities, as economists say) far greater than input.

To date, there's been little discussion of how a care economy could work in the United States, though versions of it exist in many nations. We often hear that it's "too expensive," but actually it's been hugely expensive NOT to make these investments in terms of both human cost (the care many did not receive for lack of a caregiver, the poverty of millions of unpaid caregivers, the inability of women to participate fully in society) and economic cost (the growth of the economy is slowed by not compensating caregivers for their contributions to business and society). Although much care would remain to be done in daily life, paying for key elements of care on a broader scale would be positively transformative.

Among many benefits to building a paid care infrastructure, the most direct are the following:

1. Ensuring all Americans get the care they need
2. Freeing up current unpaid caregivers to work for pay if they'd like
3. Documenting through payment the heretofore un-booked value of that care work on the ledger of human production, which adds that value directly to GDP, where, newly manifest as exchange value, it would make a hugely positive first-order impact on the economy (of 21 percent or more),[1] lifting all boats
4. Further growing GDP when the newly employed paid care workers spend their earnings, often in community businesses
5. Democratizing the civic status of people previously excluded, by marking both carer and caree as worthy of compensation and investment, respectively

Such infrastructure revises the Wages for Housework concept[2] into a Wages for Care program: one that pays skilled workers to do care (often centralized), freeing family members to take other jobs. (Federici entitled her essay "Wages Against Housework" intending that wages allow women to choose against housework by making it just one of their many job options, and not requiring that their identity be tied to their work.) Additionally, it expands care to those previously receiving none, due to lack of family caregivers available.

This chapter outlines one way of organizing an economy of care through a mixed-market approach that blends the advantages of both free markets and government intervention—of capitalism and socialism—to benefit all.[3]

Payment for the expanded care infrastructures can be supplied through a combination of

1. *increased taxation* on individuals and businesses (as in most of the developed world) that is balanced in most household and business budgets by the reduced cost of health care and lifetime care services (such as childcare and elder care) and raised levels of care; and
2. initial government investment in buildings, equipment, salaries, and other costs through *deficit spending,* to be repaid over time through increased economic growth (which will manifest in the further business development and individual earnings and expenditures that it enables, and the higher tax paid on higher incomes).[4]

Discussion, debate, and development of these and other funding options are invited!

Previously, the likelihood that such a proposal could be heard in the United States let alone spur action was minuscule, given the many barriers to innovation enforced by those invested in the status quo, but the coincidence of the two species transformations—expanded longevity and shifting fertility patterns—against a background of mounting climate catastrophe creates an unprecedented opportunity to renovate decrepit systems to meet the needs of our moment. Disgust with the recent evidence of corruption and cruelty among those in power and their failure to support basic services for Americans can create a revolutionary moment that strengthens the legal and economic frameworks for a caring democracy going forward.

GROWING THE ECONOMY THROUGH CARE

To operate most effectively, a care economy would make core care services reliable and universally affordable, across the nation. Investment in such services through taxes and deficit spending would create many new caregiver jobs; those new salaries would be spent in community businesses of all kinds. In what economist John Maynard Keynes famously called "multiplier effects," shop owner A then spends some of the cash from that purchase in shops B and C (for business and/or personal expenses), and those owners do likewise, over dozens of exchanges before the benefit disappears into savings accounts.[5] Each time the money is re-spent, it benefits both the spender and the group, as taxes are generated through each exchange, repaying much if not all of the care investment.[6] This applies directly to the deficit spending, which introduces new funds, and indirectly to the tax-funded spending, which recirculates preexistent funds, since those earning the salaries will tend to be low- and middle-income workers, who are more likely to spend than save versus higher-income individuals.

In addition to those multiplier effects, care would have many other positive effects in the economy and in society. Here are a few.

A centralized universal health care system would reduce the cost of health care overall

- by removing the profit component (cutting out the middlemen who add enormously to cost);
- by leveraging wholesale bargaining power around purchases of drugs, equipment, etc.;
- by reducing individuals' health expenditures (replaced by tax payments, lower over time);
- by preventing illnesses in the first place (saving people cost and misery and their families the burden of caring for them) and allowing them to participate more in their communities over their lifetimes; and
- by saving employers the cost of health insurance and workdays lost to illness.

Expanded childcare (including after-school and summer care) would

- allow more moms who so chose to work consistently, earning more for their families and avoiding work gaps that can undermine career progress;
- reduce economic pressure on families;
- reduce domestic violence that results from economic pressure and from isolation;[7]
- admit women's voices to policy discussions at all levels, expanding the range of available insight; and
- create opportunities for children to thrive through learning and play in centers and for families to connect.

Expanded elder care would

- ensure people have the care they need for managing health issues, including disabilities;
- create well-staffed centers for accessing multiple needed services, socializing, classes, and community service;
- provide regular home-health services;
- reduce isolation and opportunities for elder abuse; and
- begin to address the huge economic, health, and societal transformations introduced by expanded longevity.

Offering affordable care to all who need it would mean, for example, that a mom with kidney pain doesn't refrain from going to the doctor because the visit would be expensive and her growing kids need school clothes. If she can go to the doctor regularly throughout her lifetime, she is less likely to develop the pain in the first place and so will have fewer lost workdays and will spend less time in bed unable to do things with her family. Dedicated case managers would coordinate care.

Developing a government-subsidized care infrastructure to supply key segments of the necessary care work now supplied at home or not at all would take time. The process would require major investments in new buildings for childcare and elder care centers, in equipment, and in workforce training.[8] These centers, as well as home-based caregivers for people who needed those, would eventually create hundreds of thousands of good care jobs, which could be filled by caring people of all genders. Some centers could combine child and elder care elements, allowing connection across generations and including care for kids with special needs and people with disabilities. Center construction would also generate jobs and other new economic activity and add to GDP.

Such a shift would require phase-in to avoid both supply chain bottlenecks for building materials and other goods, and potential inflation from rapid increase in demand, lessons learned through COVID. Starting up would initially involve collaboration with preexistent child and elder care centers, which would benefit from added support.

A constitutional amendment could be required to add a federal care infrastructure to the enumerated powers of the federal government, overriding states' ability to underinvest in some of their people on the basis of race, gender, or class, as has been the case historically.[9] That amendment might be tied to the Equal Rights Amendment barring discrimination based on sex (written by Crystal Eastman and Alice Paul), now approved by the required thirty-eight states (on an altered schedule) and declared the law of the land by President Biden in 2024, though its status is tentative.

Such a big change would spur fierce battles (as seen in the recent oligarchic push to undo the limited redistributions of funds and power made to date) but could be addressed by electing legislators and leaders committed to democratic change and to blocking the undue influence of what Mancur Olson called "distributional coalitions" of the wealthy—special interest groups who lobby to change democratic rules for their benefit. Despite their likely objections, they too would benefit from the expanded, more delicious, and sustainable pie.

Currently, we all pay the price every day in lost individual and community benefits, as many who could be working and growing the economy are kept at home giving full-time, uncompensated care, often in poverty, when they'd love to be out earning to help their families and communities. Such funds earned would reduce family stress, so DV would also decline. And, of course, any who choose not to participate in receiving care need not.

Paying for key portions of the care work women have long done and expanding the reach of care would operate like a flywheel of value in the community—maintaining economic momentum for the long term by including the value of the newly compensated care work in the exchange markets where it can multiply and where, if there are drags on the wider economy, care could maintain economic power more consistently.[10]

Covering the costs of the expanded care systems would require dividing them among all the beneficiaries (society, business, and families), whereas previously families (and specifically women) bore the brunt, outside the monetary system. While many in business claim to fear that more public investment in care would be costly, this complaint ignores the huge economic and social gains such care would unleash. Instead, I suggest, the resistance is spurred by a different fear: that the skill gains, added revenues, and other forms of value that such investments would generate wouldn't all go into the pockets of those now in power. The rich would still have plenty in the expanded economy, but they wouldn't have (almost) all, as in the throttled economy they now defend. Businesses would all benefit from the expanded population with solid incomes to spend. (Too often shortsighted businesses see labor cuts as cost savers, without considering that they simultaneously reduce the revenue side of their budget!)

CORE CARE

So what could a care economy involve? Suggestions will vary, but along with the health, child-, and elder care mentioned above, core elements could include food security, affordable housing, reliable birth control (RBC), paid parental leave, family allowances to support and incentivize family formation, solid public education in all zip codes, affordable college tuition for those accepted, and a safe, unpolluted, sustainable environment. It would take a while to reach that full complement of benefits, but if it seems like a lot, recall that all or most are available in Denmark, France, Spain, Germany, Italy, New Zealand, Australia, Turkey, Iran, and Saudi Arabia. Many are available in India, Japan, Israel, South Korea, and China, two of which have much bigger populations.

Quality care resources would provide a solid foundation, which individuals would build upon through earnings. Various kinds of care would be called on across lifetimes, according to need. In addition to the services themselves, all would benefit from the expanded contributions of insight, skill, and innovation from fellow citizens no longer mired in debt, worry, and the traumas of poverty; from the improved environment (see chapter 11); from the economic growth; and from expanded community engagement and dialogue, which would serve as a platform for dealing fairly and forthrightly with the many issues we'll face going forward.

Providing such care in the new context of RBC would be different from past welfare systems that provided limited benefits that did not enable sufficient numbers of people to rise out of poverty. As has been the case with RBC, phased-in access to core care services would lessen Americans' desperation—and if a strong path-to-citizenship and a guest-worker immigration system were installed, that of immigrants too.

Such a change would likely lower willingness to take low-wage, unpleasant jobs. Different from "not working," holding out for a decent job would be any workers' choice if available. If no one was forced by caste to take bad or inadequately paid jobs, those jobs would change: some would be automated, some pay levels would rise, some working conditions would become less harsh, and some types of work would disappear. Some difficult jobs might be welcomed as a path by immigrant workers, as is currently the case, especially if framed within an ethically managed program and access to care benefits. Opening discussions on how to better structure work to be both productive and satisfying in a context of non-desperation could generate advances and opportunities we can't now imagine.

By committing to setting up systems to help all thrive, the federal government initially takes on the cost of capital construction of care spaces (including childcare and elder centers, nursing homes, and community clinics) and the full cost of care services for those who can't afford any sliding scale payment. But since care is dynamic, a person's relation to it may change over time. For example:

- If a family receives free childcare that enables the caregiver to work, along with any needed training for both parents to advance, soon the family moves into a stronger economic position where they pay more of the sliding-scale cost.
- If a state that previously refused Medicaid expansion shifts to providing its lifelong health care to all—or even better, if the United States moves to a national health service for all—fewer people will become ill and many with current comorbidities can come to manage them, reducing the need for care, and freeing them up to earn, pay taxes, and participate.
- If underresourced schools are brought up to par, the communities in those neighborhoods will produce more skilled workers, less crime spurred by desperation, and more tax revenues to cover school costs.

Those who can pay for sliding-scale services will, but the rates will be lower than currently and the service better, absent the profit-making impetus to raise prices, cheat, and skimp on real value—as happens too often within the current model.[11] All transitions will require strict watchdogs and penalties, to guard against the grift industry that preys on American consumers at every opportunity.[12] Which services are best covered fully and which are best sliding scale is open to analysis and discussion.

Of course, not all care could or should be outsourced and paid for. Every moment of our lives involves elements of mutual care—these interactions are the core of our lives as free beings, as Joan Tronto reminds us. Similarly, Texas feminist Genevieve Vaughan compellingly argues that mutual care among individuals is a gift, referencing the maternal care-*giving* model.[13] However, the uncompensated interaction of care with capital, whereby women have produced the workforce for employers' profit, is wage theft and political suppression. Monetizing some care so that no one is pushed into dependency or excluded from the polity repairs that inequity, grows the economy, and strengthens the society.

HOW WOULD WE PAY FOR IT?

There are varying ways to approach payment for a fully functional care infrastructure, and I'll explore the two noted above here, in overview. Others may have additional ideas. But the key recognition is that many countries (see the earlier list) already fund caring democracies that thrive because they support their people (including sliding-scale access to early childcare and health care for all). Although socialized care is portrayed as radical by conservatives in the United States, we can remind ourselves that lack of such a system is seen as demented by other developed nations—a kind of Emperor's New Clothes blindness.

If they all can do it, the United States can too. Very different from what we've known, getting there would require candid, in-depth discussions, and commitment on both sides to working through mistrust to help the group thrive. After centuries of divide-and-conquer discord, building a caring democracy through cooperation would be a process, but as Nancy Folbre and others have noted, common struggles can be coalition builders[14]—and in our moment in addition to a common need for expanded care, we have both the oligarchs who seek to steal all the value and the threat of climate change (a product of those same parties' care-less actions) to combat together. Anger against their overreach may be their gift to us all, a coalition builder that can enable system-wide change for the better.

The simplest method, as in most caring nations, would involve taxes paid by businesses and individuals for a range of types of care, with a baseline percentage due from all, additional increments above certain wealth levels, and exceptions for those needing subsidies.

For businesses, this would involve adding the cost of employee production into the corporate tax rate, thus articulating in GDP the value to business of the work of care. The expanded care that this tax on business would enable would directly pay for some of the care that families have long done. In Europe, total corporate tax rates in countries that cover or subsidize large amounts of care costs average 21.5 percent in 2025. This is smaller than the 35 percent that was the US basic corporate rate before the 2017 tax cuts reduced the rate to 21 percent (current in 2026). Additions to this rate would spur debate, but some addition seems important for corporations to acknowledge and repay the contributions of families to their profits, to reduce income disparities, both in the United States and worldwide, and limit corporations' power *over* the people, returning them to a more appropriate power *to* function well and responsibly, within a democratic framework run by the people.

For individuals, the level of added income tax would be progressive, paying the community back for the opportunities to do well its infrastructure supplies. In Europe, nations with high rates of care provision range from top marginal income tax rates of between 44 and 49 percent (the United Kingdom, Germany, Greece, Iceland, Ireland, Italy, Luxembourg, and the Netherlands) to between 50 and 56 percent (Denmark, Austria, France, Portugal, Sweden, Finland, and Slovenia). Although that is substantially more than the current United States' top rate of 37 percent, it includes a lifetime of care coverage, and most people pay lower rates. Those who earn more pay more but still have plenty. (For comparison, we can recall that in the United States in 1955, the top marginal rate [paid by few] was 91 percent, so it is not the case that paying taxes is in any way "un-American."[15])

The lack of transparent discourse around taxes in the United States over the past few decades has obscured the extent to which *low taxes mean low services* and, as a result, the harm they have done to our people and our economy, to the (limited) benefit of the few. Likewise, recalling Olson's *Rise and Decline of Nations*, high taxes on the wealthy can prevent the formation of distributional coalitions that can buy influence to further expand their wealth and power at the expense of the rest of the group and of democracy. If the recent effort to lower taxes to benefit oligarchs has the effect of opening up discussion of how taxes can make our economy more efficient and more robust while helping the people thrive and growing our democracy, then this book may arrive at a good moment to join that discussion. Part of sustaining democracy would be building safeguards against its cyclical destabilization through the coalition power grabs that Olson describes.

If, however, responsible tax restructuring still proves off the table in our moment, there are other ways to approach care funding. The simplest would be higher levels of initial government investment through deficit spending. The United States has run a deficit most years since 1970, and all years since 2001, to cover items viewed as "necessities," including principally defense and tax breaks for the very rich. As productivity increased through care, the value multiplier effects in the community and the new taxes generated would recover large portions of the investment over time.[16]

OFF THE SIDELINES—FILLING THE TEMPO LABOR GAPS

As discussed in chapter 9, the combination of expanding longevity with recent fertility declines creates demand for more workers. Related dynamics have been in play since the 1960s, and the rising demand for workers has been supplied by both immigrants (in 2022 51.6 million, or 15.6 percent, of those living in the United States were foreign born) and adults formerly on the sidelines of the labor force—including women who either didn't have kids or found care.

As we move into the dip in incoming native-born young workers created by young people's delay of first births since 2008 (the delay gap), even more demand for additional labor will emerge, requiring a response exactly the opposite of current policies that A. urge women workers to move home with kids, B. deport undocumented workers who've been doing needed jobs but who weren't offered a legal path, and C. fire people of color and women in positions of authority on baseless claims that their promotions were undeserved, often putting clearly less qualified people in their places.

Such policies aim to reestablish the old-boy caste system. But pushing these workers out will deepen labor, service, and goods shortages; deflate the economy; and raise poverty rates—creating an economy of scarcity where a few do well and most suffer (and, again, pushing people into poverty reduces the customer base and thus profits for business).

To reverse this path, investing in care infrastructure would add jobs and services, expand available workers, and spur growth. If our education system, including adult ed, were fully funded, many workers abandoned by our current systems in inner cities or rural areas who turn to crime and drug use in despair could retrain and become upright contributors (the best way to cut drug trafficking is to cut demand). The systemic underinvestment in education and other services in low-income communities and the failure to reskill Midwestern workers after NAFTA and grow opportunities in those regions grossly disserves those workers, their families, and the nation.

Those who see themselves as losing through more equitable "redistribution" of resources will object because though businesses will still profit, the disparities will be less great and other voices, including those of caregivers, will be heard at the policy table. Building and maintaining a real democracy will require compromises on all sides, just as those who've lost through wage theft for centuries have compromised. Differently, today's compromises will benefit all present and the generations to come.

Investment in care would likely also generate more births given that many people indicate they're refraining from kids not because they don't want them but because they fear they won't be able to afford the costs involved. A national commitment to lifetime health, elder, and childcare services care for current and future Americans could do much to reassure potential parents that their kids will have a chance to thrive.

Essentially, such increases in socialized care will benefit the overall economy—opposite to what we've heard for years, from sources profiting from the status quo. The particulars can be worked out equitably, with reference to models that work elsewhere. Given the current division in our nation, there would doubtless be arguments. But firm leadership that focused on building a caring democracy, allowing for success but banning oligarchs, addressing the shifting socioeconomic realities of workforce, longevity, civic voice, and climate change, and finding ways for all sectors to thrive—that could win many over.

CARE POLICY INNOVATION

Although our national narrative foregrounds democracy, our care-less economy and society have been short on equitable systems to support it. The rest of the chapter provides overviews of how three essential care systems could operate as the starting place for discussion: family support (including childcare; school/work synchrony; parental leave, sick/family leave, and family allowances), health care, and elder care. Additional systems would also be developed or better funded within a robust Wages for Care system.

FAMILY-SUPPORT INFRASTRUCTURE

A collection of family-support programs could help all the nation's children and their families thrive and contribute while simultaneously incentivizing more people to form families going forward.

Childcare As we've seen, childcare is both a gateway to women's civic participation and, contradictorily, an outcome of that participation. Women's delay of childbirth has enabled some to move into policymaking roles and increase discussion of childcare, but to date, childcare policy has not benefited as much from their ascent in the United States as elsewhere, as figure 10.1's comparison of sixteen developed nations' annual public spending on early childhood care per child suggests.

Why does Lithuania (#81) invest sixteen times more in toddler care than the United States, the wealthiest country on the earth, while Norway (#28) invests sixty times as much? Key background: multiple nations with developed childcare systems initiated them after population decimation in World Wars, which the United States has not experienced. These longer histories of care may impact the level of women's participation in policy roles today. Norway (like some others) developed its child benefit program after World War II and had a female prime minister from 2003 to 2021. Lithuania was part of the Soviet Union until 1990 and as

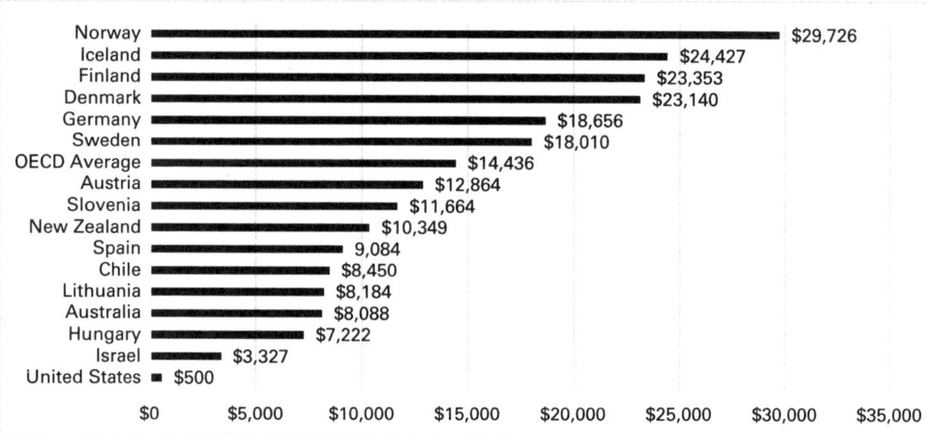

Figure 10.1 Annual public spending on childcare for toddlers in developed nations, 2021. Source: Claire Cain Miller, "How Other Nations Pay for Child Care. The U.S. Is an Outlier," *New York Times*, October 6, 2021. Data source: Organization for Economic Cooperation and Development and Elizabeth Davis and Aaron Sojourner for the Hamilton Project.

such benefited from government-sponsored public nurseries, either free or subsidized. After exiting the USSR, childcare offerings became more expensive, but Lithuania introduced a family allowance program in 1994. Since then, their female leadership has included a two-term president (2009–2019), three prime ministers, and several speakers of Parliament. Various factors enabling women's increased access to the polity interact in each national history. The process has been slower in the United States.

But we can fix that by drawing on other nations' models. France's model (inaugurated after World War I) provides a starting point (open to edits): free childcare for all children aged three to five and sliding-scale childcare for all infants and toddlers aged zero to two, their care being more expensive and less used. It would take a while to construct buildings and train teachers here, but such a system would be a boon for families, children, and employers. Kids would get the benefit of learning and socialization, and parents could work steadily to provide for their families.

School/Work Synchrony Along with childcare, after-school care and summer care programs for kids in elementary and higher grades are much needed. The asynchrony between work and school hours often bars mothers from working consistently. Fees are exorbitant and scheduling is complex for the programs that do exist. A national expansion of the public school day and calendar to provide sliding-scale wraparound care options to all families would allow parents who so choose to work full time and to move without risking their access to care.[17]

In a fit of exasperation when my youngest was small, I calculated the percentage of standard 8:00 a.m. to 6:00 p.m. work hours (including commute) that kids are in public school between birth and age eighteen. That worked out to be *just 37 percent of the time*—since many districts don't start school until kids are age five, it lets out at 3:30 p.m. (or earlier), and there's no coverage in summer. The rest of the time, care is on you (see figure 10.2).

Omitting the more self-sufficient high school years, the percentage covered falls to 33.3 percent for kids aged zero to fourteen. If you add in pre-K (for four-year-olds, available in some school districts), the percentage for those aged zero to fourteen rises back to 37 percent—meaning that during normal work hours kids are not in public school for 60 percent of the time, or more. That's why so many parents have to leave work, especially when kids are small, why employers have long viewed women as unreliable workers they can't risk investing in, and why many people feel they can't have kids.

But we can fill those workday coverage gaps by rationalizing the school schedule with optional, sliding-scale programs:

- work-synchronous childcare for kids aged three months through pre-K, centralized so costs are lower
- after-school coverage for pre-K–8: extending the school day to 6:00 p.m., with sports, arts, and tutoring
- summer camps: offering sports, arts, and learning activities in otherwise empty school buildings, while avoiding the summer skills slide

These wraparound services parallel those that many with funds now pay for. They would be optional and flexible (pickup any time after school dismissal), allowing both parents to work consistently while providing kids with fun, friends, and learning. Additional programs could be developed for the children of shift workers.

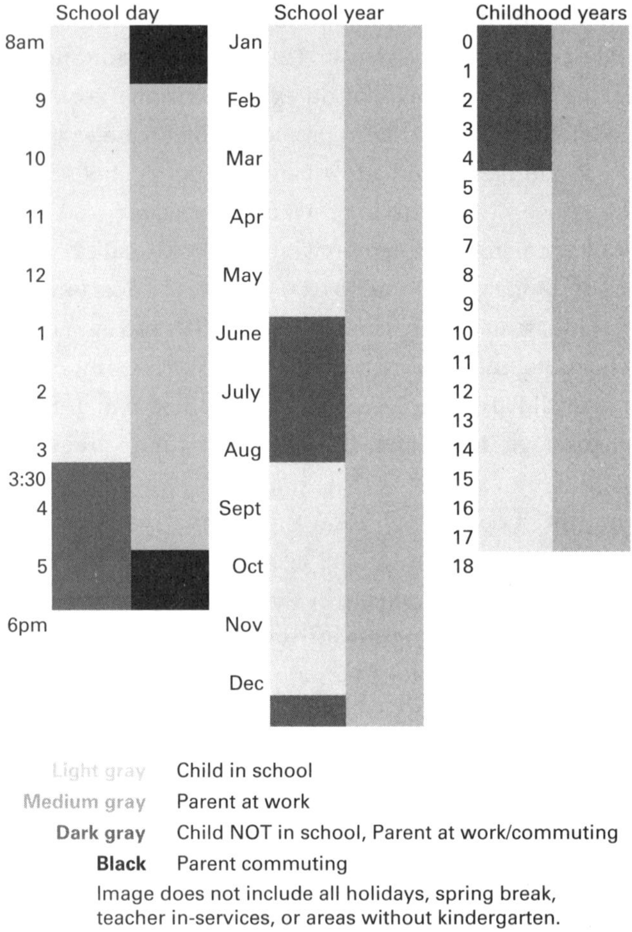

Figure 10.2 School/work asynchrony: Overview of lack of workforce support for families. Source: Author.

Although schools are funded locally, a federal program could supply initial support for this upgrade to state and local systems, which could soon absorb that cost with funds from the addition of mothers' wages to the local tax base.

The educational boon such programming would offer would be enlarged by mandating a base level of pre-K–12 education funding nationally. As noted, there are huge variations in the levels of investment in children across states and school districts. The effect of low investment in SEDM states is to consign many children to lifetimes of poverty and limited job options, while employers hire skilled workers from states that invest in education more. A full democracy would not allow such disparities.

Parental Leave, Sick/Family Leave, and Family Allowances Another feature of national care programs in Europe is paid parental leave, allowing babies and parents time to bond. Parental leaves vary from fourteen weeks of maternity leave and two weeks of paternity leave (European Union minimum, optional, with two weeks mandatory for mothers) to two years (Romania) and vary by percentage of salary covered and funder (employer, government, or combination). While long paid leaves sound great, they can be expensive to companies (especially smaller ones) because they're required to keep your job open and risk your deciding not to return. This can lead to discrimination against hiring women, seen as "unreliable workers," and/or to career delays. One Finnish study finds that paid leaves also don't benefit kids or parents.[18]

Mandatory shared leaves offer a way to mitigate gender discrimination, because they mean that employers can't anticipate that men won't also take time off for care. In the United States, fourteen weeks of paid leave to be split between parents seems a good starting place (with single parents able to access the full amount).[19]

It's predictable that children will sometimes get sick, and many employers let parents use their sick leave time to care for them. But many low-wage jobs don't offer employer-paid sick leave, so parents end up unemployed if they fall ill or if a sick child has to stay home. The Family and Medical Leave Act guarantees many workers the right to take a leave up to twelve weeks to care for their or a family member's health, but the act is unfunded, so few people use it. To date, nineteen states and Washington, DC, have implemented mandatory paid sick leave laws, requiring that employers provide some paid time off for illness (based on length of employment). A nationwide length-of-service-based, portable sick leave requirement for all employers would protect families, with small businesses and new-to-workforce employees able to apply for some subsidies.

In the face of declining fertility, increasing numbers of nations (including Australia, Canada, France, Japan, South Korea, and the United Kingdom) offer some form of regular allowance to help families support children. In the United States in 2021, the Child Tax Credit was paid as cash to families too poor to pay taxes, halving child poverty in that year, and it would do the same again if reinstated. In 2025, President Trump proposed a one-time $5,000 cash baby bonus, not an amount to convince anyone to enter the expensive world of child-rearing but useful to those already planning to. While such bonuses generally have had limited effect on incentivizing family formation, regular allowances may over the long term.

HEALTH CARE

While most developed nations offer universal health care, the United States does not, though the Affordable Care Act offered something close to that as a possibility through the Medicaid expansion option for states. Initially, however, twenty-four states did not take the option—a number reduced to ten as I write. In those ten states, the health of much of the low-income population is bad and worsening, caregivers and emergency room budgets are burdened, and residents' federal tax dollars are paying for health benefits elsewhere.

One recent study found that in Texas, 78 percent of severe maternal morbidity cases (near misses for maternal death during childbirth) were due to preexisting health conditions (comorbidities)—suggesting the need for prepregnancy (aka lifelong) access to health care for women as well as access to more nutritious (less harmful) food.[20] Saving mothers' lives and keeping them healthy has huge positive ripple effects on both their families and the economy and would be a big factor in raising interest in having children. Men, whose life expectancy is markedly lower than women's, also need health care and good food to keep them healthy long term. Which is not to say that general health is excellent in other states, just better than in the ten still opting out (seven of them in the former Confederacy).

The clear case for a centralized full care system (with savings on administrative costs and negotiated drug costs, access to all providers, and nobody skimming a profit) has been made by many, but the health care industry has consistently lobbied it away. The Affordable Care Act greatly improved health care access, but some coverage gaps remain even among states that have expanded Medicaid and overall costs are higher than needed.

Instituting a national health system like Medicare for All that guaranteed good health care to all Americans would be transformative. To date, the refusal of its proponents to include tightly regulated private insurance options, as the Canadian and European systems do, has played a role in blocking acceptance of the program. Compromising to find a workable way forward as a near term first step seems useful. Without a national health program, as Bernie Sanders, Pramila Jayapal, Elizabeth Warren, and others have emphasized, the nation with the best health care options will continue to have appalling national health outcomes.

If nationalized, a well-regulated health insurance industry could continue to exist, in smaller form, to provide services the public system doesn't. There would be cost savings on middlemen, on redundancies across providers, on waste (as there'd be no incentive to cheat for profit), and on pharmaceuticals. While lower health costs would reduce GDP initially, the savings would flow more productively into other industries.

ELDER CARE, SOCIAL SECURITY, AND LONGEVITY

The growing crowd of elders brings growing demand for elder services—with financial and workforce complications. In 2025, almost one-fifth of the US population is sixty-five and older (seventy-three million), and by 2029 that group will outnumber those under age eighteen for the first time.

Mention of elder care often spurs thoughts of illness and health care, which are a real part of aging. But the new longevity is the result of expanded elder health, and many are quite well and active. Just 5 percent of elders reside in nursing homes each year, with an average stay of two years. Alzheimer's affects 10.8 percent of those aged sixty-five and older, with 80 percent of those staying with family caregivers. There's a growing movement to offer care to their caregivers—through spelling them with in-home aides, through elder day care, and with direct compensation for the work caregivers do at home, which often blocks them from paid employment.

In addition to medical services, many elders require different kinds of interaction and services—like book clubs, sports teams, church groups,

Backroads or Road Scholar travel groups, crafts fairs, and good restaurants. The huge majority of elders "age in place," meaning they continue living in their homes postretirement (a factor in the housing crisis that is too little discussed), and many prefer in-home health care. Some move to warmer climes or move in with relatives. A growing portion move to retirement communities or senior housing where, when well run, they can access community activities and avoid loneliness.

Who lives long is largely determined by who has healthy food, habits, and environment; lifetime access to good medical care; and safety from violence. Those benefits often correlate with identity factors, which are still widely linked to labor roles, wages, and access to services. Newborns' average life expectancies at birth vary by income level and race/ethnicity (often a proxy for income). A 2016 study found that men in the top 1 percent of the income distribution between 2001–2014 had a life expectancy of 87.3, while for the bottom 1 percent it was 72.7 (a 14.6-year gap); for women, the difference was 88.9 versus 78.8 years (10.1 years).[21]

Across races in 2023, life expectancy rose by roughly one year over 2022. Non-Hispanic American Indian, Alaska Native (AIAN) men and Black men fared worst on life expectancy, at 66.7 and 70.3, respectively, and non-Hispanic Asian and Hispanic women fared best, at 87.1 and 84 each (related in part to traditional plant-based diets). See table 10.1. While everyone pays into Social Security, only those who live long get the payout, so AIAN and Black men in particular lose out. This disparity could be avoided with Medicare for All and equitable education—which shapes job prospects, wages, and safety.

Table 10.1 Life expectancy by gender and race/ethnicity, born 2023

	All	**NH AIAN**	**NH Asian**	**NH Black**	**Hispanic**	**NH White**
Male	75.8	66.7	83.2	70.3	78.5	76.0
Female	81.1	73.5	87.1	77.6	84.0	80.9

Data source: Elizabeth Arias, Jiaquan Xu, and Kenneth Kochanek, "United States Life Tables, 2023," *National Vital Statistics Report* 74, no. 6 (Centers for Disease Control and Prevention, 2025): Table A. NH: Non-Hispanic; AIAN: American Indian, Alaska Native.

As now structured, the Social Security system faces a shortfall by 2035. That's because currently the checks due to the large swath of retired baby boomers aren't covered by the smaller number of working people in younger generations paying into the system. In 1940 when the Social Security model was established, life expectancy had risen to 60.8 for men and 65.2 for women. At that point, per each retiree there were 159 workers (many of whom didn't make it to retirement age, which was then 65); today, that's one to three, and it is anticipated to be one to two by 2050.[22]

To resolve the shortfall, structural changes are needed. Among viable options are raising eligibility ages and/or the cap on wages subject to the Social Security tax ($176,100 in 2025). Many who enjoy their work are already working longer, which will help mitigate the delay gap in the workforce—but to avoid blocking the upward path of younger workers, some handing on of responsibilities by elders working long past sixty-five seems appropriate. A raised retirement age floor (granting access to Social Security payments) could vary by health status and/or by profession since desk jobs may be less wearing than physical labor or other factors. Social Security might come to be means tested, so that those who don't need the money either access it later or not at all (though contributions would be mandatory making that resource available as a fallback, if needed).

Such edits could be combined with a more transformational option: moving to the Medicare funding model, as Stephanie Kelton suggests,[23] would guarantee that any shortfall from the dedicated Social Security tax will be made up from the federal budget (including new care-tax revenues). Since the shortfall is the result of the expanded longevity of humans (a goal for most), the alternate funding model seems reasonable if most have equal chance of benefiting. Active efforts to ensure that no groups have lesser chances of survival built in due to income level (see above) would be required. Labor historian Jan Lucassen recommends that, in order to be satisfying, work involve "meaning, cooperation, fairness"; retirement should operate similarly.

Given that expanded longevity is a new experience for humanity, there hasn't been extensive dialogue on what to do with the extra time or how it could best be structured. Providing baseline supports can assist in that structuring, especially for people with fewer resources. One support could be community centers combining programming and services for elders with volunteer opportunities (such as Elder Corps, AmeriCorps Seniors, Foster Grandparents, and the Retired Senior Volunteer Program), providing them with chances to contribute and socialize while spelling their family caregivers. Ideally, such centers would combine elder care and childcare, allowing interaction across multiple generations (children's parents and elders' children would also visit) and general thriving.

But eventually, even the fittest will face illness and then death, and as boomers age, increasing numbers of health aides will be needed to assist them. Thinking ahead, everyone has an interest in ensuring that there are sufficient workers available to fill that demand by putting family-support, health, and elder care systems as well as immigration pathways in place now to allow that.

11

SAVING THE PLANET

Climate Care

All we hear from our so-called leaders are words that sound great, but so far have led to no action.

—Greta Thunberg, remarks at Youth4Climate Summit (2021)

Despite the fantasies of capitalists who wish their polluting industries had no bad effects, and who have for too long succeeded in convincing the world to let them stick with bad practices and business models, climate change is happening fast, and there is no planet B. Either climate care fuels the future or there is none.

The fantasists are often also pronatalists, calling for more births, even as they work to ensure that the earth those children inherit will be barely habitable. Pro-fossil-fuel climate "policy" lays the earth's resources waste for momentary gain, leaving a conflict-filled, diminished world.[1] Rising tides in Miami, heatwaves in Paris and Boston, disappearing polar icecaps, and intensifying storms around the globe mean that no one is fooled by the "everything's okay" narratives. But many either don't like the idea of changing their habits or haven't been given much direction on what they can do, collectively or individually. With many politicians and media moguls invested in the status quo, we need real leaders, able to provide responsible guidance.

Only *when* caregiving's essential role in addressing this crisis is recognized, and *if* caregivers' voices are not just *at* the decision-making table but running it, do we have a chance to save the world. Preserving the terrestrial environment to continue to sustain human and other animal life requires information, innovation, cooperation, and action. To date, none has been sufficiently evidenced, and the clock is ticking.

The climate crisis and care gaps, though different in scale of negative effect, result from the same model of exploitation of resources and failure to provide care. To address and reverse climate decay, we can adopt the Haudenosaunee people's model of considering all decisions in light of their effects on the environment that future generations will inherit, extending at least seven generations ahead.

Humans have created climate change by burning fossil fuels—coal, oil, and gas—for energy. These fuels emit carbon dioxide and nitrous oxide, which rise and encircle our atmosphere like a blanket, trapping the sun's heat, warming the earth, and altering many of the earth's systems. A 3-degree Celsius (5.4-degree Fahrenheit) rise above the pre-industrial norm would cause catastrophic harm. Between 1850 and 2024, the earth's average temperature has risen by 1.55 degrees Celsius (2.8 degrees Fahrenheit), and the rate of rise has been three times faster after 1982 than before.[2] Increasing weather emergencies—including droughts that among other things feed forest fires, hurricanes, floods, and changes to once stable seasonal patterns—are already pushing people out of coastal areas. As these proliferate and sea levels rise, we can anticipate major migrations, rising food insecurity, and housing crises—as, along with wildlife, humans struggle to locate supportive ecosystems. If not forestalled, all these outcomes will give rise to conflict; we must prepare ourselves to respond equitably while also working to avoid them, and we have to work fast.

In parallel to these changes, the human population on earth has quadrupled over the past one hundred years from two billion to eight billion (up from one billion in 1825), as noted, and we're on path to add a new billion every twelve to fifteen years for some time, further pressuring the environment. Figure 11.1 portrays the recent population rise. Now imagine how that chart would look without birth control.

Women's use of reliable birth control has been steadily helping the planet over the past two hundred years.[3] The worldwide lowering of the fertility rate has lessened the burden on the earth's ecology at exactly the time when most needed. With more members of multiple generations on the planet simultaneously, growing the load on the environment and changing our social dynamics in ways we have not contemplated, addressing the fallout will require intergenerational partnerships.

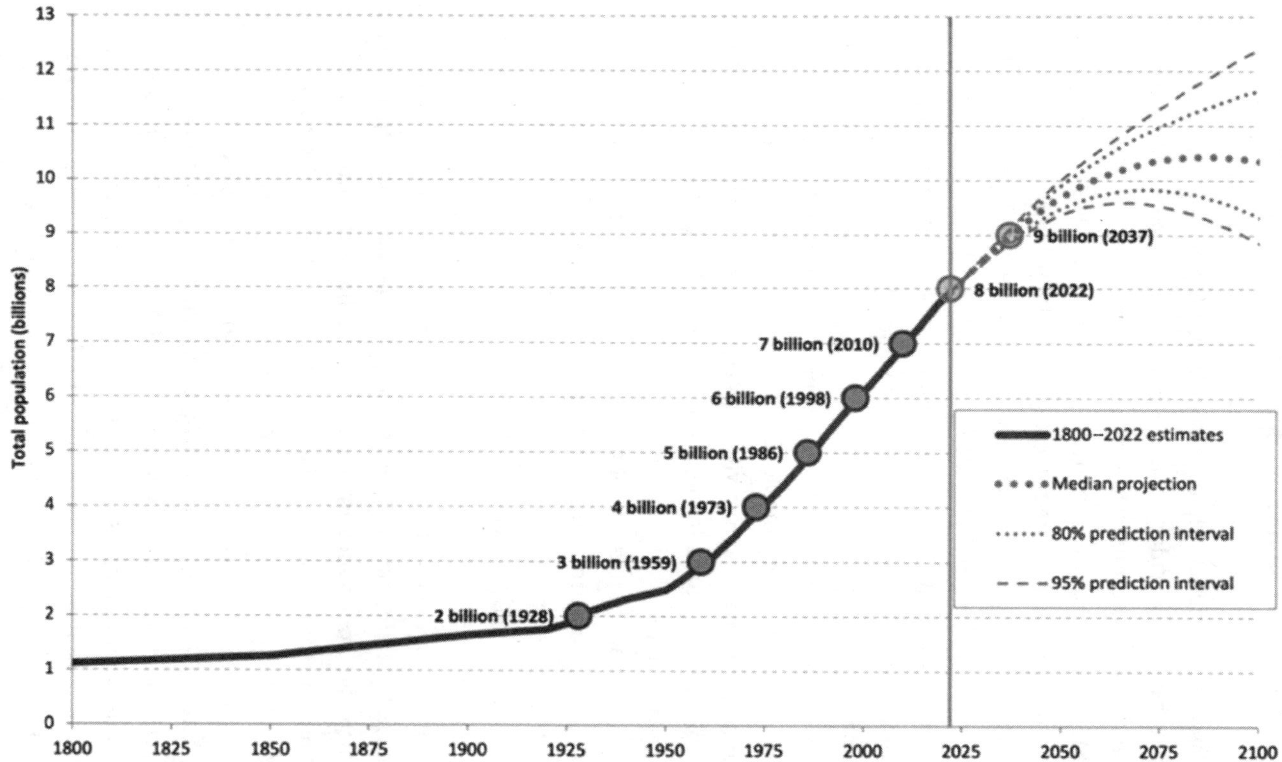

Figure 11.1 World population estimates, 1800–2022, and projections to 2100 (medium-variant projection with 80 and 95 percent prediction intervals). Data source: United Nations, Department of Economic and Social Affairs, Population Division, *World Population Prospects 2022* (United Nations, 2022).

Fertility control has limited our population growth to so-far sustainable levels of food demand, but the burden of nonsustainable energy use has initiated major climate changes, requiring a collaborative mitigation effort that has largely failed to materialize, even as renewable energy sources and carbon-capture technologies show progress.

Wildlife is hurt by land-use change, as habitats are converted to farming and housing, and temperature rise also ruins habitats. Both are factors in the 73 percent decline in the average size of wildlife populations over the fifty-year period 1970–2020[4] and the full extinction of five hundred vertebrate species in the past century. Along with these harms to the animals, cuts to biodiversity undermine the ecosystems humans operate within. While longevity may not itself be responsible for these changes, its ripple effects cause harm, especially while energy sources and consumption patterns are not made sustainable. These effects must be considered and managed, going forward, along with radical reworking of global relations and of economic structures through the UN and other bodies.

Along with diminishing the available workforce, the sidelining of female workers advocated by pronatalists would create climate harm by denying the world their insight. In her 1977 Nobel Prize acceptance speech, physicist Rosalyn Yalow, co-developer of the radioimmunoassay technique that revolutionized diabetes treatment, emphasized that "the world cannot afford the loss of the talents of half of its people if we are to solve the many problems which beset us." Along with many insights, the great value of differing perspectives is lost through such shortsightedness.

Of particular importance in our climate-challenged moment will be insights and perspectives on care and repair. Women have long been at the forefront of environmental activism—from Rachel Carson, Wangari Maathai, Ynestra King, Winona LaDuke, and Vandana Shiva to more recently Greta Thunberg, Xiye Bastida, and many other Gen Z and Millennial activists. Their voices must be part of the efforts to shift the global focus toward valuing and enacting climate care. Women's almost total historical absence from the policy tables in the O&G industry has fed the huge amount of harm that has been allowed to occur in that realm.

While historically the extraction of value from subordinated people and from the earth could continue over many generations, there was always a built-in end point. When humans began to actively destroy their environment, the time for reversing the harm went on a very limited clock. If business continues as usual, it will destroy its customer base. Of course, climate catastrophes will create new opportunities for preying on the fears and vulnerabilities of others. In such a dystopian context, caregivers will be even more stretched and even more essential.

Only if businesses collaborate with climate caregivers (by choice or requirement), shift their models to include investment in the people's thriving, and create a bulwark against further exploitation of and care-less-ness toward the planet and its people, of all genders, will they grow real value for all parties for a much longer term.

As Margaret Mead observed, the gender binary has never adequately defined anyone. Since her day, society has been moving toward the world she imagined in 1935, where each person can express their own combination of assertive and nurturing/attentive qualities according to their temperament, without disparaging or discounting the work of others in order to find value in themselves. That progress has brought us nearer to a world of thriving.

Likewise, progress has been made in breaking down old race/ethnicity barriers, which long kept huge groups in low-wage, low-status jobs and out of policymaking roles—causing great suffering and the further loss of insight to society. The backlash we've seen recently indicates the displeasure of some who long held unfair advantages at the undoing of the systems that sustained those advantages. To identify and reject divide-and-conquer strategies requires strong leadership, honest dialogue, and commitment to finding solutions that serve all.

Can an embrace of a bigger sense of human community be expanded and sustained by combining benevolence with self-interest, such that we can all contribute to mutual welfare and to a sustainable future for the next generations? That will require new narratives that imagine healthy societies, not just dystopian catastrophe stories and endless whodunits; stories that portray relationships of interdependence and mutual respect across lines of gender, race/ethnicity, sexuality, and nativity, where the drama rotates around finding solutions to long-term climate health and human thriving. These are the struggles and mysteries that matter.

While the UN and some nations have been proactive around initiating responses to climate change, others have done little. Carbon taxes were a start toward emissions reduction, and carbon border taxes that put financial pressure on companies and nations to police emissions could be a next step. As temperatures rise (in summer 2025, Boston was hotter than Houston on some days), constituents must take the reins to elect leaders committed to climate progress.

It's another project to outline the specifics of a road to global collaboration on climate repair. But after the backward steps around green energy forced on us recently, leadership committed to proactive, informed national and global cooperation to reduce climate harms will be essential to adjusting our systems quickly and handling the economic complexities that will follow. At home, a network of local and regional climate boards would be vital to sharing information and innovations, initiating and running projects that reduce carbon emissions, rebuild ecosystems, rehouse dislocated families, support small local farms that reduce the need for long supply chains (even within big cities), and settle disputes. Such mutual aid efforts can build trust and community and reinforce the family-support care infrastructure to grow the thrive. There's much to be done, and everyone's contributions are needed.

CODA

Building (Human) Capital

I am participating in the creation of yet another culture, a new story to explain the world and our participation in it, a new value system with images and symbols that connect us to each other and to the planet.
—Gloria Anzaldúa, *Borderland/La Frontera* (1987)

As humanity moves into a tenuous future, our diverse insights and skills are our common resource. Rather than doubling down on harmful, exploitative patterns, we can work to build a thriving future for all within a caring democracy that invests in everyone, sustainably.

That first requires caring for democracy and protecting the systems that allow all to participate, but that anti-democratic forces have actively undermined. We can do that by (as a start) reupping and strengthening the Voting Rights Act to end voter suppression and gerrymandering in all states; funding political campaigns federally to give each candidate's ideas equal media play; overriding states' "rights" that disserve citizens' rights; requiring a referendum option in all states; and investing equitably in solid education for all so that all Americans understand the issues and have the skills they need. Our twin emergencies around democracy and climate require no less to enable full participation in finding real solutions.

Another essential step toward that thriving future is reaffirming women's rights to full citizenship, beginning with restoring their right to make their own reproductive decisions throughout the nation, without exception. As those historically assigned the work of care, their participation in all levels of decision-making is key to forward movement.

These projects involve big changes, as do those outlined in chapters 10 and 11, and there will be disagreements at every turn. But there's no choice but to work them through if we're not ready to give up the struggle for democratic ideals or to accept that "it's just our mass extinction event, mom," as my youngest once told me calmly, putting things in paleontological perspective.

We can make the change we need only if we throw out the divide-and-conquer narratives that have undermined our collaboration across labor categories over centuries and work together toward the mutual thrive—building an economy that grows through investment in human capital and in the community, not extractive discounts based on gender, race/ethnicity, nativity, and class.

That includes doing the hard work to develop systems for acknowledging the full extent of the real domestic product in economic terms, abandoning the pretense that care work is not essential labor, and compensating people fairly for that labor in terms of funds, status, and access to civic voice within a democracy.

By putting all brains on our many problems, we can invest in two extremely fertile and interactive endeavors: democratically caring for the other real domestic product—the people—and for the earth, the domestic space we all share—our common home. That pair of care projects together contain all the world's value, if we can collaborate to keep it.

ACKNOWLEDGMENTS

Heartfelt thanks to all who have talked with me about the issues addressed herein over the decades: those conversations have been inspiring. In particular, the insights and accounts of all who struggle against biased systems have been informative and motivating. Special gratitude to my amazing husband, family, and friends. The views expressed here are my own and do not reflect those of my employer. Any errors are my own. Some of the arguments in this book appeared previously in *The Nation, The Houston Chronicle, NANO, The Daily Beast, Rewire, The New York Times,* and *The Atlantic.*

APPENDIX

Poverty, Confederacy, Abortion Access, and Teen Fertility, by State

State	Percent in poverty (2022–2024 average)	Confederate or not	Legal v. Bans (prior to 22 weeks) 2024*	Minimum wage 2024[†]	Teen fertility rate 2024	Teen fertility rate 2007
Louisiana	**19.5**	Confederacy	Ban Full	7.25	**21.28**	**55.20**
Mississippi	**17.4**	Confederacy	Ban Full	7.25	**22.77**	**70.06**
New Mexico	**17.2**	no	Legal	12.00	**18.04**	**63.95**
Kentucky	**15.4**	no	Ban Full	7.25	**20.41**	**52.57**
Alabama	**14.7**	Confederacy	Ban Full	7.25	**19.08**	**52.07**
Arkansas	**14.5**	Confederacy	Ban Full	11.00	**22.18**	**60.14**
North Carolina	**14.0**	Confederacy	Ban - 12	7.25	14.31	**47.95**
West Virginia	**14.0**	no	Ban Full	8.75	**17.81**	45.84
Oklahoma	**13.8**	no	Ban Full	7.25	**19.59**	**58.50**
Nevada	**12.6**	no	Legal	12.00	12.50	**51.65**
Georgia	**12.4**	Confederacy	Ban - 6	7.25	**15.97**	**53.38**
Texas	**12.3**	Confederacy	Ban Full	7.25	**18.47**	**61.76**
Florida	**12.1**	Confederacy	Ban - 6	14.00	11.84	42.96
Michigan	**11.9**	no	Legal	12.48	10.31	33.48
South Carolina	**11.9**	Confederacy	Ban - 6	7.25	**17.36**	**51.90**
New York	11.6	no	Legal	16.50	8.04	26.04

State	Percent in poverty (2022–2024 average)	Confederate or not	Legal v. Bans (prior to 22 weeks) 2024*	Minimum wage 2024†	Teen fertility rate 2024	Teen fertility rate 2007
Arizona	11.5	no	Ban - 15	14.70	13.91	**59.61**
California	11.1	no	Legal	16.50	8.67	39.58
Ohio	10.5	no	Legal	10.70	14.05	39.90
Illinois	10.3	no	Legal	15.00	10.36	40.17
Missouri	10.2	no	Ban Full	13.75	**15.90**	44.03
Pennsylvania	10.2	no	Legal	7.25	9.69	30.69
Tennessee	10.1	Confederacy	Ban Full	7.25	**19.90**	**53.37**
Alaska	10	no	Legal	13.00	14.5	42.87
Oregon	9.7	no	Legal	15.05	9.00	34.53
North Dakota	9.3	no	Ban Full	7.25	11.75	29.25
Rhode Island	9.3	no	Legal	15.00	7.52	29.23
Connecticut	9.2	no	Legal	16.35	6.54	23.05
Massachusetts	9.2	no	Legal	15.00	5.44	21.40
Washington	9.2	no	Legal	16.66	9.28	33.27
Indiana	9.1	no	Ban Full	7.25	**15.02**	43.01
New Jersey	9.1	no	Legal	15.49	7.31	24.90
Kansas	8.9	no	Legal	7.25	14.72	42.47
Montana	8.7	no	Legal	10.55	11.11	35.26
Hawaii	8.6	no	Legal	14.00	11.00	38.70
South Dakota	8.6	no	Ban Full	11.50	**15.30**	41.26
Virginia	8.6	Confederacy	Legal	12.41	10.67	34.17
Delaware	8.5	no	Legal	15.00	13.05	39.22
Idaho	8.5	no	Ban Full	7.25	9.94	39.86
Iowa	8.4	no	Ban - 6	7.25	12.23	32.76
Wisconsin	8.3	no	Legal	7.25	9.67	31.11

State	Percent in poverty (2022–2024 average)	Confederate or not	Legal v. Bans (prior to 22 weeks) 2024*	Minimum wage 2024†	Teen fertility rate 2024	Teen fertility rate 2007
Maryland	8.2	no	Legal	15.00	10.30	34.28
Colorado	8.1	no	Legal	14.81	11.19	41.55
Maine	8.1	no	Legal	14.65	7.83	26.05
Wyoming	8.1	no	Legal; Ban Blocked	7.25	14.70	**49.87**
Nebraska	8.0	no	Ban - 12	13.50	13.96	35.46
Vermont	7.6	no	Legal	14.01	6.35	20.98
Minnesota	7.3	no	Legal	11.13	7.34	27.92
New Hampshire	6.8	no	Legal	7.25	4.58	19.31
Utah	6.6	no	Ban - 18	7.25	8.20	35.37

* Summary of access in most of 2024: Arizona's ban was ended on November 25, 2024.

† Twenty states default to the federal minimum wage: $7.25 since 2009.

Listed in order of poverty rates, with the top fifteen poverty and fertility rates bold. Eleven of the states with the highest poverty rates also had among the top fifteen highest teen fertility rates in 2024, and twelve did in 2007. Fertility rates have fallen markedly since 2007 due in large part to improved access to RBC. Poverty rates have also declined in many states recently, due in part to the decline in teen fertility rates. The Confederacy included only the eleven states indicated, but in Kentucky, Oklahoma, West Virginia, and Missouri slavery was legal through 1865 and in New Mexico Native American peonage was legal post-1865.

Data sources: Poverty percentage from Emily Shrider and Christina Bijou, "Poverty in the United States: 2024," Table of Interrelationships of Three-Year Average State Poverty Rates: 2022–2024, U.S. Census Bureau, September 9, 2025; Abortion ban/legality status from Allison McCann and Amy Schoenfeld Walker, "Tracking Abortion Laws Across the Country," *New York Times*, accessed November 15, 2025, and other summaries of 2024 bans; minimum wages from Paycom.com, "Your 2025 Guide to Every State's Minimum Wage," July 3, 2025; fertility rates for women aged 15–19 by state for 2007 and 2024 gathered via the Wonder Database, at https://wonder.cdc.gov.

NOTES

PREFACE

1. A self-rooting migrant, Sikander has suggested. Letters on the frame suggest both the Urdu word for wind and the Hebrew and Arabic names of the wife of Adam (Havah/Hawa).

2. Previously Mohammed stood on the tenth plinth but was removed in 1955 after protests by Muslims against representing the prophet.

3. Ross Douthat, "Be Open to Spiritual Experience. Also, Be Really Careful," *New York Times*, February 1, 2023; Shahzia Sikander, "My Sculpture Was Beheaded. Here's Why I'm Not Fixing It," *Washington Post*, July 30, 2024.

4. The fragmented visage was removed from the grass and the remaining figure topped with a blue tarp against rain damage, leaving only the lower half visible. The tarp muted the statement the artist intended for passersby, a step toward the protesters' Virgin Mary aesthetic. Several events on the beheading followed, and the artist gave an inspiring talk on campus on the installation's last day. The story still resonates here.

INTRODUCTION

1. See Claudia Goldin's field-defining publications on birth control's role in women's progress into civic life; including (with Lawrence Katz), "The Power of the Pill: Oral Contraceptives and Women's Career and Marriage Decisions," *Journal of Political Economy* 110, no. 4 (2002): 730–770. See also Martha J. Bailey, "More Power to the Pill: The Impact of Contraceptive Freedom on Women's Life Cycle Labor Supply," *Quarterly Journal of Economics* (2006): 289–320.

2. That right was already limited for many before Dobbs by cost and state restrictions.

3. Allison McCann and Amy Schoenfeld Walker, "Tracking Abortion Laws across the Country," *New York Times* (updated January 6, 2026). Although 99 percent of abortions occur at or before twenty-one-weeks' gestation, severe fetal anomalies or threats to maternal life or health may arise later, as may other issues, requiring later access. See Ivette Gomez, Alina Salganicoff, and Laurie Sobel, "Abortions Later in Pregnancy in a Post-Dobbs Era," KFF, February 2, 2024.

4. Of course, gay couples have children through other means.

5. The amendment passed in only thirteen because though the Florida amendment received 57 percent of the vote, passage required 60 percent. The fourteen with majorities in favor were Arizona, California, Colorado, Florida, Kansas, Kentucky, Maryland, Michigan, Missouri, Montana, Nevada, New York, Ohio, and Vermont; the two that fell short of 50 percent (Nebraska and South Dakota) were confusingly presented. In Arkansas, officials removed their amendment on a technicality.

6. For more expansive analysis, see Nancy Folbre, *Rise and Decline of Patriarchal Systems: An Intersectional Political Economy* (Verso, 2021): chapter 6.

7. Gerda Lerner, *The Creation of Patriarchy* (Oxford University Press, 1986); Angela Saini, *The Patriarchs: The Origins of Inequality* (Beacon, 2023).

8. Jan Lucassen, *The Story of Work: A New History of Humankind* (Yale University Press, 2021), 32–35.

9. Sarah Blaffer Hrdy, *Mothers and Others: The Evolutionary Origins of Mutual Understanding* (Harvard University Press, 2009).

10. Scholars propose a range of dates, depending on which factors they foreground.

11. Friedrich Engels, *The Origin of the Family, Private Property and the State* (Verlag Otto Meissner, 1884).

12. Heidi Hartmann, "The Unhappy Marriage of Marxism and Feminism: Towards a More Progressive Union," *Capital and Class* 3, no. 2 (1979).

13. Some societies' rules have accepted gay relationships if there's also a procreative straight relationship (see chapter 7).

14. Lucassen, *The Story of Work*.

15. This evidence includes material objects, archaeological evidence, and surviving matriarchal societies that carry forward prehistoric social organizations.

16. Marija Gimbutas, *The Living Goddesses* (University of California Press, 2001).

17. Gimbutas, *The Living Goddesses*, 113; Jo Lawson-Tancred, "Archaeologists Uncover Evidence of First Women-Led Society in Europe," artnet, January 21, 2025.

18. Heidi Goettner-Abendroth, *Matriarchal Societies: Studies on Indigenous Cultures Across the Globe* (Lang, 2013).

19. Albert B. Lord, *The Singer of Tales* (Harvard University Press, 1960).

20. Elaine Pagels, "What Became of God the Mother?," *Signs: Journal of Women in Culture and Society* 2, no. 2 (1976): 293–303.

21. The poems evolved through recitation over ages, until transcribed by Homer circa 700 BCE. In their palimpsestic account of the culture's development, remnants of old worlds peek from beneath the new.

22. Although Priam is a patriarch, Troy also represents an older world where women have options. See Elizabeth Gregory, "Unravelling Penelope: The Construction of the Faithful Wife in Homer's Heroines," *Helios* 23, no. 1 (1996): 3–20.

23. Isabel Wilkerson, *Caste: The Origins of Our Discontents* (Random House, 2020).

24. Mancur Olson, *The Rise and Decline of Nations: Economic Growth, Stagflation, and Social Rigidities* (Yale University Press, 1982); Mancur Olson, *Power and Prosperity: Outgrowing Communist and Capitalist Dictatorships* (Basic Books, 2000). For additional discussion of free riders and stationary (restrained) and roving (destructive) bandits, see Folbre, *Rise and Decline of Patriarchal Systems*.

25. Claudia Goldin and Lawrence Katz, "The Power of the Pill: Oral Contraceptives and Women's Career and Marriage Decisions," *Journal of Political Economy* 110, no. 4 (2002): 730–770.

26. Increasingly, "right-to-life" suits challenge employer mandates to cover birth control, referring, for example, to "abortifacient contraceptives, *including, inter alia*, emergency contraception and intrauterine devices" (*Cedar Park Assembly of God of Kirkland Washington v. Washington State*, ongoing suit); cited in Jessica Valenti, "Attacks on Birth Control," *Abortion, Every Day* (July 31, 2025).

27. Brooke Schultz, "Trump Admin. Cuts Program that Brought Local Food to School Cafeterias," *Education Week* (September 11, 2025).

28. Loretta Ross et al., eds., *Radical Reproductive Justice: Foundation, Theory, Practice, Critique* (Feminist Press, 2017); Dorothy Roberts, *Killing the Black Body: Race, Reproduction, and the Meaning of Liberty* (Pantheon, 1997).

29. Gallup Poll, "Legality of Abortion Demographic Tables: Americans' Views on Legality of Abortion [Survey Dates May 1–18, 2025], 2025, gallup.com.

30. Current birth timing dynamics occur within the context of no family-support infrastructure; were there such infrastructure, more women who started families early could take public roles.

31. The energy industry is among the least gender diverse, at 15.5 percent female; see Sebastian Shehadi, "These Are the Most (and Least) Male-Dominated Industries in the US," *Investment Monitor* (January 9, 2023).

32. Janet Yellen, "The History of Women's Work and Wages and How It Has Created Success for Us All," *19A: The Brookings Gender Equality Series* (Brookings Institution, 2020).

33. See Marilyn Waring, *Counting for Nothing: What Men Value and What Women Are Worth* (Harper & Row, 1988); Vandana Shiva, *Staying Alive: Women, Ecology, and Development* (South End Press, 2016).

34. At least since Mary Wollstonecraft (1792), Sarah Grimké (1838), and Sojourner Truth (1851), feminists have critiqued the economics of gender.

35. Views on what to measure vary: The Gender Development Index compares male and female life expectancy at birth, years of schooling, and command over economic resources. The Genuine Progress Indicator includes twenty-six factors.

36. Although they also benefit the children importantly, one study found that the greatest impact of childcare programs was as a high-return active labor market policy for adults, emphasizing the benefit to workers' earnings. See John E. Humphries et al., "Parents' Earnings and the Returns to Universal Pre-Kindergarten," Working Paper No. 33038 (National Bureau of Economic Research, October 2024).

37. Paying for home care work is another model.

38. At least 169,000 women did so in 2023 and another 155,000 in 2024, up from 81,000 in 2020. See Guttmacher Institute, "Abortion in the United States: Fact Sheet," April 2025.

39. Andrea Suozzo et al., "Texas Won't Study How Its Abortion Ban Impacts Women, So We Did," *ProPublica*, February 20, 2025.

40. Lizzie Presser and Kavitha Surana, "A Third Woman Has Died Under Texas' Abortion Ban as Doctors Reach for Riskier Miscarriage Treatments," *Texas Tribune*, November 27, 2024.

41. Benjamin Thornburg et al., "Anxiety and Depression Symptoms After the *Dobbs* Abortion Decision," *JAMA* 331, no. 4 (2024): 294–301.

42. Alex Morin et al., *The Texas OB/GYN Physician Workforce: Early Assessment of the Impact of Abortion Restrictions on the Workforce Pipeline* (Manatt Health, 2024).

43. CDC WONDER database (https://www.wonder.cdc.gov), accessed October/November 2025. Small rises occurred in the following states with bans or gestational limits below twenty-four weeks in all or part of 2023 and 2024: Idaho, Indiana, Missouri, Nebraska, South Dakota, Utah, and West Virginia. Rates in states without restrictions (Colorado, Montana, New Mexico, Oregon, Virginia, and Wyoming) were already relatively low.

44. However, per our analyses, rates fell less in ban states than in ban-free sectors; see Elizabeth Gregory and Zachary Hough, "Post-Dobbs Fertility Rates: US, TX, CA," IRWGS, October 2024. See also Suzanne Bell et al., "US Abortion Bans and Fertility," *JAMA* 333, no. 15 (2025): 1324–1332. Abortions rose by 11 percent between 2020 and 2023; see Isaac Maddow-Zimet and Candace Gibson, "Despite Bans, Number of Abortions in the US Increased in 2023," Guttmacher Institute, March 19, 2024.

45. Lindsey Dawson and Jennifer Kates, "Policy Tracker: Youth Access to Gender Affirming Care and State Policy Restrictions," KFF, last updated August 12, 2025, https://www.kff.org/lgbtq/gender-affirming-care-policy-tracker/.

46. Amanda Baumle et al., "Effects of State-Level Abortion and LGBT Laws and Policies on Interstate Migration Attitudes," *Population Research and Policy Review* 42, no. 6 (2023): article 90; Daniel Dench et al., "Are People Fleeing States with Abortion Bans?," NBER Working Paper No. 33328 (National Bureau of Economic Research, January 2025).

47. "Gender Differences in 2024 Vote Choice Are Similar to Most Recent Presidential Elections," Center for American Women and Politics, last updated December 28, 2024, https://cawp.rutgers.edu/blog/gender-differences-2024-presidential-vote.

CHAPTER 1

1. See Houstonsuffragists.org for an account of failed voter suppression efforts in Harris County in 1920.

2. Crystal Eastman, "Now We Can Begin," *Liberator*, December 1920.

3. Sanger invited Dr. Gregory Pincus to extend his research on hormones to contraception, and engaged McCormick to fund the project. The science was assisted by Drs. Chang Min-Chueh, John Rock, and others.

4. *Planned Parenthood of Southeastern Pennsylvania v. Casey*, 505 U.S. 833 (1992).

5. Among the members of Congress past and present who have publicly reported having abortions are Representatives Cori Bush, Pramila Jayapal, Barbara Lee, and Jackie Speier. See Madison Feller and Rose Minutaglio, "Our Abortion Stories," *Elle*, June 24, 2022.

6. See Susan J. Tolchin and Martin Tolchin, *Clout: Womanpower and Politics* (Coward, McCann & Geoghegan, 1974).

7. Martha J. Bailey found that women's gains in the paid labor market accrue only to those who delayed childbearing; see Bailey, "More Power to the Pill: The Impact of Contraceptive Freedom on Women's Life Cycle Labor Supply," *Quarterly Journal of Economics* (2006): 289–320.

8. While all states have some childcare subsidy access for the very poor, the funds don't match demand. Although their goal is to allow mothers to work more consistently and earn higher wages, that's undermined in states where if parents' income rises beyond an income threshold they first lose the subsidy and access to childcare, then often their new job, returning them to poverty, renewed eligibility, and the end of the waitlist.

9. Affordable childcare reduces abuse both by reducing financial stress and by ensuring that more eyes on kids and moms mean problems are spotted sooner. Children learn and socialize, and parents often learn child-rearing strategies.

10. Gosta Esping-Andersen, *The Incomplete Revolution: Adapting to Women's New Roles* (Polity, 2009).

11. Charlotte Perkins Gilman, *Women and Economics* (Small, Maynard & Co., 1898).

12. Delay isn't required for representation: with a real family-support infrastructure and more dads who share care, women could have children while younger if they chose, while also completing schooling and pursuing careers.

13. Elizabeth Gregory, *Ready: Why Women Are Embracing the New Later Motherhood* (Basic Books, 2007/2012).

14. See bell hooks, *Understanding Patriarchy* (Washington Square Press, 2004); Uma Narayan "Contesting Cultures," in *The Second Wave: A Reader in Feminist Theory*, ed. Linda J. Nicholson (Routledge, 1997). Over millennia, mothers have lectured their daughters to accept abuse, seeing no other option, and mothers-in-law have tortured their son's brides, exercising the ounce of power they have in that relationship and nowhere else. See also Karissa Haugeberg, *Women Against Abortion: Inside the Largest Moral Reform Movement of the Twentieth Century* (University of Illinois Press, 2017) and the film *Shiny Happy People: The Duggar Family Secrets* (Netflix, 2023).

15. Jeet Heer, "The Revolt of the Republican Women," *The Nation*, December 5, 2025.

16. Sandra Grey, "Numbers and Beyond: The Relevance of Critical Mass in Gender Research," *Politics and Gender* (2006): 492–502.

17. David Leonhardt, "Decoding Joe Manchin," *New York Times*, December 22, 2021.

18. See Elizabeth Gregory, "Jobs for Men but Not for Women," *The Nation*, December 14, 2021.

19. Think Reps. Rosa DeLauro and Nancy Pelosi, the Squad (Reps. Cori Bush, Summer Lee, Alexandria Ocasio-Cortez, Ilhan Omar, Ayanna Pressley, Delia Ramirez, Rashida Tlaib—and their allies Jamal Bowman and Greg Casar), Sen. Elizabeth Warren, and quite a few others on the Democratic side, as well as some Republican women, like Nancy Mace of South Carolina, who advocates for increased access to birth control and maternal health care.

20. Jessica Calarco, *Holding It Together: How Women Became America's Safety Net* (Random House, 2024).

21. Silvia Federici, "Wages Against Housework" (Power of Women Collective, 1974), 4. Virginia Woolf similarly described submissive women as magnifying mirrors for men; see Virginia Woolf, *A Room of One's Own* (Hogarth Press, 1929).

22. See discussion in Isabel Wilkerson, *Caste: The Origins of Our Discontents* (Random House, 2020).

23. See Mary Inman, "The Housewife's Role in Social Production," in *In Women's Defense* (Committee to Organize the Advancement of Women, 1940) and the work of Marxist feminists of the 1970s and 1980s.

CHAPTER 2

1. James Mohr, *Abortion in America: The Origins and Evolution of a National Policy* (Oxford University Press, 1979).

2. Massachusetts passed the first abortion ban in 1845; thirty states enacted laws between 1866 and 1877. See Mohr, *Abortion in America*, 120–123, 200, 229.

3. Mohr, *Abortion in America*, 253.

4. Federal Reserve Economic Data (FRED) for male and female labor force participation over time. I cite twenty-five to fifty-four data instead of all adults 16+ because more people now attend college and enter the workforce later and live longer in retirement, which makes current and prior adult data not comparable.

5. Bureau of Labor Statistics, US Department of Labor, "Current Population Survey: Household Data Annual Averages: 2023," table 8.

6. Reproductive Health Access Project, "The History of Mifepristone," April 18, 2023.

7. Isaac Maddow-Zimet and Candace Gibson, "Despite Bans, Number of Abortions in the US Increased in 2023," Guttmacher Institute, March 19, 2024; Maddow-Zimet and Kimya Forouzan, "Stability in the Number of Abortions from 2023 to 2024 in US States without Total Bans Masks Major Shifts in Access," Guttmacher Institute, April 2025.

8. Jacqueline E. Ellison et al., "Changes in Permanent Contraception Procedures Among Young Adults Following the Dobbs Decision," *JAMA Health Forum* 5, no. 4 (2024).

9. Xiao Xu et al., "Tubal Sterilization Rates by State Abortion Laws After the Dobbs Decision," *JAMA* 332, no. 14 (2024).

10. Julie Strasser et al., "Tubal Sterilization and Vasectomy Increased Among US Young Adults After the Dobbs Supreme Court Decision in 2022," *Health Affairs* 44, no. 1 (2025): 99–107.

11. Mike Schneider, "Changing Face of America Revealed by Census Bureau," *Fortune* (September 11, 2025).

12. Peter McDonald, "Low Fertility in Australia: Evidence, Causes and Policy Responses," *People and Place* 8, no. 2 (2000): 6–21.

13. The TFR estimates the number of children women would bear on average if they all went through their childbearing years experiencing the age-specific birth rates in effect for that year. The TFR sums the age-specific birth rates per 1,000 women for all five-year age groups (in 2023 that was 324.2), multiplies that by five (324.2 × 5 = 1621.0), and divides by 1,000 (for 2023, that's 1.621 children each). TFRs before 1917 were based on the decennial Census.

14. From 179 million in 1960 to 341 million in 2024.

15. Claudia Goldin and Lawrence Katz, "The Power of the Pill: Oral Contraceptives and Women's Career and Marriage Decisions," *Journal of Political Economy* 110, no. 4 (2002): 730–770.

16. US Census Bureau, *Daytime Care of Children: 10.1974 and 2.1975*, Current Population Reports, Series P-20, No. 298 (US Government Printing Office, October 1976). One study found that in 2024 33 percent of parents with children under six used paid childcare, and 53 percent used unpaid childcare; see Board of Governors of the Federal Reserve System, *Economic Well-Being of US Households in 2024* (Federal Reserve, 2025).

17. On how requirements for "good motherhood" intensified as the average number of children declined, see Sharon Hays, *The Cultural Contradictions of Motherhood* (Yale University Press, 1998).

18. Arlie Russell Hochschild with Anne Machung, *The Second Shift: Working Parents and the Revolution in the Home* (Viking, 1989).

19. In 2021, dads represented 18 percent of stay-at-home parents, up from 11 percent in 1989; see Richard Fry, "Almost 1 in 5 Stay-at-Home Parents in the United States Are Dads," Pew Research Center, August 3, 2023. Per the Bureau of Labor Statistics, on an average day, 48 percent of women did housework such as cleaning and laundry, compared with 22 percent of men. (BLS, "American Time Use Survey News Release," June 27, 2024, table 1).

20. Conversation with author, May 2025.

21. Author's calculation: While mothers of children under age five tend 1.5 preschool children on average, childcare workers average roughly 11 children per worker, across state-mandated teacher/child age ratios, assuming parity in numbers of children in care across age bands. While 1,000 parents at home care for 1,500 children, in centers 1,000 could care for 11,000 (or, where 1,000 previously cared for

1,500, now 137 would do so, freeing 863 to take jobs in other industries), meaning that of home caregivers moving into jobs, roughly 13.7 percent would be needed to take the new jobs their children created in childcare centers, while 86.3 percent could go into jobs in other industries. Numbers would vary with other ratios.

22. For detailed discussion of odds at various ages, see Elizabeth Gregory, *Ready: Why Women Are Embracing the New Later Motherhood* (Basic Books, 2007/2012). See also the discussion of gametogenesis in chapter 7 of this book.

23. Amalia Miller, "Motherhood Delay and the Human Capital of the Next Generation," *American Economic Review: Papers and Proceedings* 99, no. 2 (2009): 154–158.

24. Data on average ages for 2024 per CDC Wonder online database (https://wonder.cdc.gov).

25. John Bongaarts and Griffith Feeney, "On the Quantum and Tempo of Fertility," *Population and Development Review* 24, no. 2 (1998): 271–291.

26. In 2023, the average number of own children under age eighteen in families with children was 1.94." US Census Bureau, Historical Families Tables FM-1 (November 2024).

27. Miller, "Motherhood Delay and the Human Capital of the Next Generation."

28. Elizabeth Gregory and Zachary Hough, "Post-Dobbs Fertility Rates: US, TX, CA," IRWGS, October 2024.

29. Molly Cook Escobar et al., "171,000 Traveled for Abortions Last Year, *New York Times*, June 13, 2024; Nisha Verma and Daniel Grossman, "Self-Managed Abortion in the United States," *Current Obstetrics and Gynecology Reports* 12, no. 2 (2023): 70–75; Emily Schmall, "Sterilizations Among Women Rose After Roe Was Overturned, Study Finds," *New York Times*, September 11, 2024; Kavitha Surana, "Abortion Bans Have Delayed Emergency Medical Care. In Georgia, Experts Say This Mother's Death Was Preventable," *ProPublica*, September 16, 2024.

30. United Nations, *World Fertility 2024* (United Nations, 2025).

31. Nancy Folbre, "Children as Public Goods," *American Economic Review* 84, no. 2 (1994): 86–90; Jenny Brown, *Birth Strike: The Hidden Fight over Women's Work* (PM Press, 2019).

32. Tucker Carlson and JD Vance, "JD Vance Discusses the Childless Left on Tucker Carlson Tonight," Fox News, October 11, 2021. Project 2025's focus on keeping women at home raising families shows the underlying concern.

33. Heritage Foundation, *Mandate for Leadership: The Conservative Promise* (Heritage Foundation, 2023), 486.

34. Elizabeth Gregory, "Are Women Full Citizens?: The Abortion Debate, and the 'Gifts' of Life and Poverty," *NANO* no. 11 (2017).

35. Vegard Skirbekk and Catherine Bowen, "The Low Fertility Fallacy: Why Panic About Birthrates Is Overblown," *Foreign Affairs*, November 6, 2024; Vegard Skirbekk, *Decline and Prosper!: Changing Global Birth Rates and the Advantages of Fewer Children* (Palgrave Macmillan, 2022); David Miles, "Macroeconomic Impacts of

Changes in Life Expectancy and Fertility," *Journal of the Economics of Ageing* 24 (2023).

CHAPTER 3

1. United for ALICE, *The State of ALICE in the US* (United Way, 2025).

2. When one parent doesn't contribute to supporting a couple's children, family members or others sometimes step in to assist, also generating work.

3. In 1798 Thomas Malthus proposed a form of birth control to limit population growth: delaying marriage, sex, and children until your late twenties, thus reducing the number of children born, to avoid what he considered the otherwise inevitable outpacing of food supply by population, creating famine and poverty. See Thomas Mathus, *Essay on the Principle of Population* (J. Johnson, 1798). Almost two hundred years later, Gary Becker connected having fewer children to higher human capital investment among the wealthy but did not explore how that would affect the class system if lower fertility spread across women in all class positions. In her analyses of birth control's effect on women's workforce participation, Claudia Goldin has focused on the gains to the pool when better-educated women entered the workforce but not on the losses to the low-wage workforce (including losses of male workers) created by fewer unplanned births.

4. That continues at a steeper angle a downward trend in teen rates since 1991. The previous decline did not coincide with an overall decline, since it was balanced by increased later births. Those followed big declines post–baby boom among women in their thirties who felt they didn't need more children. The increases in births to older women in the mid-1970s and onward reflect tempo effects for women who came of age after the introduction of the Pill and delayed first births.

5. National Center for Health Statistics, "Births: Final Data for 2022," *National Vital Statistics Reports* 73, no. 2 (2024): 30 (table 10).

6. Carter Sherman, *The Second Coming: Sex and the Next Generation's Fight over Its Future* (Simon & Schuster, 2025).

7. Jeffrey M. Jones, "LGBTQ+ Identification in US Rises to 9.3%," Gallup Poll, February 20, 2025. The poll only surveyed adults aged eighteen and over. Fifty-six percent of the 23.1 percent identified as bisexual.

8. Sarah S. Brown and Leon Eisenberg, *The Best Intentions: Unintended Pregnancy and the Well-Being of Children and Families* (National Academies Press, 1995).

9. "Unintended Pregnancy in the United States (Fact Sheet)," Guttmacher Institute, January 2019.

10. The Earned Income Tax Credit, housing assistance programs, and SNAP benefits have all been expanded, as have benefits in states that recently expanded Medicaid under the Affordable Care Act. Many of these gains will be reduced by the 2025 tax bill.

11. The data compared employ the Supplemental Poverty Measure (undocumented families didn't receive stimulus payments or a Child Tax Credit). See Columbia

University Center on Poverty and Social Policy, Historical SPM Data tables, utilizing Anchored SPM (2012) with Taxes and Transfers, https://povertycenter.columbia.edu/historical-spm-data. See also Dana Thomson et al., *Lessons from an Historic Decline in Child Poverty* (Child Trends, 2022), using the Historical SPM.

12. Douglas Harris, "Are American's Rising High School Graduation Rates Real—or Just an Accountability-Fueled Mirage?," Brookings Institution, March 2, 2020.

13. Author's calculations based on CDC Wonder online database for 2007 and 2024 (https://wonder.cdc.gov).

14. Kiley Hurst, "US Women Outpacing Men in College Completion," Pew Research Center, November 18, 2024.

15. *State of Missouri; State of Kansas; State of Idaho v. U.S. Food and Drug Administration et al.*, United States District Court, Northern District of Texas (Docket No. 2:22-cv-00223-Z; filed October 11, 2024): points 746–752, https://storage.courtlistener.com/recap/gov.uscourts.txnd.370067/gov.uscourts.txnd.370067.195.1.pdf (revised in later filings). A South Carolina senator made related claims about a state's interests in population during its abortion ban debate in 2022 and 2023.

16. Jacqueline Froelich, "New Law Weakening Child Labor Protections in Arkansas Takes Effect," KUAF Public Radio, August 2023.

17. Some unions are stronger, but many barriers to unionization persist. Private-sector unionization rose to 6.9 percent in 2023, while public-sector unionization declined to 36 percent. Per one study, "more than 50 years of efforts to block access to unions have taken a heavy toll on workers' rights" (Heidi Shierholz et al., "Workers Want Unions, but the Latest Data Point to Obstacles in Their Path," Economic Policy Institute, January 23, 2024). The Protecting the Right to Organize (PRO) Act (yet unpassed) attempts to fix that.

18. *Idaho Statesman* livestream, discussion with Sen. Chuck Winder (R-Boise), Rep. Lauren Necochea (D-Boise), and Rep. Wendy Horman (R-Idaho Falls), January 5, 2024, https://www.youtube.com/watch?v=obBtFvNfccE&t=1950s. Per Necochea, 50 percent of maternal/fetal medicine specialists had left the state by then.

19. Jenny Brown, *Birth Strike: The Hidden Fight over Women's Work* (PM Press, 2019).

20. Chandra Childers, "The Evolution of the Southern Economic Development Strategy," Economic Policy Institute, May 6, 2024.

21. Edward E. Baptist, *The Half Has Never Been Told: Slavery and the Making of American Capitalism* (Basic Books, 2016).

22. Baptist, *The Half Has Never Been Told.*

23. Racial privilege means that white and Black workers are less likely to unite against employers who exploit both.

24. See Caroline Kitchener, "Texas Teen Who Wanted an Abortion Now Has Twins," *Washington Post*, June 20, 2022.

25. See, for example, James Barragan, "In Roe Decision, Clarence Thomas Invites New Legal Challenges to Contraception and Same-Sex Marriage Rights," *Texas*

Tribune, June 24, 2022; Scott Yenor and Jennifer Galardi, "RFK Should Grill the Pill" *Heritage Foundation* (October 2025).

26. These views are echoed in the Project 2025 *Mandate for Leadership*.

27. Lydia Saad, "Gender Gaps on Abortion Reach Historic Highs," Gallup.com, June 9, 2025.

28. Carrie Blazina, "Key Facts About the Abortion Debate in America," Pew Research Center, July 15, 2022.

29. Ava Sasani, "These 1,572 US Politicians Have Helped Ban Abortion Since Roe Fell. They're Mostly Men," *The Guardian*, June 22, 2023. These figures include only representatives who approved bans in effect by the article's publication. KFF, "Population Distribution by Sex, 2022," kff.org.

30. About two-thirds of women legislators were Democrats in 2022, including a slight majority of Democrats in ban states (394 D to 390 R), while about three-fourths of women legislators in nonban states are Democratic. See Center for American Women and Politics: https://cawp.rutgers.edu/.

31. Diana Greene Foster, *The Turnaway Study: Ten Years, a Thousand Women, and the Consequences of Having—or Being Denied—an Abortion* (Scribner, 2020).

32. Elizabeth Gregory, "Texas & Harris County Reproductive Health Update: 2022 Fertility Rates, Post 2021 Six-Week Abortion Ban," IRWGS, January 2024.

33. Elizabeth Gregory et al., "Houston Area Domestic Violence Providers Study and Initial Local DV Data Aggregation," IRWGS, February 2023.

34. Annamaria Milazzo, "Racial Disparities in Maternal Health: The Role of Preexisting Health Conditions," IRWGS, June 2024.

35. "Abortion: Historical Trends," Gallup, May 2025.

36. Carrie N. Baker, "Forced Pregnancy Is Involuntary Servitude, Violates the 13th Amendment," *Ms. Magazine*, May 23, 2022.

CHAPTER 4

1. Margaret Mead, *Sex and Temperament in Three Primitive Societies* (William Morrow & Company, 1935).

2. See discussion of archeological analyses of the Neolithic city of Çatalhöyük in Anatolia (flourished in 7000 BCE) in Saini, *The Patriarchs*, 56–80.

3. Silvia Federici, *Caliban and the Witch: Women, the Body and Primitive Accumulation* (Autonomedia, 2004), 181.

4. Not coincidentally, some who want to deny women fertility control, insisting that fetal "rights" supersede those of female citizens, also seek to reverse the suffrage amendment, such as Defense Secretary Pete Hegseth and his pastor (Mariel Padilla, Grace Panetta, Mel Leonor Barclay, "Who's Questioning Women's Right to Vote?," *The 19th*, August 12, 2025). The discussion of voting by household doesn't explore the loss of votes that would entail for joint households relative to single-adult households.

5. Ben Barres, *The Autobiography of a Transgender Scientist* (MIT Press, 2018); and Joan Roughgarden, cited, p. 100. Barres cites a comment on a talk he gave after transitioning: "his work is much better than his sister's" (9).

6. Marilyn Waring, *Counting for Nothing: What Men Value and What Women Are Worth* (Harper & Row, 1988). See also Margaret Gilpin Reid, *Economics of Household Production* (Wiley, 1934), discussed in Claudia Goldin, *Career and Family: Women's Century-Long Journey Toward Equity* (Princeton University Press, 2021).

7. Per author's discussion with labor negotiator Elsa Flores, Houston, 2025.

8. See Mother (Mary) Jones, "Girl Slaves of the Milwaukee Breweries," *United Mine Workers Journal* 20, no. 47 (1910).

9. Leopoldina Fortunati, *The Arcane of Reproduction: Housework, Prostitution, Labor and Capital* (Autonomedia, 1996), 33.

10. Social caste systems share three structural parallels: assignment of those in the lower caste to limited work options, low wages, and rationales for why things can't change (tradition/custom).

11. See the huge literature on competition. Caste may function similarly to monopsony in limiting workforce options.

12. Nancy Chodorow, *Reproduction of Mothering: Psychoanalysis and the Sociology of Gender* (University of California Press, 1978).

13. Paula England, "The Case for Comparable Worth," *Quarterly Review of Economics and Finance* 39 (1999): 743–755.

14. Ruth Milkman, *On Gender, Labor, and Inequality* (University of Illinois Press, 2016), 77.

15. Salary negotiations are subject to distortions due to bias. But the prime issue is profit: if an employer knows women will take less (because they have no union, insufficient information, or a higher level of desperation), they may offer that.

16. Sebastian Shehadi, "These Are the Most (and Least) Male-Dominated Industries in the US," *Investment Monitor* (January 9, 2023).

CHAPTER 5

1. Silvia Federici, "Wages Against Housework" (Power of Women Collective, 1974), 1.

2. Melissa Murray, "Children of Men: The Roberts Court's Jurisprudence of Masculinity," *Houston Law Review* 60, no. 4 (2023).

3. Julie Suk, *After Misogyny: How the Law Fails Women and What to Do About It* (University of California Press, 2023).

4. Ann Fessler, *The Girls Who Went Away: The Hidden History of Women Who Surrendered Children for Adoption in the Decades Before Roe v. Wade* (Penguin, 2006).

5. "'Baby in a Dumpster.' A Spate of Abandoned Newborns Unsettles Texas," *Washington Post*, December 30, 2024.

6. See Elaine Pagels, "What Became of God the Mother?," *Signs: Journal of Women in Culture and Society* 2, no. 2 (1976): 293–303.

CHAPTER 6

1. Fifteen billion dollars is a conservative estimate. See John Naughton, "The Growth of Internet Porn," *The Guardian*, December 30, 2018.

2. Silvia Federici, "Wages Against Housework" (Power of Women Collective, 1974), 4.

3. Matthew Goldstein, "In Epstein Case Follow the Money," *New York Times* (January 17, 2025).

4. See Kimberlé Crenshaw, "Mapping the Margins: Intersectionality, Identity Politics, and Violence Against Women of Color," *Stanford Law Review* 43, no. 6 (1991): 1241–1299.

5. Claire Goudreau, "Looking Back at the Violence Against Women Act After 30 Years of Protection," Johns Hopkins, September 27, 2024. Since those without recourse generally don't report DV, rate changes are extrapolated from trends in reported abuse. VAWA was instigated by feminists and introduced by Senator Biden. It's been reaffirmed and expanded several times, though approval has been blocked several times by Republicans who did not want to expand its protections to people in LGBTQ+ relationships or to close the "boyfriend loophole," which would deny guns to abusive boyfriends. Although laws prohibiting known abusers from owning firearms have passed, National Rifle Association–funded efforts to defang those laws are ongoing. The Supreme Court denied one such effort in 2024 (*U.S. v. Rahimi*).

6. Elizabeth Gregory et al., "Houston Area Domestic Violence Providers Study and Initial Local DV Data Aggregation," IRWGS, February 2023.

7. Rachel Louise Snyder, *No Visible Bruises: What We Don't Know about Domestic Violence Can Kill Us* (Bloomsbury, 2019).

8. Cristina Rivera Garza, *Liliana's Invincible Summer: A Sister's Search for Justice* (Hogarth, 2023).

9. Arkadi Gerney and Chelsea Parsons, *Women Under the Gun: How Gun Violence Affects Women and 4 Policy Solutions to Better Protect Them* (Center for American Progress, 2014).

10. Carol Gilligan, *In a Different Voice: Psychological Theory and Women's Development* (Harvard University Press, 1982).

11. bell hooks, *Understanding Patriarchy* (Washington Square Press, 2004).

12. Angelique Chrisafis, "Gisèle Pelicot Tells Mass Rape Trial 'It's Not for Us to Have Shame—It's for Them,'" *The Guardian*, October 23, 2024.

13. Amy Sherman, "In Context: What JD Vance Said About Rape, Abortion and 'Inconvenience,'" *Politifact*, October 12, 2022.

14. Samuel L. Dickman et al., "Rape-Related Pregnancies in the 14 US States with Total Abortion Bans," *JAMA* 184, no. 3 (2024): 330–332. They found that even in

the few states with rape exceptions abortions are hard to access, especially if parents won't help.

15. Leopoldina Fortunati, *The Arcane of Reproduction: Housework, Prostitution, Labor and Capital* (Autonomedia, 1996), 27.

16. Largely through the efforts of Laura X; see "New Laws Recognizing Rape as a Crime," *New York Times*, December 29, 1984.

17. "Sex Worker Statistics by Country, Gender," International Union of Sex Workers, 2024, https://iusw.org/sex-worker-statistics/.

18. Frances H. Ampt et al., "Incidence of Unintended Pregnancy Among Female Sex Workers in Low-Income and Middle-Income Countries: A Systematic Review and Meta-Analysis," *BMJ* 8, no. 9 (2018).

19. Emma Goldman, "The Traffic in Women," in *Anarchism and Other Essays*, ed. Emma Goldman (Mother Earth Publishing, 1910).

20. See Sarah Luna, *Love in the Drug War: Selling Sex and Finding Jesus on the Mexico-US Border* (University of Texas Press, 2020).

21. NOMAS, "Prostitution: Key Facts and Analysis, in Brief," nomas.org; Michel Carael et al., "Clients of Sex Workers in Different Regions of the World: Hard to Count," *Sexually Transmitted Infections* 82 (2006): iii26–iii33.

22. Nikolas Westerhoff, "Why Do Men Buy Sex," *Scientific American*, October 1, 2012.

23. NOMAS, "Prostitution."

CHAPTER 7

1. Breast removal ("top") surgeries among queer people born female are less common than breast augmentation surgeries among straight people: 304,181 breast augmentations in 2023 (up 2 percent from 2022) and 27,187 breast removals from 2016 to 2020—though the numbers are growing. "Chestfeeding" is possible for those who give birth after breast removal.

2. April Maria Ortiz, "Trans in the Heart of Texas, *San Antonio Current*, December 21, 2024.

3. Jeffrey M. Jones, "LGBTQ+ Identification in US Rises to 9.3%," Gallup Poll, February 20, 2025.

4. Henry Berg-Brousseau, "Anti-LGBTQ+ Grooming Narrative Surged More than 400% on Social Media Following Florida's 'Don't Say Gay or Trans' Law, as Social Platforms Enabled Extremist Politicians and Their Allies to Peddle Inflammatory, Discriminatory Rhetoric," Human Rights Campaign, August 10, 2022. The content was driven by ten individuals, including Governor DeSantis's press secretary, Representatives Marjorie Taylor Greene and Lauren Boebert, among others, and got forty-eight million views.

5. Masha Gessen, "Chase Strangio's Victories for Transgender Rights," *New Yorker*, October 12, 2020.

6. "A Survey of LGBT Americans," Pew Research Center, June 13, 2013.

7. Danielle Taylor, "Same-Sex Couples Are More Likely to Adopt or Foster Children," US Census Bureau, September 17, 2020.

8. "LGBTQ Family Building Survey," Family Equality, February 6, 2019.

9. The first sperm bank to support lesbians and single women opened in 1982 (the Sperm Bank of California). See Dana Rudolph, "A Very Brief History of LGBTQ Parenting," Family Equality, October 20, 2017. Gestational surrogacy began in 1985.

10. Nestor Hernandez, "Percentage of Married and Unmarried, Same-Sex and Opposite-Sex Couple Households with Children Down from 2019 to 2023," United States Census Bureau, November 13, 2024. See also "Household Characteristics of Same-Sex Couple Households by Relationship Type: 2023," table 2, American Community Survey.

11. Bethany G. Everett et al., "Sexual Orientation Disparities in Pregnancy Risk Behaviors and Pregnancy Among Sexually Active Teenage Girls: Updates from the Youth Risk Behavior Survey," *LGBT Health* 6, no. 7 (2019): 342–349.

12. Yun Zhang et al., "Family Outcome Disparities Between Sexual Minority and Heterosexual Families: A Systematic Review and Meta-Analysis," *BMJ Global Health* 8, no. 3 (2023). The article surveys studies from 1989 to 2022.

13. Pierre Dupreelle et al., "A New LGBTQ Workforce Has Arrived—Inclusive Cultures Must Follow," Boston Consulting Group, 2021.

14. Although the right to marry is no longer linked to sexuality, the proportion of LGBTQ+ couples who are married is still lower than among straight couples. See "LGBT Americans Married to Same-Sex Spouse Steady at 10%," Gallup, February 10, 2022. In part this is because more than 50 percent of those identifying as LGBTQ+ are under age thirty.

15. Rebecca Glauber, "Trends in the Motherhood Wage Penalty and Fatherhood Wage Premium for Low, Middle, and High Earners," *Demography* 55 (2018): 1663–1680. See also Rakesh Kochhar, "The Enduring Grip of the Gender Pay Gap," Pew Research Center, March 1, 2023.

16. Ceylan Engin et al., "Socioeconomic Inequalities in the Lesbian and Gay Male Populations," in *International Handbook of Demography of Poverty and Inequality*, ed. Joachim Singelmann and Dudley L. Poston Jr. (Springer, 2025), 75–88.

17. Amanda Baumle, *Same-Sex Partners: The Demography of Sexual Orientation* (SUNY Press, 2009).

18. Jeff Frank, "Gay Glass Ceilings," *Economica* 73, no. 291 (2006): 485–508; Yunus Aksoy et al., "Demographic Structure and Macroeconomic Trends," *American Economic Journal: Macroeconomics* 11, no. 1 (2019): 193–222.

19. John M. Blandford, "The Nexus of Sexual Orientation and Gender in the Determination of Earnings," *ILR Review* 56, no. 4 (2003): 622–642; Dan A. Black et al., "The Economics of Lesbian and Gay Families," *Journal of Economic Perspectives* 21, no. 2 (2007): 53–70.

20. bell hooks, *Understanding Patriarchy* (Washington Square Press, 2004).

21. Jesse Watters, "White Dudes for Harris," *The Five*, Fox News, July 30, 2024.

22. See John Boswell, *Christianity, Social Tolerance, and Homosexuality: Gay People in Western Europe from the Beginning of the Christian Era to the Fourteenth Century* (University of Chicago Press, 1980).

23. Michel Foucault, *The History of Sexuality, Volume 1: An Introduction* (Pantheon, 1978), 43.

24. Per the Human Rights Coalition, in 2024, 42 percent of trans victims with a known killer were murdered by a romantic/sexual partner, friend, or family member; 78 percent were people of color, and 56 percent were Black trans women. ("Fatal Violence Against the Transgender and Gender-Expansive Community in 2024," https://www.hrc.org/resources/fatal-violence-against-the-transgender-and-gender-expansive-community-in-2024). See also Samantha Schmidt et al., "Surviving as a Black Transgender Woman in Baton Rouge," *Washington Post*, June 29, 2021.

25. Katharine A. Phillips, "Suicidality in Body Dysmorphic Disorder," *Primary Psychiatry* 14, no. 12 (2007): 58–66.

26. Jody L. Herman et al., "How Many Adults and Youth Identify as Transgender in the United States?," Williams Institute, June 2022.

27. Jones, "LGBTQ+ Identification in US Rises to 9.3%."

28. Carla Pfeffer, *Queering Families: The Postmodern Partnerships of Cisgender Women and Transgender Men* (Oxford University Press, 2017).

29. Jacey Fortin, "Texas Law Bill Bans Care for Minors in Transition," *New York Times*, June 3, 2023, sec. A, p. 15.

30. Landon D. Hughes et al., "Gender-Affirming Medications Among Transgender Adolescents in the US, 2018–2022," *JAMA Pediatrics* 179, no. 3 (2025): 342–344. Only those with health insurance were tracked, so the percentage in the full population is lower.

31. Katherine L. Kraschel et al., "Legislation Restricting Gender-Affirming Care for Transgender Youth: Politics Eclipse Healthcare," *Cell Reports Medicine* 3, no. 8 (2022): 100719.

32. Daphna Stroumsa et al., "Pregnancy Outcomes in a US Cohort of Transgender People," *JAMA* 329, no. 21 (2023): 1879–1881.

33. Eleanor Klibanoff, "After Texas Banned Puberty Blockers and Hormones for Trans Kids, Adults Lost Care, Too," *Texas Tribune*, December 4, 2024.

34. Harry Barbee et al., "Postoperative Regret Among Transgender and Gender-Diverse Recipients of Gender-Affirming Surgery," *JAMA Surgery* 159, no. 2 (2024): 125–126.

35. Charlie Baker, Testimony before the US Senate Judiciary Committee, December 18, 2024.

36. Heath Fogg Davis, *Beyond Trans: Does Gender Matter?* (NYU Press, 2017).

37. Kazutoshi Takahashi Shinya Yamanaka, "Induction of Pluripotent Stem Cells from Mouse Embryonic and Adult Fibroblast Cultures by Defined Factors," *Cell* 126 (2006): 663–676; Anne Le Goff, Robbin Jeffries Hein, Ariel N. Hart, Isaias Roberson, and Hannah L. Landecker, "Anticipating *In Vitro* Gametogenesis: Hopes and Concerns for IVG Among Diverse Stakeholders," *Stem Cell Reports* 19 (2024): 933–945; Mitinori Saitou and Katsuhiko Hayashi, "Mammalian In Vitro Gametogenesis," *Science* 374, no. 6563 (2021).

38. Rob Stein, "New Research Could Change the Landscape of Human Reproduction," NPR, July 18, 2023; Rob Stein, "A Reproduction Revolution Is on the Horizon: In Vitro Gametogenesis or IVG," NPR, September 28, 2023; Rob Stein, "Infertile People, Gay and Trans Couples Yearn for Progress on Lab-Made Eggs and Sperm," NPR, September 13, 2023.

39. Angela Davis, "Outcast Mothers and Surrogates: Racism and Reproductive Politics in the Nineties," in *American Feminist Thought at Century's End*, ed. Linda Kauffman (Blackwell, 1993).

40. Amanda Baumle et al., "Effects of State-Level Abortion and LGBT Laws and Policies on Interstate Migration Attitudes," *Population Research and Policy Review* 42 (2023): 90.

CHAPTER 8

1. Deborah Sontag, "Once a Pariah, Now a Judge: The Early Transgender Journey of Phyllis Frye," *New York Times*, August 29, 2015. Frye's conferences explored legal options around issues like employment, identity (as stated on birth certificates and driver's licenses), housing, and health access.

2. Houston, Dallas, and San Antonio have all had many years under female mayors; Los Angeles, Chicago, and Boston fewer and more recently; and New York and Philadelphia zero.

3. The Republic of Texas (1836–1845) was a stopgap between settlers' exit from Mexico and their acceptance into the United States. The state also has the most experience belonging to other nations: Mexico, Spain and France (as a colony), and the would-be Confederate nation.

4. Of the foreign-born, 65 percent come from Latin America, 24 percent from Asia, and 6 percent from Africa. Texas Legislative Study Group, "U.S. and Texas Immigration Background (Part I)" (February 16, 2024).

5. Coda Rayo-Garza, "New Census Data Reflect Rising Challenges in Texas on Health Insurance, Poverty, and Income Inequality," Every Texan, September 11, 2025; United for ALICE, "The State of ALICE in Texas," United Way, 2025; Jeffrey S. Passel and Jens Manuel Krogstad, "U.S. Unauthorized Immigrant Population Reached a Record 14 Million in 2023," Pew Research Center, August 21, 2025; Caitlin Carter, "Health Insurance Coverage by State: 2023 and 2024," *American Community Survey Briefs*, September 2025.

6. "Texas Ranks 29th in Teacher Pay; 47th in Per-Pupil Spending," *Texas Education News*, April 30, 2025; *Kids Count Data Book* (Annie E. Casey Foundation, 2025); Michael Karlis, "Texas Has Most Toxic Air and Polluted Water, Study Finds," *San Antonio Current*, May 23, 2025.

7. Nina Banks, "Black Women in the US and Unpaid Collective Work, Theorizing the Community as a Site of Production," *Review of Black Political Economy* 474 (2020): 343–362.

8. Texas's incarceration rate was 751 per 100,000 people in 2023 (including prisons, jails, immigration detention, and juvenile justice facilities); see "Texas Profile," Prison Policy Initiative, 2023, https://www.prisonpolicy.org. Some smaller states have higher per capita rates, but Texas has the largest number of prisoners at 219,000, with 437,000 on probation or parole. Although there are many white prisoners, a disproportionate number are non-Hispanic Black (12 percent of the population and 33 percent of those incarcerated).

9. Nazgol Ghandnoosh, "One in Five: Racial Disparity in Imprisonment—Causes and Remedies," *The Sentencing Project*, December 7, 2023.

10. Robin McDowell and Margie Mason, "Prisoners in the US Are Part of a Hidden Workforce Linked to Hundreds of Popular Food Brands," *AP News* (January 29, 2024).

11. Elizabeth Gregory et al., "Houston Area Domestic Violence Providers Study and Initial Local DV Data Aggregation," IRWGS, February 2023.

12. As of 2024, the current gerrymander meant that Democrats would need to win 58 percent of the statewide vote to flip seats from the active 24–14 congressional split, and a similar split in the state legislature. The 2025 mid-decade gerrymander tilted an additional five seats Republican, meaning that a greater majority would be required to flip the balance. See Michael Li and Julia Boland, "Anatomy of the Texas Gerrymander," Brennan Center for Justice, December 2021.

13. As a big state, Texas has room for in-migrants while keeping land costs low. If the state didn't undercompete on labor, taxes, regulations, etc., other states would see fewer business exits and workforce issues.

14. The state has recently reduced homeowners' property taxes, further limiting funds for services—while not helping renters.

15. The 7.3 figure represents the average among the forty-six states with a sales tax in 2023; see Miranda Crace, "Sales Tax by State: State and Local Sales Tax Rates for 2023," Rocket Money, December 22, 2023.

16. Andrea Suozzo et al., "Texas Won't Study How Its Abortion Ban Impacts Women, So We Did," *ProPublica*, February 20, 2025.

17. See, for example, Stephania Taladrid, "The Texas OB/GYN Exodus," *New Yorker*, November 25, 2024.

18. Kavitha Surana and Lizzie Presser, "Ticking Time Bomb": A Pregnant Mother Kept Getting Sicker. She Died After She Couldn't Get an Abortion in Texas," *ProPublica*, November 19, 2025.

19. Alex Morin et al., *The Texas OB/GYN Physician Workforce: Early Assessment of the Impact of Abortion Restrictions on the Workforce Pipeline* (Manatt Health, 2024).

20. The Trevor Project, *2023 US National Survey on the Mental Health of LGBTQ Young People* (The Trevor Project, 2023); Amy Novotney, "'The Young People Feel It': A Look at the Mental Health Impact of Anti-Trans Legislation," American Psychological Association, June 29, 2023; Wilson Y. Lee et al., "State-Level Anti-Transgender Laws Increase Past-Year Suicide Attempts," *Nature Human Behavior* 8 (2023).

21. Amanda Baumle et al., "Effects of State-Level Abortion and LGBT Laws and Policies on Interstate Migration Attitudes," *Population Research and Policy Review* 42 (2023): 90.

22. "Texas Daily Population Growth and Components of the Change, 2020–2025," Texas Demographic Center, 2026.

23. Daniel Dench et al., "Are People Fleeing States with Abortion Bans?," NBER Working Paper No. 33328 (National Bureau of Economic Research, January 2025).

24. Evan Symon, "Oracle Moving Headquarters Out of Austin," *California Globe*, April 26, 2024.

25. Saul Elbein, "Dozens of Texas Businesses Back Challenge to Abortion Ban," *The Hill*, December 14, 2024; Rebecca Weaver, "The Texas Abortion Ban Is a Huge Business Mistake—And More Companies Need to Say So," HRuprise, September 23, 2021.

26. Francesca D'Annunzio, "How Mass Deportations Would 'Devastate' Texas," *Texas Observer*, October 21, 2024; Alejandra Martinez, Alejandro Serrano, Berenice Garcia, Carlos Nogueras Ramos and Joshua Fechter, "Some Texas Business Leaders Are Apprehensive about Trump's Pledged Deportations," *Texas Tribune*, January 8, 2025.

27. "Undocumented Immigrant Offending Rate Lower than US-Born Citizen Rate," National Institute of Justice, US Department of Justice, September 12, 2024.

28. "The Latino Face of Human Trafficking and Exploitation in the US," Polaris Project, April 24, 2020.

29. Reese Oxner, "78% of Texas Voters Think Abortion Should be Allowed," *Texas Tribune*, May 4, 2022; Will Fritz, "Poll Shows Most US Adults Agree That Politicians Use Attacks on Trans Rights to Distract," *Wisconsin Independent*, June 21, 2024.

30. Passel and Krogstad, "U.S. Unauthorized Immigrant Population."

31. Southern politicians make it difficult to vote for citizens they think will support the opposition, by reducing polling places and mail-in ballot drop boxes, limiting early voting, and, recently, outlawing drive-through voting (which worked beautifully, but that was the flaw). These tricks are clear, yet they continue without federal intervention. Poverty also reduces turnout—among residents working multiple jobs, who feel their vote won't matter or encounter too many barriers. Such vote limiting constitutes a modern version of the antebellum Census that counted slaves as three-fifths of a person, so they counted toward each state's congressional representation; however, since they couldn't vote, their "representatives" felt no call to advocate for them. A positive step could be honest public discussion of economic and social issues, avoiding knee-jerk narratives.

32. Center on Budget and Policy Priorities (CBPP), "How States Spend Funds Under the TANF Block Grant: State Fact Sheets," CBPP, September 23, 2024. See also Chandra Childers, "The Evolution of the Southern Economic Development Strategy," Economic Policy Institute, May 6, 2024; Ife Floyd et al., "TANF Policies Reflect Racist Legacy of Cash Assistance," CBPP, August 4, 2021.

33. Diana Azevedo-McCaffrey and Ali Safawi, "To Promote Equity, States Should Invest More TANF Dollars in Basic Assistance," CBPP, January 12, 2022.

34. *State of Missouri et al. v. Food and Drug.*

35. This is trackable when women deliver babies, many of whom don't have health care until they become pregnant, when it becomes available through Medicaid in Texas. See Annamaria Milazzo, "Racial Disparities in Maternal Health: The Role of Preexisting Health Conditions," IRWGS, June 2024.

36. Kim Krisberg and David Leffler, "Why Texas Republicans Still Oppose Medicaid Expansion," *Texas Tribune*, November 7, 2022. In North Carolina, Governor Roy Cooper, as part of the state's Medicaid expansion in 2024, "negotiated a deal with 99 hospitals . . . to forgive about $4 billion in medical debt owed by nearly 2 million people in exchange for the medical institutions receiving federal funding tied to Medicaid expansion." See Karen Tumulty, "Roy Cooper Showed Democrats How to Govern and Win. And He's Not Done," *Washington Post*, December 24, 2024.

37. Texas Advisory Committee to the U.S. Commission on Civil Rights, "Racial Outcomes in Maternal Mortality," September 2025, 5; Milazzo, "Racial Disparities in Maternal Health."

38. Mel Leonor Barclay and Jasmine Mithani, "Without the Federal Government Almost No Money Exists to Fight Domestic Violence," *The 19th*, October 31, 2025; Katherine Hapgood, "Trump Administration Policy Change Makes Deep Cuts to Homeless Permanent Housing Program," *Politico*, November 14, 2025.

39. Benjamin Thornburg et al., "Anxiety and Depression Symptoms After the *Dobbs* Abortion Decision," *JAMA* 331, no. 4 (2024): 294–301.

40. Texas Freedom Network, "Health and Sex Education in Texas: A Troubled History," 2019, https://tfn.org/sex-ed/Factsheet_TroubledHistory_LH_2019.pdf.

41. As do the other participants in the SEDM described in chapter 3 but on a smaller scale.

42. The British East India Company held sway from 1757 to 1858, and the British Raj from 1858 to 1947.

43. Utsa Patnaik, *Agrarian and Other Histories: Essays for Binay Bhushan Chaudhuri* (Columbia University Press, 2017).

CHAPTER 9

1. It was one billion in 1825. For in-depth discussion of demographic trends, see Jennifer Sciubba, *Eight Billion and Counting: How Sex, Death and Migration Shape Our World* (Norton, 2022).

2. Richard Reeve notes that jobs in traditionally male fields involving manufacturing and heavy lifting have declined due to automation and offshoring, leading some to leave the workforce. He urges male workers to consider work in traditionally feminine fields—a move to degender work from the other direction that will be most effective if accompanied by raises in pay and status for all in those jobs. See Richard Reeve, *Of Boys and Men: Why the Modern Male Is Struggling, Why It Matters, and What to Do About It* (Brookings Institution Press, 2022).

3. Per CDC National Vital Statistics reports, male life expectancy was 60.8 in 1940, 65.6 in 1950 (the point at which most people could be expected to retire), and 74.3 in 2000.

4. This assumes a workforce entry age range of eighteen to twenty-five years, depending on level of education.

5. See the Federal Reserve Bank of St. Louis, "Labor Force Participation Rate Female: From 25 to 54 Years for United States," https://fred.stlouisfed.org/.

6. Andrew Park and Pooja Slahotra, "Republican Voter Turnout Far Outpaces Democrat Turnout in 2024 Primaries," *Texas Tribune*, March 3, 2024, figure captioned "Young voters noticeably absent in this year's primaries."

7. Emily Guskin et al., "Exit Polls from the 2024 Presidential Election," *Washington Post*, December 2, 2024. See "Voting and Registration in the Election of November 2024," US Census Bureau, April 2025.

CHAPTER 10

1. Estimates vary from 21 to 50 percent, including different kinds of care.

2. Silvia Federici, "Wages Against Housework" (Power of Women Collective, 1974); Leopoldina Fortunati, *The Arcane of Reproduction: Housework, Prostitution, Labor and Capital* (Autonomedia, 1996). See also discussions in chapters 4 and 5.

3. This would involve some redistribution of assets over time, repaying the wage theft long imposed as poverty on low-income workers by our economic system (all the free labor of reproduction and maintenance that families have done, and the access to education and other services denied to the poor, blocking their access to opportunity). But the group overall benefits from the expanded thriving, including that enabled by climate care (see chapter 11).

4. Although deficit spending is compounded by interest, the government can also cover the interest on deficit. Building on Keynes, Modern Monetary theorists argue that, where needed to grow national value, this can be done without issue up to the point at which the new funds in people's pockets raise demand beyond what business can meet, causing inflation at too high a rate. In combining new taxes with deficit spending, the Wages for Care model damps potential inflation while also adding the values of new pay and expanded care services to the community.

5. John Maynard Keynes, *The Means to Prosperity* (Macmillan, 1933).

6. A reverse multiplier may occur when new taxes are added that reduce some people's available disposable income. However, if the new taxes paid cover salaries

for the newly hired and services for all (like health care, etc.) that cost more previously, the effect on disposable income will still be positive over the long term, since it works out to additional income and/or expanded services.

7. Elizabeth Gregory et al., "Affordable Childcare Could Reduce Domestic Violence," IRWGS, April 2025.

8. For many, the ability to work would depend on first having childcare.

9. Without SEDM discounts, employers would no longer have that reason to migrate from other states, and SEDM states would begin to have better-educated workforces, reducing their need for skilled migrants.

10. The possibility of reaching full employment could in itself be a goal, as a form of economic care for workers.

11. See, for instance, Maureen Tkacik, "'So Much Evil Had to Happen for This Bill to Pass': Oregon Just Made Corporate Medicine Illegal, Again. Here's How It Happened," *The American Prospect* (June 13, 2025); and "The Obamacare Boiler Room: Perhaps No Florida Health Care Scam Has So Concisely Illustrated the Burning Need to Rethink Our Broken Health Care System," *The American Prospect* (November 18, 2025).

12. Consumer Financial Protection Bureau (CFPB), "Twelve Years of Protecting Consumers and Honest Businesses," CFPB, July 20. 2023; Callum Jones, "'She's Going to Prevail': FTC Head Lina Khan Is Fighting for an Anti-Monopoly America," *The Guardian* (March 9, 2024).

13. In *The Maternal Roots of the Gift Economy* (Inanna Publications, 2018), Vaughan explores alternatives to patriarchal methods of valuation. She views childbearing and child-rearing as gifts to the community inherent in motherhood, expecting no transactional return from the child, and understands that prepatriarchal economies worked through similar gifts. Led by mothers animated by principles of child nurture, she postulates that such economies shared what they needed from each member. Vaughan advocates a care model different from what I offer here, which involves monetization of some care to allow caregivers into the polity and expand the economy. Vaughan views the biological production of children as a gift to the community, not just to the baby. Without disputing the view that communities of mutual care might operate without money, I don't see that as likely soon, so my efforts focus on near-term solutions, but I share her view that community thriving is key.

14. See, for instance, Nancy Folbre, *Rise and Decline of Patriarchal Systems: An Intersectional Political Economy* (Verso, 2021).

15. Reasons included paying down World War II debt and avoiding inflation from expanded consumer purchasing power.

16. John E. Humphries et al., "Parents' Earnings and the Returns to Universal Pre-Kindergarten," Working Paper No. 33038 (National Bureau of Economic Research, October 2024).

17. To date, thirteen states plus the District of Columbia have instituted mandatory paid leave programs for maternity or other family care needs, funded through

a small tax on all employees (California, Connecticut, Massachusetts, New Jersey, Rhode Island, Washington, Colorado, Delaware, Maine, Maryland, Minnesota, and Oregon) or through mandated private insurance for employers (New York). See "State Paid Family Leave Laws Across the U.S.," Bipartisan Policy Center, February 20, 2025.

18. A recent study in Finland found that paid childcare improves child outcomes (Jonathan Gruber et al., "Paying Moms to Stay Home: Short and Long Run Effects on Parents and Children," NBER Working Paper 30931, February 2023).

19. Fourteen states and Washington, DC, currently have paid parental and disability leave programs (variously funded).

20. Annamaria Milazzo, "Racial Disparities in Maternal Health: The Role of Preexisting Health Conditions," IRWGS, June 2024.

21. Raj Chetty et al., "The Association Between Income and Life Expectancy in the United States, 2001–2014," *JAMA* 315, no. 16 (2016): 1750–1766.

22. 1940 longevity data from Elizabeth Arias and Jiaquan Xu, "United States Life Tables, 2019," *National Vital Statistics Report* 70, no. 19 (Centers for Disease Control and Prevention, 2025): table 19; "Ratio of Social Security Covered Workers to Beneficiaries, 1940–2013," Social Security History, https://www.ssa.gov/history/ratios.html.

23. Stephanie Kelton, *The Deficit Myth: Modern Monetary Theory and the Birth of the People's Economy* (Public Affairs, 2020).

CHAPTER 11

1. The United States' 2025 decision to withdraw from the Paris Climate Accord, the simultaneous declaration that we face an energy crisis that can only be fixed by extracting more oil and coal, and the widely endorsed boostering of crypto (a grift that not only robs people but also requires enormous levels of polluting energy) make no sense in a moment when the price of gas is low and solar power installations are growing the economy.

2. World Meteorological Organization, "WMO Confirms 2024 as Warmest Year on Record at about 1.55 °C Above Pre-Industrial Level," January 10, 2025; Rebecca Lindsey and Luann Dahlman, "Climate Change: Global Temperature," NOAA, January 18, 2024.

3. Although without birth control longevity might not have expanded to quite the same extent because women would not have seen the health benefits of fewer births.

4. *Living Planet Report 2024: A System in Peril* (World Wildlife Fund, 2024).

INDEX

The letter *f* following a page number denotes a figure.